WHEN *the* GOOD NEWS GETS
EVEN BETTER

REDISCOVERING THE GOSPELS THROUGH
FIRST-CENTURY JEWISH EYES

NEB HAYDEN

A 12-WEEK BIBLE STUDY

David C Cook
transforming lives together

WHEN THE GOOD NEWS GETS EVEN BETTER
Published by David C. Cook
4050 Lee Vance View
Colorado Springs, CO 80918 U.S.A.

David C. Cook Distribution Canada
55 Woodslee Avenue, Paris, Ontario, Canada N3L 3E5

David C. Cook U.K., Kingsway Communications
Eastbourne, East Sussex BN23 6NT, England

David C. Cook and the graphic circle C logo
are registered trademarks of Cook Communications Ministries.

Unless otherwise noted, Scripture quotations are taken from the *New American Standard Bible*, © Copyright 1960, 1995 by The Lockman Foundation. Used by permission. Scripture quotations marked TLB are taken from *The Living Bible*, © 1971, Tyndale House Publishers, Wheaton, IL 60189. Used by permission; PH are taken from J. B. Phillips: *The New Testament in Modern English*, revised editions © J. B. Phillips, 1958, 1960, 1972, permission of Macmillan Publishing Co. and Collins Publishers; MSG are taken from *THE MESSAGE*. Copyright © by Eugene H. Peterson 1993, 1994, 1995, 1996, 2000, 2001, 2002. Used by permission of NavPress Publishing Group; and NKJV are taken from the New King James Version. Copyright © 1982 by Thomas Nelson, Inc. Used by permission. All rights reserved.

ISBN 978-1-4347-6700-4

© 2009 Neb Hayden
First edition published by McFarland Publishing, LLC in 2006 © Neb Hayden, ISBN 0-9778443-0-7

The Team: John Blase, Sarah Schultz, and Jack Campbell
Cover Design: Amy Kiechlin
Cover Photo: Shai Ginott/Corbis

Printed in the United States of America
Second Edition 2009

1 2 3 4 5 6 7 8 9 10

041409

CONTENTS

PREFACE

How is it possible to make the good news of the gospel better? How can truth be enhanced? How can Jesus Christ be improved upon? Impossible! Then, why the title *When the Good News Gets Even Better*? The good news gets even better only when it's understood as it was intended by the Author.

Many years ago my wife, Susan, and I went on the first of several two-week study seminars in Israel with Dr. Jim Martin. As we gathered with him on our first day, Jim said, "You will never understand the Scriptures until you learn how to think like a Jew." Thinking simple but profound thoughts became the impetus for a personal journey that eventually became this study.

I began reading and studying everything I could concerning Jewish history, culture, and customs but had no real hooks to hang it all on until a dear friend told me of a fascinating study he was engaged in. Bob Warren, a former professional basketball player and fantastic teacher told me of a similar experience he had in Israel and that he was studying the Gospels from a Jewish perspective. With Bob's encouragement, I began a similar journey in the Gospels.

That which began as a personal quest later became a study course that I taught, and finally this ninety-day study book. Seeing the four gospels through first-century Jewish eyes gave me a perspective I had never seen, though I had studied and taught the Gospels for many years. We have the study arranged according to "days," to which you can make this a ninety-day (or three-month study). However, there are eleven sections, so with those and factoring in a week for introductions and setting ground rules for a group, this arrangement allows for a twelve-week study.

I wrote *When the Good News Get Even Better* from the following perspectives:

◆ **Through First-Century Jewish Eyes:** The Bible is a Jewish book, written to Jewish people, in a Jewish culture, about a Jewish Messiah. The Jewish history and religious instruction framed and dramatically influenced everything a first-century Jew saw Jesus do or heard Him say. As Gentiles, we read and study the Gospels from a twenty-first-century Gentile perspective. This study book is my attempt to help bridge the gap.

◆ **Through an Empathetic Understanding:** The Gospels are *your story.* The people you read about were real. They had the same emotional issues that you have. We will step into their sandals and try understanding these life events autobiographically. We will become a Samaritan woman who lost hope as Jesus reshapes her whole world. We will get inside the life of a rich little tax collector named Zaccheus as he encounters Jesus and has dinner with Him. We will feel the desperation of a woman with a hemorrhage as she pushes through the crowd to touch Jesus' robe. If we understand the circumstances of their Hebrew lives and apply our own similar emotions, we can empathetically engage the account.

♦ **Through the Window of Grace:** Most believers hear the word *grace* throughout their lives but are taught a law-based perspective. *Should, must, ought to,* and *duty* are the constant companions of most believers as we seek to live out our faith. In the Gospels, we find a new freedom where *desire* replaces *obligation*. Jesus changes hearts, and we experience a new motivation. We no longer *have* to study the Scriptures, pray, and share our faith.... We *get* to do those things. This is the flavor of our study in the Gospels.

♦ **Through Chronological Study:** I used the outline of A. T. Robertson's *A Harmony of the Gospels* as a guideline. To see the four gospels as one as the events occurred will add a new spice and excitement to the greatest story ever told.

This study is designed for both individual and group study. Following the day-by-day sequence will take you through the Gospels in twelve weeks or three months (ninety days) at an average of twenty to thirty minutes per day. In a small group, two to three days of material can be studied depending on your time constraints. I highly encourage you to read individually in advance the passages listed for the next section before your weekly gathering and to take notes on what you learn.

The Gospels are the foundation of our faith and will give you a unique opportunity to walk the dust roads with Jesus and to be there as a participant rather than simply an observer. Every move Jesus made and every word He spoke has direct implications for your life in the twenty-first century.

My hope is that this study will not simple be new information to ponder but a new discovery of the life of Jesus through Hebrew eyes. It is my hope that you will come to more deeply know and enjoy the One who wrote the Gospels. This is *When the Good New Gets Even Better.*

—Neb Hayden

GETTING THE MOST OUT
OF THIS STUDY

Aerial View: We will obviously not be able to deal with every event in the Gospels, but the connection between the events as they happen is critical to understand. We will take an aerial view or brief summary of the passage before moving on.

Through Hebrew Eyes: Understanding Jewish culture and history is critical for a full appreciation of the emotions, issues at stake, and reactions of people in the Gospels. When you see the star of David we will try to help you think as a Jew would have thought in that day based on his background, teaching, history, and culture.

Insight into the Passage: The light bulb indicates my brief commentary on the passage. These are insights I have gleaned from my more than thirty-four years of ministry. They have made a deep impact in my life and have been the result of my studies as well as the contributions of many wonderful people along the way.

Snapshot: Context is very important in studying the Scriptures. When you see the camera icon, I will give a brief picture of the current atmosphere—the circumstances and issues leading to the passage or event we are about to study. This will help you gain a feel for the setting in which everything is taking place.

Directions: This is application time when we check our compass. It might be a statement or question concerning where we go from here. It is the "So what? What difference can this make for me right now?" part of this study. This is a place for personal reflection and application of what we have learned.

PART I: BEGINNINGS

God's unique and abiding love for the Hebrew people is unparalleled in human history. Throughout the Old Testament, Israel is called the "bride of God." These nomadic wanderers suffered greatly at the hands of their enemies and for most of their existence have lived under the continual dominance of other nations. Freedom and autonomy is the brass ring they have longed to grasp. They, like each of us, have loved God and yet have disobeyed Him, often trusting in their own abilities rather than in His faithfulness and sovereignty. God's beloved *bride* sought other lovers, yet He continues, even to this day, to pursue them with His unfailing love.

But, God had been strangely silent during the four hundred years from the end of the writing of the Old Testament until the beginning of the New Testament. The flow of communication to His people through the prophets during this period came to a halt, but the Hebrew people continued to anxiously await the coming of *the* Prophet spoken of by Moses (Deut. 18:18–19) and more specifically by Isaiah, the psalmist, Daniel, and others.

As we begin this fascinating adventure in the Gospels, Rome has been in control of Israel since 63 BC. Bitter hatred exists between the Jews and their captors. In the minds of many, God appears to have abandoned His people. Many Jews quietly echo the sentiment of Job, who, amidst great agony of body and soul, cries out to God in his pain. Symbolically shaking his fist to the heavens, he in essence thunders, "God, You know nothing of suffering; You have never experienced the loss of sons as I have. You have never experienced shame and rejection, being abandoned by friends. You sit in Your heaven surrounded by Your holy hosts, but You have no notion of what it is like on this earth. Is there anyone in this vast universe who can identify with my pain? Is there anyone who knows what it's like to be a man?"

And so, in the fullness of time, God responds to the cries of Job and all of His people. At the right time, He wraps Himself in human skin and pitches His tent in the midst of humanity and lives among those He created, identifying with every human emotion and every human hurt. Never again would a man or woman be able to say, "God, You don't understand what it's like to be me." And so we begin the story of God's answer to the dilemma of all humankind....

DAY 1

LUKE EXPLAINS HIS METHOD OF RESEARCH.

READ: Luke 1:1–4

Probably during the early 60s AD, some thirty years after the crucifixion, a passionate follower of Jesus Christ and traveling companion of the apostle Paul took pen in hand and wrote a biography about the Savior. Though others already had written accounts by that time (1:2), Luke apparently wanted to make certain that an orderly and historically accurate account of Jesus' life and ministry was rendered chronologically. Luke was a medical doctor, easily identifiable because he always wore a golf hat (just kidding). As a physician, he places great emphasis on the healing ministry of Jesus. Luke was also a meticulous historian who took great pains to record events *as they happened*. He was the only gospel writer who was *not* a Jew. He writes to fellow Gentiles, specifically Greeks, who were consumed with the concept of the "ideal man." Rather than attack this humanistic flow of thinking, Luke gives great attention to the person of Jesus, as if to say, "You want to hear about a real man? Then listen up!" He wants his Gentile readers to see that Jesus' great message of truth and liberation is now wide open to Gentiles and Jews alike. Luke was not part of the original twelve, but he had interviewed many eyewitnesses who walked with Jesus. Like the no-nonsense Sergeant Friday in the *Dragnet* series of the 1960s, Luke wants "just the facts, ma'am … just the facts." His focus on the chronology of events is unique. (The other accounts record events in keeping with a particular theme that they wanted to underline to specific groups of people.) Luke's theme is simply *Jesus, the Son of Man.*

Luke comes right out of the chute in verses 1–2 by assuring his readers that he wants to set the record straight through the eyes of those who had actually been there and seen it all happen. He writes specifically to a man named Theophilus, also a Gentile, who was probably a Roman official and a new believer. Based on his meticulous research, Luke wants to reassure Theophilus, and us, that the *exact truth* is available to all honest seekers who have *ears to hear.*

THE GOSPEL WRITERS

• There are 89 chapters within the 4 Gospels.

• Only 4 chapters deal with the birth and first 30 years of Jesus' life.

• 85 chapters deal with the last 3 years of Jesus' life.

• 27 of the 89 chapters deal with the last week in Jesus' life.

Theophilus means "one who loves God." Luke refers to him as "most excellent." This indicates that he was probably a Roman official or at least a person of wealth or high position.

THE GOSPEL OF MATTHEW: Matthew was a converted customs agent (Matt. 9:9) and one of the original twelve apostles. He writes a detailed account of Jesus' life. Lies were being spread by Jesus' enemies, and many sought personal gain from this new "movement." Matthew shows that the events of Jesus' life were powerfully foretold by the prophets hundreds of years prior to His coming. Writing to Greek-speaking Jews, Matthew shows them that Jesus is the fulfillment of their dreams and their history. Sixty-two times he quotes the Old Testament, arguing that Jesus is the completion to their greatest longings. Matthew's theme is *Jesus, the King of the Jews.*

THE GOSPEL OF MARK: Mark was also called John Mark in Acts 12:12. Peter refers to him as his "son in the faith" (1 Peter 5:13). Mark would later accompany Paul and Barnabas on Paul's first missionary journey. He deserted the team and returned home (Acts 13:13) but became helpful to Paul in later years. Though he was not among the original apostles, Mark gained much personal insight and information from Peter, with whom he shared a special closeness. Mark writes to Romans with an unflinching sense of immediacy. He wants his readers to get off the beach and dive head first into the waters of life. Mark is an action guy with a great sense of aliveness and enthusiasm. He uses the word *immediately* (Mark 1:12) at least forty times in his account, stressing the urgency Jesus felt and knowing that this would appeal to Roman thinking. Probably written in the late 50s or early 60s AD, Mark's theme is *Jesus the Messiah, the Servant of Jehovah.*

THE GOSPEL OF JOHN: John is thought to have written his gospel while in exile on the Isle of Patmos, sometime around AD 90. He writes much concerning the deity of Jesus. Unlike the Synoptic Gospels (Matthew, Mark, and Luke), John writes more concerning the things Jesus said (His discourses) rather than what He did (His miracles). As the eldest of the four writers, John probably read the other accounts many times, and his maturity and the wisdom of his years may have made him more intent on communicating the *heart* of Jesus to his readers rather than His *works*. Ninety percent of the content in John's gospel is not found in the parallel accounts. John's gospel is the only book in the Bible written primarily for the nonbeliever. John's theme is *Jesus, the Son of God.*

John Pictures Jesus as the Word.

READ: John 1:1–18

John wants his readers to know that Jesus (*Yeshua*) is unlike anyone who ever set foot on the planet. The Word existed from the beginning of time. In fact, the Word was another way of referring to God. The Word is, therefore, a Person. The Word is not simply information *about* Jesus, the Word *is* Jesus. Every created thing finds its origin in the Person, Jesus. Within this living, breathing personal Word is the sum total of everything concerning life. This Word even has the ability to scatter darkness and illuminate everything and everyone He touches.

In order to prepare the world for His coming, God sent a Jew named John (*Yohnanan*) to ready the hearts of people for this new *Light* that was to follow. This living Word became flesh and lived among those to whom He came to give life. He came to His own people, the Jews. Most of them rejected Him, but many Gentiles accepted His free gift of life and became sons of God.

Notice that "Word" is capitalized, indicating a proper name. The Greek rendering is *logos*, a person possessing intellect, emotion, and will. To a Jew, it was a way of referring to God. Therefore, John is saying that God came to earth as the living Word. Everything the ancient rabbis taught about the Word was fulfilled in this person, Jesus Christ.

> *Write a brief definition of the "gospel" as it is typically used today. ("We left our former church because the minister didn't preach the gospel.")*

If the Word is a person and not simply doctrinal information, can we not properly conclude that the "gospel" is also a person? Most believers speak of the "gospel" as if it is certain theological principles and doctrinal facts that must be included if we are to be true to the Scriptures. Consider the definition you just wrote. Have you left anything out? Have you added something that

---

You may wonder how these men could have remembered exact conversations and teachings of Jesus 30–60 years after the fact. There were no pens and notebooks so memorization was a critical discipline of the ancient Jews. However, this is not a story 4 guys glued together and called "the Gospels." Every word is from the very breath of God. How can we know they were accurate? In John 14:26, Jesus tells them that the Holy Spirit will give them perfect recall. (He will "bring to your remembrance all that I have said to you.")

What is the most important verse in the Bible? A friend asked me that once. "I believe that it is John 1:1," he said. I've come to believe he is right. If the Word (Jesus) was not God and did not come and dwell among us, the rest is just a good idea and really doesn't matter all that much. Every doctrine rests on the person of Jesus as God. Without this person as the living Gospel, we are left with high-sounding rhetoric with no power to make it come alive within us.

need not be there? Are you positive? Is it compatible with biblical truth? What about sincere, godly men and women who would render a somewhat different definition than yours? You can see the problem. If the Gospels were basically doctrinal information about Jesus (His birth, His life, His teachings, His miracles, His death, His resurrection, His ascension, and His return, etc.), all of this and more would have to be specifically stated every time someone spoke or taught. If anything is left out, the *gospel* will not have been preached according to someone's or some denomination's definition. What would your former pastor have had to actually say each Sunday for you to feel he had "preached the gospel"? We will never all agree on every point, but we can agree that the gospel *is* this unique, God-man, Jesus Christ, fully and completely, and believe if He is lifted up as the centerpiece, the whole world will feel welcome to gather around Him, explore His free gift of life, and become His companion.

GENEALOGIES LISTED BY MATTHEW (1:1–17) AND LUKE (3:12–38)

READ: Matt. 1:1–17; Luke 3:12–38 (What would possess Luke and Matthew to list all of these unpronounceable names?)

READ: Luke 1:5–25

Matthew lists Joseph's family line to make a strategic point that Joseph was not Jesus' father. Joseph did not beget Jesus but was simply the husband of the woman who was His mother. Luke shows in his gospel that Jesus is a descendant of the house of David and *could* therefore qualify as king.

The Jews have always stressed the importance of understanding their uniqueness, of knowing where and from whom they have come. Roots have critical importance, for Israel's faith was deeply imbedded in their history and culture. Knowledge of their Hebrew beginnings is central to biblical thought. To a Jewish person in the time of Jesus, reading the Holy Scriptures was like reading a family album. The destruction of the temple in AD 70 was so traumatic, because in addition to the loss of 1.1 million lives, all of the genealogical records stored there were destroyed by fire, and that precious information was lost forever.

No doctrine and no religion can bridge the gap that separates people across the globe. Only the person of Jesus can "draw all men" to Himself (John 12:32). Doctrine is a tool that God uses to change our perception of reality, but only the person of Jesus can change the heart. Everything was intended to revolve around this person. Life is a person (Col. 3:4); Truth is a person (John 14:6); Love is a person (1 John 4:16). A particular theology may draw some, but only the person of Jesus can draw every human being. If we gather around the centrality of Jesus, our theological differences will slowly dissipate because our desire will change from wanting to be right to wanting only Him.

Five women appear in Matthew's genealogy:

- *Tamar:* A Jew *Rahab:* A Gentile prostitute

- *Ruth:* A Moabite

- *Bathsheba:* A temptress who brought down a king

- *Mary:* A simple peasant girl

Matthew is telling us that a new age is coming; a time when Jews and Gentiles, men and women, saints and sinners will all be on equal footing with God. The Messiah will make no distinctions. This would have been revolutionary.

Important to know here is that Matthew and Luke are showing, in different ways, that Jesus was the stepson of Joseph, not a biological son. They both seem to be saying to their readers, "Whatever else you may be thinking, let's agree on this as a beginning thesis: Jesus is fully qualified to be the Messiah. He fits every standard proclaimed by God through the voice of the prophets. He is the legitimate candidate."

PART II: THE BIRTH AND GROWTH OF JOHN THE BAPTIST AND JESUS

The great drama begins! The angel Gabriel announces to Zacharias that his wife, Elizabeth, will have a son who will prepare the Hebrew people for the coming of the Messiah. Six months later, Gabriel visits a teenage girl named Mary and tells her that she will be the mother of the long-awaited Messiah. We will see the amazing circumstances surrounding Jesus' birth and the family's subsequent escape from Herod into Egypt. As Jesus grows into manhood, God the Father will wake Him each morning and teach Him (Isa. 50:4–9). In His deity, Jesus knew all things, but in His humanity He would learn as He grew in manhood (Heb. 5:8).

DAY 2

THE BIRTH OF JOHN THE BAPTIST

READ: Luke 1:5–25

Herod is a very complex character. He was born an Arab, his religion was Jewish, he was culturally Greek and politically a Roman. As a young man he personally led his army in 10 wars. He had sided with Anthony and Cleopatra against Octavian, who became Augustus Caesar. After Anthony lost the battle, Herod forcefully and confidently went in to face Octavian, whom he had fought against giving food, weapons, and ships to the enemy. Without flinching, he said to Octavian, "Let not Caesar ask whose friend I was. Let Caesar ask what kind of friend I was. Caesar decided Herod was a man who would be loyal and trustworthy, so he placed him in authority over the Jews.

Herod the Great was the reigning king in Jerusalem, but when John was born, he was nearing the end of his reign. His reign over Israel began in 37 BC and lasted until his death in 4 BC. He was appointed by the Romans and was viewed as a sort of caretaker monarch who would keep the Jewish people under control. He suffered from paranoia, always fearful that his crown would be stolen from him. Ruthless and bloodthirsty, he put to death anyone he even mildly suspected of usurping his authority. Married to ten wives during his life, Herod had three of them and at least three of his sons killed for that very reason. He was an elaborate builder, mostly for the edification of himself and for places to protect him from the wrath of his enemies. He was deeply hated by the Pharisees because of his contempt for the laws of God and by the Sadducees, who resented him for severely curtailing their power and influence. Herod was an Edomite of Arab descent who supposedly converted to Judaism but was never considered a true Jew. His paranoia about losing his position is clearly seen when he hears that a child has been born in Judea who is said to be the King of the Jews. Calculating that the Christ-child is around two years old, he ordered all male children of that age throughout the district to be killed.

Herod was well aware of his unpopularity among the Jews and feared that no one would mourn on the day he died. He ordered that prominent families (men, women, and children) be gathered together and herded into the Hippodrome (a large stadium arena) and put to death the moment he died so that there would be mourning throughout the land on that day. Upon his death, his wife mercifully released all of the people, subverting his evil wishes. Rather than Herod the Great, Herod the *Paranoid* may be a more fitting title for him at the end of his life.

Zacharias and Elizabeth were a devout couple, advanced in years and childless. Zacharias was a member of one of twenty-four priestly divisions who rotated serving in the temple for a week at a time. By the casting of lots, Zacharias is chosen to enter the temple and offer the sacrifice at the altar. Because no one but the priest may enter into the Holy of Holies, a rope would have been tied around his waist in order to pull him out in the event that he died performing his duties. While the priest was inside, the people gathered outside to pray that the offering would be acceptable to God. As Zacharias enters the temple, he immediately becomes fearful. Why? He sees an angel, but where the angel stood was the cause of his great fear.

Remember that God had been strangely silent for 400 years between the writing of the Old and New Testaments. All of a sudden, He speaks through the angel Gabriel to Zacharias. If the shock of that encounter wasn't enough, he is now told that his elderly and barren wife is pregnant.

Entering the Holy of Holies always carried with it a sense of great anticipation and honor mixed with fear. Jewish tradition stated that if the priest entered the Holy of Holies and an angel appeared at the right side of the altar, God was displeased with the offering and the priest would die. Though there is no record of this ever happening, the possibility was always on their mind. On the other hand, a feast would immediately follow the priest's exit to celebrate his safe return.

The angel tells Zacharias that he and Elizabeth will have a son who will be great in the sight of the Lord and filled with the Holy Spirit, even while in his mother's womb. He will prepare the way for the Messiah. This declaration was too much for Zacharias to process; his faith had never been tested at this level. Because of his unbelief, the angel Gabriel removes Zacharias's ability to speak. He emerges from the temple deeply shaken and remains mute for the next nine months.

Keep in mind as you study that so much myth has grown up around familiar stories and passages in the Bible that we often confuse cultural ideas with biblical truth. We are attempting to, in a sense, rescue the truth from familiarity. It is easy to hear so much, so often that truth is lost in the process.

Zacharias was a victim of tradition. It kept him from believing the truth. Just for fun, put a B beside only the following quotations that are from the Bible.

1. _____ "Charity begins at home."
2. _____ "Above all, to thine own self be true."
3. _____ "God helps those who help themselves."
4. _____ "Never a borrower or a lender be."
5. _____ "Cleanliness is next to godliness."
6. _____ "The Devil can cite Scripture for his own purpose."

Answers on next page

Can you think of any Christian traditions that are more cultural than biblical?

Throughout the Gospels, we will observe in the Jewish mind-set a *cause-and-effect* mentality. If a baby was born deformed, for instance, there must be a specific reason for God's displeasure with that child. In John 9, the disciples, who had grown up under pharisaic Judaism, ask Jesus if the man born blind was caused by *his* sin (in his mother's womb) or by *the sin of his parents*, illustrating the prevalent Jewish thinking.

Consider the fact that Elizabeth is childless. Her barrenness would have been considered a great shame in first-century Jewish culture. This *cause-and-effect* mentality would foster the natural assumption that she and her husband had secretly sinned against God and were paying the price. Many believers still think that way today.

Imagine being saddled with this kind of guilt all your life. Consider for a moment what God is doing here. This faithful couple painfully accepts their plight of childlessness. At the point where they have finally given up the dream of having children, God comes through against all odds. What does this say to you about *learning to give up?* We are taught always to persevere and to persist; however, it is often when we finally give up our desires and dreams that God comes through in miraculous ways. Can you think of any personal examples of this?

Write and discuss (if in a group) what it means to "die to your dreams."

Answers
from previous page
None are from the Bible.

*1, 3, and 5 are quotes
coined by Benjamin
Franklin, 2 and 4 are
from Shakespeare's*
Hamlet, *6 is from* The
Merchant of Venice.

DAY 3

GABRIEL TELLS MARY THAT SHE IS PREGNANT WITH GOD'S SON. SHE VISITS HER COUSIN ELIZABETH AND IS OVERWHELMED WITH GRATITUDE.

READ: Luke 1:26–58

Six months after his appearance to Zacharias, the angel Gabriel tells a young Jewish virgin, presently engaged to a young man named Joseph, that she is pregnant with the long-awaited Messiah. It is interesting to contrast the reaction of Zacharias, an elderly man and religious leader, and Mary, a fourteen-to-sixteen-year-old teenager, when they are both confronted with Gabriel's news. Zacharias, an elderly man and a religious leader, and Mary, a teenager, were both understandably startled when confronted by the angel Gabriel. Mary questions the angel, as does Zacharias. However, there was an obvious difference in that Zacharias was punished by losing his speech until the birth of his son, and Mary was not.

Read and compare the two encounters with Gabriel and the difference between Zacharias's response (1:11–22) and Mary's response (1:28–38).

The great surprise to Mary would not have been that the Messiah would not come in the natural manner of birth.

Jews knew the Scriptures and would be quite familiar with the manner of the Messiah's coming. Read Isa. 7:14; 11:1–2; 40:3–5; Mal. 3:1; Isa. 52:13–53:12.

The astonishment would have been that she was the chosen girl to be the catalyst in His coming. Dating back 700 years to the time of Isaiah, all Jewish girls dreamed of possibly being "the one."

What would have been the one prophecy about the Messiah that would probably have caused Mary to think she would not be the one? (See Mic. 5:2.)

_____
_____
_____

An engagement back then was far more binding than today. It was sealed by a wedding contract called a *ketubah*. This engagement contract was practically equivalent to marriage and could be broken only by a "bill of divorcement." *Take a guess from the following options at what age a young man and a young woman would be considered ready for marriage.*

A Jewish girl:	*A Jewish boy:*
a) 12	a) 13
b) 12 yrs. + 1 day	b) 14
c) 13	c) 16
d) 14 ½	d) 18

Answers
on next page

17

The angel Gabriel is highly regarded in Jewish theology as a messenger from God. He is pictured in rabbinic writings as standing before the throne of God. For Gabriel to be sent specifically to Zacharias implies that he was a major topic of discussion in the "board room" in heaven, an incredible honor for him.

STAND IN MARY'S SANDALS: You are a young teenage girl. In the months to come, your pregnancy will become obvious public knowledge. No word would be articulate enough and no connections with the right people would be adequate enough to explain away the obvious. You are powerless over the dilemma that confronts you. You will need to learn a new level of trust that God will protect you in at least three basic relationships:

- You will have to entrust yourself to God for your relationship with your fiancé. *Describe your emotions after you begin to process what you have been told.*

- You will have to trust God to protect you from slander within your community. *How will your child be viewed as He grows up?*

- You will have to trust God for your personal safety. *The penalty for a betrothed virgin found with child was* _____ *(Lev. 20:10).*

A creative way to study this passage autobiographically is to write (on a separate page) an imaginary dialogue between Elizabeth and Mary as they thought and dreamed together over those 3 months. Keep in mind their age difference, their fears, their joy, and all the unanswered questions before them.

This great news is a heavy load for anyone, especially a young girl Mary's age. The implications are unprecedented and overwhelming. Often God does things that may seem illogical to us at the time because He thinks so differently that we do. Consider Joshua being told the battle plan to take Jericho. Marching in circles around the city and blowing a horn would hardly be included in any military strategy manual, yet Joshua obeyed this illogical command and God came through.

Can you think of a way God has done this sort of thing in your life or in the lives of others? (Write and discuss.)

Mary visits her cousin Elizabeth, who is six months pregnant. As Mary arrives, John jumps within Elizabeth's womb at the presence of the unborn Savior within Mary's womb. Mary is overwhelmed with gratitude to God and praises Him (Luke 1:46–56), referring to Him as "God my Savior." Mary knew she was not sinless and needed a Savior (v. 47). She stays with Elizabeth almost three months until just prior to John's birth.

BE THE WOMEN: Think about the conversations these two women must have had during those three months. Be Mary and Elizabeth. With what you are learning about Jewish society, their circumstances, and what they know from their teaching about the coming Messiah, use your imagination and write down the thoughts and questions they must have had.

◆ "You're What?!" Mary Returns Home to Tell Joseph (Matt. 1:18–25).

DAY 4

JOHN'S BIRTH, CHILDHOOD, AND TIME IN THE WILDERNESS

READ: Luke 1:57–80

Eight days after John's birth, according to Jewish law, he is taken to the temple to be circumcised and dedicated. It was Jewish custom for the father to name the child after a relative, living or dead. Finally, after nine months, Zacharias's speech returns to him, and he firmly says that the child's name shall be John, although no relative on either side of the family bore that name.

The name John means "grace," indicating that God is now planning to do a whole new thing. From now on, God's faithful will no longer follow Him out of *duty* and *obligation*, but out of *desire*, which is the essence of grace.

> *Be honest. On a scale of 1 to 10 (1=lowest amount of obligation; 10=highest), how much of your spiritual walk is out of obligation?* _____

John will spend much of his life in the wilderness preparing for his great calling. Though obviously instructed by godly parents, they were very old

Consider this: Jesus was the only person who was ever born as a result of His own choice. The rest of us were born because someone else made the choice. In fact, Jesus most certainly sat in on the meeting to decide whom His mother was going to be.

by the time of his bar mitzvah at age thirteen. Luke says he lived in the wilderness until he began his ministry at age thirty. Why? Probably to be kept apart from the erroneous teaching of pharisaic Judaism, which permeated Jewish society. There, in the wilderness, he was probably being privately instructed by God in a similar manner to Jesus (Isa. 50:4–9).

John will not merely be a forerunner, but he will have the office of a *prophet*. The Hebrew word for prophet is *navi*, and it signifies a spokesperson or one who speaks for a divine power to human beings. *The idea of prophecy is based on a belief in a God on whom the destiny and the well-being of humankind depends.*

The Birth of Jesus

READ: Matt. 1:18–25; Luke 2:1–7

It would have been a painful time for Mary and Joseph after she returns from her three-month visit with Elizabeth. Joseph is confused and believes he should end the engagement quietly to protect Mary. Finally, an angel intercedes and explains that the Holy Spirit has planted the seed in her womb and that she will bear a Son named Immanuel ("God with us"). Imagine, God is coming to earth and out of all of the women in the world, you have been personally picked by God to be the vehicle of His coming.

Notice how binding an engagement was in Jewish life as Matthew refers to Joseph as Mary's _____ in verse 19 even before they were married.

THOUGHTS FOR DISCUSSION

1. As Jesus grew, do you think He was ever confronted directly with the false charge of being illegitimate?

2. How would *you* answer the charge that Jesus was born out of wedlock?

As descendants of David, Joseph and Mary were required to return to Bethlehem. Since Mary was also of the house of David, she, too, was probably required to enroll. In Syria, the Roman province in which the Holy Land was located, girls twelve years and over were required to pay a poll tax. When viewed from a human perspective, the couple came to Bethlehem because it was required by the law. From the divine perspective, however, God was acting providentially to bring them to the place where Micah had prophesied that the Messiah would be born (Mic. 5:2–5).

THE DATE OF JESUS' BIRTH

There has been much speculation concerning the date and season of Jesus' birth, but we can get fairly close through some basic deductions.

- Historians are relatively certain that Herod the Great died in the year 4 BC. The Bible tells us he was alive when Jesus was born; therefore, Jesus had to have been born before 4 BC.
- We also know that Herod spent the year prior to his death in Jericho, which would have been 5 BC.
- When Herod met with the magi, he did so in Jerusalem, pushing the time to possibly late 6 or early 5 BC. Herod's order to kill all male babies two years of age confirms that his calculations at that time were that Jesus had been alive up to two years.
- We also know that the decree of Cyrenius, governor of Syria, concerning taxation began in 8 BC and continued for several years.

BORN ON CHRISTMAS DAY?

Most scholars also agree that December would not have been the month of Jesus' birth. We can rule out springtime because Caesar would have realized that in an agrarian society, the Jews would never have been willing to leave their crops during planting and harvesting season for a census. Also Caesar would have avoided such sacred festivals as Pentecost, Passover, and the Feast of Tabernacles, which occurred during that time of year. Winter would have made traveling difficult. Also in winter the shepherds would not have been "in the fields keeping watch over their flocks" (except for the temple sheep used for sacrifices). One window of opportunity for an agricultural tax would have been late summer when harvesting was complete, planting had not begun, travel was easier, and there were no religious festivals. So, it appears that late August or early September may have been a plausible time for the birth of Jesus to have occurred.

All of this about dates and times of Jesus' birth is a matter of great conjecture. It is not something to get bent out of shape over. Our problem is the myths and traditions that have developed around the Christmas celebration. Sometimes the myths are harmless, but other times understanding the true biblical, cultural, and historical realities will help us see a fuller and more accurate picture of the events and of God Himself.

DAY 5

THE BIRTH ANNOUNCEMENT TO THE SHEPHERDS

Imagine being a peasant with a job that ranks at the bottom of the social ladder, in a country and among a people who have been oppressed for generations. Got the picture? Now imagine the angel Gabriel, the greatest angel of them all, appearing to you and your friends one night and telling you that a Savior has come to "save" you and your people. "Why would Israel need saving?" you would wonder. "We're the ones who are oppressed. It's those jerks who run the Roman Empire who have got their foot on our necks. They are the ones who need saving." You'd have a point, if you were a Jew. It is difficult to go into any oppressed culture and have people be receptive to "being saved" because they naturally think in terms of "level of offense" rather than the "condition of the heart."

READ: Luke 2:8–20

♦ **The Glory of God Surrounds a Group of Obscure Shepherds.**

After telling us where the shepherds were and what they are doing, Luke says that "an angel of the Lord suddenly stood before them, and the Glory of God shone around them; and they were terribly frightened." Have you ever considered what the "Glory of God" was? Was it just an extremely bright light and some sort of mystical presence? The Old Testament really makes this passage come alive.

The *Glory of God* had not been seen by anyone on the earth in almost six hundred years. During the wanderings of Israel in the wilderness, the Glory of God appeared as a *cloud by day* to shelter the Hebrews from the sun and *fire by night* to keep them warm. The *Glory of God* had last been seen by Ezekiel in a vision when he was held captive in Babylon. Solomon's temple, where the *Glory* was then residing, was burned to the ground by the Babylonians in 586 BC. Before its destruction, God allowed Ezekiel to see the *Glory* depart from the temple, move to the threshold of the temple, then move to the eastern gate of the city, then hover over the Mount of Olives, and go back to heaven (Ezek. 9—11). The *Glory of God* had not been seen by any human being for almost six hundred years. Is it any wonder that the shepherds were so frightened?

Shepherds made up the bottom rung of the social ladder. They were considered untrustworthy, and their testimony was not valid in a court of law. How interesting that God chose these men to be the first Jews to see the Messiah. Why would anyone try to fabricate something like this?

♦ **The Shepherds Are Given a Specific Sign.**

After telling the shepherds the amazing news of the Savior's birth, the angel gives them what sign to help them identify the baby (of the following choices)?

a) That He would be lying in a manger.

b) That He would be wrapped in cloths.

c) Both.

Many scholars believe that the "cloths" were actually *burial cloths* used for wrapping a deceased body in preparation for burial. That being so, the uniqueness of the sign would have been the burial cloths, not the manger. The sign would point to the fact that this child was "born to die" (see John 12:27). But Dr. Ken Bailey, an expert on Middle Eastern culture, asserts that the significance of the wrapping cloths was that it actually freed these simple peasants to do what the angel had said. He states that these simple shepherds would never have felt comfortable entering the home of a person or family of royal lineage. Since the baby was wrapped in these common strips of cloth, these men would identify the family as peasants, just as they were. The *cloths* gave the shepherds the green light to feel welcome, and it also made a statement that the Messiah will open the doors of salvation and acceptance to everyone, regardless of status, gender, or nationality.

◆ **The Baby Would Be Lying in a Manger.**

Many homes were built over caves where the animals stayed under the house at night and during bad weather. The house was called a *kataluma*, containing one or two guest rooms. Apparently, those rooms were occupied, so the owner, probably a family friend, allowed Mary and Joseph to stay in the family room. But why the term *manger*? At the end of this room would have been a few steps that allowed the owner to put feed in a wooden trough for the animals under the house. Mary would have been at the end of this main room, not giving birth among the cow chips.

In his book *Jesus Through Middle Eastern Eyes*, Dr. Ken Bailey states that through our Western perspective we have assumed that Mary went into labor shortly after or during the couple's arrival in Bethlehem. Read Luke 2:6 in several translations. What does it indicate? "While they were there, the days were completed for her to give birth." Dr. Bailey asserts that Mary and Joseph could have been there from several days to a week or more before Jesus was born. Why is this important? First, Joseph was from Bethlehem, the city of David. Second, he was of David's royal line. Third, Middle Eastern people are extremely hospitable.

Therefore, there is no _____ for those in Christ Jesus (Rom. 8:1).

Though your sins are as scarlet, they will be as _____ as snow (Isa. 1:8).

One day all believers will stand in God's presence _____ and with _____ (Jude 24).

Our identity does not come from what we have done, whether good or bad. Our identity comes from what God has done on our behalf.

Had the conditions been like our traditional manger scenes, dozens of relatives and friends would have known of her whereabouts. The most likely scenario is that the guest room was occupied, so the host took the young couple into the main room where the family lives. When the time came, the men would have left the house, and Mary would have given birth in the main room of the home and then laid the baby in the wooden manger on fresh straw, just slightly below the surface of the living area.

◆ Peace Is Guaranteed to Those with Whom God Is Pleased.

Because we seldom read these passages except during the euphoria of the Christmas season, it is easy to miss the critical impact of what is implied as well as stated. Do you find it interesting that the angel links *peace* with *God's favor?* It makes sense, but it should make you nervous if you view it the way most of us have been taught. Let's illustrate: Answer the following questions as honestly as you can:

As God looks at you, is He pleased with what He sees? (yes or no) _____

How would you rate His pleasure with you on a scale of 1–10? _____
(1=low, 10=high)

What was the basis for the number you wrote? "My rating was based on
_____._"

Does your number reflect (a) your behavior or (b) who you are as a person? _____

Unless we are firmly convinced of our identity, we will never be able to adequately deal with temptation. We will see this clearly in the life of Jesus when He is baptized and then goes head to head with Satan himself. God spoke at His baptism saying, "This is my Son in whom I am well pleased." This was as much for Jesus' sake as for the crowd's. The assurance of who He was would have been crucial when Satan questioned His identity as the Son of God.

Even as devoted followers of Jesus, our tendency is to always see ourselves through the avenue of what we *do* or *don't do.* "I'm a doctor, I'm a teacher, I'm a banker." None of these define who we are; they simply tell how we earn a living. When asked if God is pleased with you, most have been trained to immediately think of what we what have done lately. "I've had lustful thoughts, I lied to my spouse, I haven't had a quiet time this week," etc. We think of our *behavior,* but that was not the question. Is God pleased with you—your person, the heart and essence of who you are from God's point of view?

The Scriptures say some fascinating things about people who know Jesus. There are scores of verses about the believer's identity, but here are a few to look up.

I am a _____ of Jesus Christ (John 15:15).

I have been made _____ (Col. 2:10).

I am _____ for all time (Heb. 10:14).

I am _____ and _____ (Eph. 1:4; Col.1:22).

I am totally _____ (Col. 2:13).

I am _____ in His sight (Isa. 43:4).

I am the _____ of God (2 Cor. 5:21).

I am a _____(Eph. 1:1; Col. 1:2).

If we define ourselves by our performance, we are never free to fail. We must succeed at all times. Success becomes our rite of passage. We then will discover that we have, out of necessity, redefined success to mean accomplishment rather than the biblical notion of faithfulness.

OUR NEW IDENTITY: From the moment we receive Jesus into our lives, our identity changes. God never defines us by our *behavior* but sees us just as we were the day we were completely "cleansed by His blood." God always sees us as *holy, blameless, forgiven saints,* regardless of how awful our behavior may be or has been. Does behavior matter? You bet it does! Sin is serious business to God. He hates it! (The same could be said of our independence, disobedience, and attempts to be in control, but He is never displeased with *who we are.*)

If the glory of God is now present in the life of the believer, how can we ever again think of ourselves as worthless?

Let's go one step further. Are you (a) a sinner saved by grace or (b) a saint?

_____

The apostle Paul said, "For I have not shunned to declare unto you all the counsel of God" (Acts 20:27 KJV).

Which of the above statements reflects more humility, a or b? _____

ME A SAINT? Seeing myself as a *saint* is both the more *biblical* and the more *humble* of the statements. It is more biblical because the Bible continually refers to believers as *saints* (1 Cor. 1:2; 2 Cor. 1:1; Eph. 1:1; Phil. 1:1). It's true that we were *sinners* before we met Jesus and we were also *saved by grace,* but as a "new creation" we no longer can be defined by what we *were* even though we still commit sin. Why? Because sins are *what you do, not who you are. Who you are* is a *saint* who sometimes messes up. To see yourself as a saint is more *humble* because it has nothing to do with anything you achieved or earned. You didn't make yourself a saint or even come up with the title. God did!

Why is considering your identity so important? Because what you believe about yourself will determine your behavior.

THE OBJECTION: Paul called himself *chief of sinners* (1 Tim. 1:15). Correct! But you can't just pull a verse like this out of context. What had Paul been speaking of in verses 13–14? What a jerk he had been. He had been a despicable sinner! Now, in verse 15 he is saying that *we can fully trust the fact that Jesus came into the world to save people like this, and he personally tops the list.* This is not a statement of how he sees himself now. If that were so, the verses you looked up on the previous page plus dozens more would be contradictory. We have to study the Scripture based on the full counsel of the Scripture. In other words, a principle must be traced through sixty-six books, not pulled out of context and a theology built on a single verse.

Why is understanding what the angel said to the shepherds so critical? If you do not believe God is pleased with you as a person, you will spend the rest of your life trying to make yourself pleasing to Him. There are not enough verses you can memorize, Bible studies you can attend, or sins that you can avoid for you to ever feel deserving of God's favor. You will become disillusioned, cynical, and dissatisfied with everything about your life and will never understand or experience *peace.* How can a believer be at peace if he or she can never do enough to achieve God's favor? It's impossible!

The Glory of God returned to earth as the shepherds stood in awe. During His time on earth, the Glory resided in Jesus. When He ascended into heaven the Glory of God left with Him, but the Glory later returned at Pentecost (Acts 2). Where does the Glory of God now dwell? _____ _____ (Col. 1:27)

How can a believer have the living God take up residence inside of him and still be determined to define himself by the sins he commits rather than by the Glory that lives within him?

DAY 6

The Wise Men Visit Jesus.

READ: Luke 2:21–38; Matt. 2:1–12

Just as we saw with John the Baptist, Jesus is taken to the temple on the eighth day after His birth to be circumcised, according to Jewish law (Luke 2:21). Two basic reasons for circumcision were (1) identity as a Jew and descendant of Abraham and (2) it pointed to a person's submission to the law. A woman was considered impure for forty days after the birth of a son (eighty days for a daughter). Mary goes to the temple to take a purification bath and as the firstborn, Jesus was offered to the Lord as well (Ex. 13:2, 12).

At the dedication of a Jewish baby, typically a lamb would be sacrificed at the temple. However, Jewish law allows for a pair of turtledoves or two young pigeons to be substituted if the couple doesn't have the financial means to buy a lamb. Mary and Joseph exercised that option due to their limited resources.

◆ **In Babylon, Some Astrologers (Magi) See a Hovering Star.**

Who were these people and why would they travel six to seven hundred miles to pay homage to a Jewish baby? There are many myths surrounding the magi. They were *not* kings. They were astrologers, men of wisdom who were well versed in medicine and natural science. They served as advisers to the king not unlike a presidential special council would do today. The fact that there were three gifts brought to Jesus has led us to generally accept the notion that there were three wise men. In fact, some scholars speculate that several hundred may have traveled in the caravan. People were safer traveling in large groups and never traveled at night, as robbers and thieves were abundant. The magi were not Jews but worshipped Zoroaster, a pagan god. They were interested in spiritual things and would often interpret dreams. What would cause them to leave home and family and make a journey of this magnitude? How did they know to follow the star and where it would lead? The answer is found in the Old Testament.

 AN AMAZING STORY: In 606 BC, King Nebuchadnezzar invaded Jerusalem, the capital of the southern kingdom of Judah. He took

Some scholars believe the magi may have come from southern Arabia based on their interpretation of the phrase "from the east." They state that for a Roman to read that, east would have meant Babylon. However, others argue that as a Jew, east would have meant the other side of the Jordan, which is the Arabian desert. We may never know for certain, but Babylon seems more likely when linked with other events in Scripture.

The astrologers would have known, after Jesus' birth, about a star from the writings of Daniel. Also, Balaam, who was from Babylon (Num. 22:5; Deut. 23:4) had spoken of the star (Num. 24:15–17; Dan. 9:24–25).

the first of three waves of Jews back to Babylon as his slaves. Nine years later, thousands more were taken. Among them was a handsome young man named Daniel. He refused to eat the diet ordered by the king for all of the slaves and was forced to enroll in the school of astrology, but his solid grounding in the truth of God could not subvert his beliefs. In 536 BC, Nebuchadnezzar took the final wave of Jews into captivity and burned Solomon's temple to the ground. One night the king has a dream that causes him great distress. He calls together his advisers who were astrologers (wise men) and demands that they interpret his dream. But the king is smart. He also demands that they tell him what the dream is about so that he can not be tricked with a false answer. If these wise counselors could not deliver, they were to be killed. One night God speaks to Daniel in a vision concerning the dream. Daniel goes in and tells the king both the content and meaning of the dream. His action saves all of the astrologers from death and he becomes a kind of folk hero among generations of grateful "wise men" and their families. Because of their admiration for Daniel and because most of the book of Daniel was written in Aramaic (the common language of Babylon), the wise men would have been able to calculate the number of years until the coming of the Messiah and the appearance of the star (see Dan. 9:24–25). (NOTE: A week of years was equal to seven years. They would have also been aware of Numbers 24:17: "A star will come forth from Jacob.") So these astrologers, because of their gratitude to Daniel for saving their ancestors and their deep interest in his writings, would have spent much time looking into the skies as the appointed time drew near.

♦ **After Being Received by Herod in Jerusalem, the Magi Visit Jesus.**

A military escort would undoubtedly have met this sizable caravan of visitors at the outskirts of the city and brought them to Herod. As mentioned earlier, Herod was extremely paranoid about losing his position and authority. As rumors fly, he is fearful that the birth of a baby said to be the long-awaited king is a direct threat to him. His inquiries about the baby's location are thinly disguised attempts to launch a concerted campaign to kill the baby Jesus just as he had done with several of his wives and sons whom he believed threatened his throne.

The trip from Babylon to Jerusalem and on to Bethlehem, some seven hundred miles, could have taken months. A day's travel in antiquity would have been about seventeen miles. When Herod calculates the age of the child based on the time when the magi first saw the star, He orders the death of every male child up to two years old. Note that Jews calculated the age of a child from the time of conception, not the actual birth. Therefore we are probably talking about fifteen months old in terms of our modern-day understanding.

◆ **The Magi Bring Gifts for the Christ Child.**

- *Gold* signifying _____. (The means for Mary, Joseph, and Jesus' flight to Egypt. They stayed up to two years until Herod's death in 4 BC.)
- *Frankincense* signifying _____. (A resin from the bark of a tree that grows in southern Arabia; stipulated by Moses for use in "sacrificial fumigation." Jesus would be our perfect sacrifice [Dan. 9:26] being "cut off," which means sacrificially killed.)
- *Myrrh* signifying _____. (Myrrh was used for embalming.)

◆ **Two Dreams Foil the Scheme of Herod (Matt. 2:12–13).**

Two warnings from God find their mark: The magi are warned to return home by an alternate route than the one first planned, and Joseph is warned in a dream to flee to Egypt and stay there until the death of Herod. The escape of the magi is seldom discussed but is fascinating as we learn about Herod and his obsessive need for control. During that time, military guards would have been posted at every exit leading from the country. This caravan of men would have been under heavy surveillance.

Herod knew he had been tricked. How then do you imagine the magi were able to escape his wrath?

Sovereignty of God or simply coincidence? Two teenagers and a newborn infant are forced to flee to a strange land without the means to support their family. Was the gold brought to them by the magi simply a happy coincidence or was an all-knowing God aware six hundred years prior that a financial pledge would be critical for the young couple as they fled abroad? Was Daniel's heroic answer to the king's dream, which saved the lives of those magi's ancestors, causing them to revere Daniel and his descendant, the Christ child, merely happenstance? *Write your thoughts.*

DAY 7

JESUS IS TAKEN FROM EGYPT TO NAZARETH WHERE HE WILL GROW INTO MANHOOD.

READ: Matt. 2:19–23; Luke 2:39–40

Why did Jesus and His parents not return to Judea? After Herod dies, his son Archelaus was appointed tetrarch of Judea. His brother Herod Antipas ruled Galilee. Archelaus was even more bloodthirsty than his father and equally paranoid. The family would be safer in Galilee.

After the death of Herod the Great in 4 BC, Mary and Joseph return to their homeland. Notice that they don't settle in Judea, but in Galilee, in the little town of Nazareth.

Why does the Bible say they moved to Nazareth rather than to Judea (Matt. 2:19–23)?

Until His death, Jesus would consistently be known as a _____.

We will discover in our study that because Jesus grows up in Nazareth, the Pharisees and Sadducees will wrongly assume He was originally from there rather than Judea. Were this true it would disqualify Him from being the Messiah. Judeans viewed Galileans as inferior people who lacked wisdom and were only obsessed with money. They were even despised by other Galileans (Ps. 22; Isa. 53; Dan. 9:26).

Thirty years later, who does Philip ask to come and meet Jesus and asks the question "Can anything good come from Nazareth?" (John 1:46)? _____ Where do you think he was from?

JESUS' CHILDHOOD IN NAZARETH

READ: Luke 2:40–52

Herod Antipas is tetrarch of Galilee throughout all but the first year or two of Jesus' time on earth. Neighbors in the small town of Nazareth would scarcely have been aware of anything unique about Jesus. His respect and obedience to His godly parents would surely have been obvious, but He would otherwise have been raised very much like the other children in the community in terms of His schooling and social life.

Though we have almost no information concerning Jesus' childhood, the Mishnah gives us the typical training and development of a male child:

- *At five years of age, begins to learn the text of the Scripture*
- *At age ten, to study the Mishnah or traditions*
- *At age thirteen, to study the commandments (bar mitzvah)*
- *At age fifteen, to study of the Talmud*
- *At age eighteen, to be offered in marriage*
- *At age twenty, to pursue a vocation*
- *At age thirty, to enter into "one's full vigor"*

In order to understand Hebrew thinking and culture, we must understand the role of the Mishnah in daily Jewish life. The Mishnah is a compilation of laws that the Jews believe were given orally by God and handed down through Israel's great leaders. These laws were compiled into one text around AD 200. They were also called "hedge laws" because they were intended to form a hedge or wall of protection around the Mosaic law. It was these laws, which were actually created by the Jewish leaders, that Jesus railed against. The intent had been to help the Jewish people, but by Jesus' day, they had become a tremendous burden and were impossible to obey.

Textbooks were not available, so all learning was done by memorization. Obviously Jesus had the instruction and example of parents who loved God and understood the importance of their input into Jesus' life as He grew.

How did Jesus learn and develop the wisdom we observe in the Gospels?
Read Isaiah 50:4–9 and write the answer in your own words.

We can find Jesus' attitude toward His parents in Hebrews 1:8. In Jesus' submission to His parents, we clearly see the superior (God) placing Himself under the authority of the inferior (man). It is said that Francis of Assisi would regularly submit himself under the authority of the youngest member of his order. Why would he do that? Consider what taking this bold step would do in Francis's life. Consider also what this would do in the young man to whom Francis submitted.

What would Francis stand to gain personally from such an action?

Respond to the principle that the key to authority is submission.

What if the apostle Paul came to you and said he wanted to submit himself to your care and guidance. *When you regained consciousness, what would be your first thoughts in terms of how this might help you mature and grow?*

The one episode in Jesus' early life that is recorded in Scripture was when His parents took Him, probably along with a large cluster of friends, to His first Passover. On the return home, obviously thinking Jesus was among the large group of friends, Mary and Joseph suddenly become aware of His absence. They return to Jerusalem and find Him at the temple, astounding the Jewish leaders with His insight and wisdom. Jesus is obviously aware of His identity and His mission even at this young age.

A Jewish boy was required to attend his first Passover after his twelfth birthday. Parents were responsible for the boy's sins until he was thirteen. At thirteen the boy would be responsible. Bringing him to the Passover was to prepare him for his coming bar mitzvah.

DAY 8

THE MINISTRY AND MESSAGE OF JOHN THE BAPTIST

READ: Matt. 3:1–10; Mark 1:1–6; Luke 3:1–20

John spent a significant part of his adult life living in the wilderness. Some scholars have speculated that he may have been raised by the Essenes at Qumran. Josephus writes that these people often adopted children and raised them according to their principles. This is unlikely considering John's radical message, which cuts cross-grain to the conventional thinking of the time. He could only have learned what he taught from the Father Himself. The educated elite thought John was a crazed, unsophisticated wild man. This was far from the truth. John had a keen mind but lived a very humble and frugal lifestyle, basically isolated due to his preparation for his mission. When his unconventional manner intersected with the radical message of repentance and grace, the assessment of him as being fanatical and eccentric is more understandable. John preached a message of repentance in preparation for the kingdom, which was at hand. The word *baptism* means "dye." When a white cloth is placed in a colored dye, the cloth *identifies* with the dye. People who came to John for baptism were not only repenting of their sins, but were also expressing by immersion into the Jordan "We want to identify ourselves with this message and with the coming kingdom."

Baptism was not invented by John. It goes back to the time of Abraham. The priests performed ritual immersion in the temple, but this differed from John's practice. John's baptism was the practice of *tevilah,* which indicated a desire to "come back to God." It had to be performed in a natural running spring, so John chose the Jordan River. It was said that the convert had experienced "new birth."

You might wonder why John would begin a ministry of preparing people for the coming of the Messiah way out in the desert. Why not choose the most populated areas of the city? Furthermore, why would people journey so far in such an uncomfortable and difficult place to hear him? It would seem like a self-defeating strategy! However, the Jews knew the Scriptures and they would certainly have known what Isaiah had said concerning the area where the Messiah would first appear.

Read Isaiah 40:3 and paraphrase:

♦ **Pretending an Interest in Baptism, the Pharisees Come to Investigate.**

This is our first encounter with the Pharisees. Much will be uncovered about these men during our study, but the most critical things to know now are the following: The two main sects during the time of Jesus were the Pharisees and the Sadducees. The Sadducees were the priestly group, while the Pharisees were guardians of the law. (We will look at the Sadducees later in the study.) The Hebrew word for Pharisee means "separated ones." Pharisees were primarily from middle-class families, while the Sadducees were more from the wealthy aristocracy. In Jesus' day

Had John simply been a preacher, he would have caused minor concern among the Jewish leaders. But baptizing people was a different matter. The leaders knew from Isaiah's writings that baptism could have great significance to the coming of the Messiah.

You will notice that as John preaches and baptizes, the Jewish leaders do not debate him or ask questions. They will do the same during the first part of Jesus' ministry. This was by design. The Sanhedrin had sent groups of Pharisees on fact-finding missions to gather evidence with which to decide if John and Jesus were a threat worth taking seriously. They appear friendly and interested, but neither John nor Jesus were fooled by this strategy.

the Pharisees numbered about five thousand. When Herod was appointed king by Rome in 37 BC, one of his goals was to reduce their power and influence, which was considerable with the people. The Hellenistic influence of the Greeks had slowly crept into Jewish thinking, and the Pharisees were determined to maintain the purity of Judaism and the Mosaic law. They had influenced all of the eighty-plus synagogues in Judea and Galilee and had exercised great control over the people. By Jesus' time, they were ultra-pious, self-righteous, and hypocritical to an extreme. Power was very important to them, and their desire for control irresistibly leads them to the desert after hearing of the popularity and influence that John was having among the Jews. What we will see throughout the Gospels, and especially during the last week of Jesus' life, is that these zealous guardians of the law lived for their *position* and *authority*. They will do anything to avoid losing even if it means breaking their own laws, which they were honor bound to protect.

A group of Pharisees come to see John under the pretense of being interested in his message and baptism. They were on a fact-finding mission having been instructed by the Sanhedrin not to ask questions or to argue with John, but only to observe. They would then return with their findings, and the council would decide if this new *movement* was a threat worthy of their attention and concern.

♦ **John Sees Through Their Pretense and Challenges Them to Prove Their Claim (Matt. 3:8–10; Luke 3:7–9).**

The Pharisees immediately dislike John for two main reasons:

1. John drew huge crowds and it took the spotlight off them. Notice the contrast between the Pharisees and John:

Pharisees	*John*
The establishment	Revolutionary, nonconformist
Prestige conscious	Secure and confident in his identity
Image conscious, rule oriented	Free spirit, inner directed
Arrogant and prideful	Humble
Lovers of money and fine things	Frugal, nonmaterialistic

2. John was a man with a Jewish pedigree, and yet he was operating outside the realm of Jewish authority. He was considered a renegade!

John the Baptist was called "greater" than the earlier prophets because he preached a fuller message. And yet, in a few words, his statement echoes what we know intuitively of our own lives: "I am not the Christ." His message compelled crowds and angered those unwilling to repent and believe: "I am not the standard," he insisted, "but I know there is One who is.

John's rebuke of the Pharisees tears at the heart of traditional Jewish theology. The Pharisees considered themselves "children of Abraham." This secured their salvation and favor with God. John tells them to "think again" (Luke 3:7–9).

John had an unusual blend of strength and boldness mixed with a humble, receptive spirit. Many begin with such an intent but lose their cutting edge along the way. How do you think a believer can maintain this?

PART III: JESUS' PUBLIC MINISTRY BEGINS

Jesus is now at least thirty years old and is ready to fulfill His mandate as the promised Messiah. We have seen Him at His most vulnerable point until He hangs on a Roman cross: as a newborn infant in His mother's arms. Why spend a week on His birth and growth as a Jewish boy? Everything about God is relational. He doesn't simply appear in a blaze of glory and thereafter reside in a large office being seen by appointment only. Who could relate to a God like that? He makes Himself approachable and available to anyone at anytime. He submits Himself to the same frailties as man. He has become one of us, and in doing so, He invites us into every corner of His life so we can see and feel what He sees and feels. Only with a God such as this will we feel comfortable walking with and sharing our deepest longings and dreams. Only when we see Him develop and grow in His humanity can we truly call Him Father.

Now we move into the beginning of Jesus' earthly ministry. He will be baptized, tempted by Satan, perform His first miracle, and begin calling His disciples. Meanwhile, the Jewish leaders are carefully watching His every move, trying to determine the level of threat He poses to their authority. The multitudes will be intrigued by His words and His miracles but are waiting on their leaders to tell them what to believe about this new and fascinating rabbi who has suddenly burst onto the scene.

DAY 9

TEMPTATION IMMEDIATELY FOLLOWS BAPTISM.

READ: Matt. 3:13–17; Mark 1:9–11; Luke 3:21–23

◆ **Jesus' Baptism Initiates His Public Ministry.**

How was John's baptism of Jesus different than that of the multitudes?

 As the Spirit of God descends as a dove, God speaks and identifies Jesus as His beloved Son in whom He is well pleased (Luke 3:22). Why does God say this? Was it for John's benefit to validate that he had tapped the right man? Was it for the multitude to give them assurance? Both of these may be true, but another reason seems very likely considering what Jesus will soon encounter. Remember our discussion concerning the announcement of the angel to the shepherds about Jesus' birth? He used the word *pleased*. Now God uses the same word in relation to His Son. Jesus had not even begun His ministry, and yet God was *pleased*. He had not taught or healed or done anything significant to this point except mature physically, mentally, socially, and spiritually (Luke 2:52). God was pleased with who He was, just as He is pleased with who we are when we are rightly related to Him. Jesus will face forty days alone without food or drink and will engage in hand-to-hand spiritual combat with Satan. It will be critical that Jesus is *certain* of His identity in order for Him to deal with the temptations He is about to face.

How can we deal with temptation effectively unless we know who we are? Let's say that I have bought into the idea that I have transferred ownership of my life to Jesus and am a new creation. Am I still a *dirty rotten sinner*? I am constantly told that I am a *sinner* and so I think of myself in that manner. All of a sudden I stand face-to-face with a very attractive and enticing temptation. I am alone. No one will know. Yet, it's wrong and I know it. I wrestle with the thought. It pulls and tugs at me. Well, who am I anyway? *I'm just a rotten sinner,* I say to myself. *Why not just go ahead and give in … just this once,* I reason. *After all, that's who I am.*

Can't say it enough: How you see yourself will determine your behavior.

If I consider myself a liar, a thief, or a cheat, what would be the natural way to play out those perceptions of myself? To lie, steal, and cheat. But, what if I believed God about my *person* rather than defining myself by the occasional stupid and harmful sins I commit? What if I looked at that temptation, and as appealing to my flesh as it is, I said, "As good as that looks and as vulnerable as I feel right now, that is not who I am! It is not worthy of me. It doesn't fit! I am the righteousness of God in Christ (2 Cor. 5:21), I am God's possession (2 Tim. 2:19), I am dead to sin (Rom. 6:2–10; Eph. 1:7). The Enemy cannot defeat me as I realize he has already been defeated (Rev. 9:9–12). Convinced of that, why wouldn't I spin on my heel and walk away?

Look at the contrast in these two perspectives. Can you see the problem? This may be a little different than you have been taught about yourself, but it may well be the reason so many of us live in defeat and with tremendous guilt. Record your honest impressions as you consider this and review Day 9.

DAY 10

JESUS IS TEMPTED IN THE WILDERNESS.

READ: Matt. 4:1–11; Mark 1:12–13; Luke 4:1–13

Be sure to always read the parallel accounts when you study the Gospels. Matthew may add a key thought or piece of information that Luke did not include, etc. You will gain a much fuller perspective of seeing these accounts through more than one pair of eyes.

Immediately on the heels of this monumental encounter at the Jordan River, the greatest moment of His life to this point, Jesus is put through the wringer. How many times have you floated away on a spiritual high from a retreat or time with friends or family, only to be cut off at the knees by an avalanche of issues or temptations? Jesus was not exempt from such an experience. On a high mountain, He is tempted by Satan in the same three fundamental areas in which we all are tempted.

From 1 John 2:16, those three areas are the lust of the _____, the lust of _____, and the _____ .

Notice how in the first two temptations Satan questions Jesus' identity ("If You are the Son of God"). If we do not understand who we are from God's perspective, we are up for grabs when temptation comes calling. If I don't know who I am, then I could be anybody, depending on the circumstances.

♦ **The Three Temptations of Satan and How Jesus Deals with Them**

1. "If You are the Son of God, command that these stones become bread."
   This temptation appeals to the lust of the _____.

2. "If You are the Son of God, throw Yourself down" (for angels will catch you).
   Satan appeals to Jesus' _____ to fully reveal Himself.

3. Satan offers to deliver to Jesus all the kingdoms of the world in exchange for His worship.
   Satan appeals to the lust of the _____.

In the first two temptations, Satan questions Jesus' identity ("*If* you are the Son of God"). If Satan can confuse us concerning who we are in Christ, then collapsing in the face of temptation is pretty much a done deal … game over! Can you now see why God personally affirms that Jesus is His beloved Son and that He is pleased with Him?

◆ Consider the First Temptation.

What if you hadn't eaten in forty days? Wouldn't it be a huge enticement to use your power to turn stones into bread? What would be sinful about doing that? Just think of how wonderful it would be for starving humanity across the globe if a miracle like that could be performed. So why would it have been a sin if Jesus had done it?

Read John 14:10. Notice the last few words. Paraphrase what Jesus says.

The secret of Jesus' life was that *He didn't live it!* How does that grab you? The truth is that every miracle He performed and every word He uttered was done by God the Father *through* Jesus the Son. Read John 14:10 again. To put it another way, *Jesus lived by the life of Another.* You see the total dependence of Jesus on His Father with every breath He took. Now, go back and consider the *first temptation* of making stones into bread. Is bread really the issue? The temptation rested in Satan's hope and desire to get Jesus to do a harmless deed through His own strength and energy rather than in total dependence on God the Father. We will deal with this principle further on in our study, but give some thought to the implications of *living by the life of another* in terms of living your own life by the life of Jesus within you. *Discuss what this would mean.*

◆ Consider the Second Temptation.

Here Satan offers Jesus a deal ... a deal that would test His Father by creating an action that was unnecessary. To do a swan dive from the pinnacle of the temple and have angels catch Him would appeal to Jesus' pride to reveal who He was and to show His power. Would the Father come through if He jumped? Jesus never doubted it, but He had no need whatsoever to prove anything to Satan or to entertain him.

◆ Consider the Third Temptation.

The issue that tends to elude most of us as believers is that God's desire is not to take a weak person and make him strong so that he can operate in strength. God's idea is for us to realize that we are weak and yield ourselves to Jesus within us to be our strength and therefore overcome our weakness. It's all about Him ... not about us being gallant and courageous on His behalf.

What is your take on the "God is My Co-Pilot" philosophy? This was a book written during WWII by an American pilot. The sentiment was sincere and hopeful, but that perspective is one of the main reasons why many believers live frustrated lives and sink without a trace. Jesus did not come simply to help us. He came to live His life through us! There is a huge difference.

If you are in a group, take a few minutes to discuss this.

Jesus answers each temptation with the truth of Scripture, not like some magic wand to protect Himself, but with the assurance that truth will always triumph.

Satan tries to tempt Jesus with the kingdoms of the world. But isn't God in control of the kingdoms of this world? Look around you. Does God appear to rule in the hearts of men and women today? If Jesus already had control of the kingdoms of the world, there would have been no temptation.

This third temptation is about *ownership* without the *payment of the cross.*

What do the following passages say about Satan's current position in the world?

Satan is _____ (2 Cor. 4:4).
Satan is _____ (Eph. 2:2).
Satan is _____ (John 12:31; 16:11).

This doesn't mean God is weak or submissive to Satan but that as a loving Father, He forces no one to follow Him. Satan is the current but temporary "god" of this world, but the good news is in Revelation 11:15–16.

People often express the cliché "Have faith"; but the question is "In what?" Faith is only as valid as its object and has no real value by itself. Strong faith in thin ice equals a bad day on the lake. In the same way, weak faith in thick ice ensures a dry crossing. Real faith, biblical faith, rests on revealed truth (thick ice), not on information. We live in an information age and believe that unlimited knowledge is the brass ring to a complete and satisfying life. The flaw in this thinking is that *knowledge* through information *is not necessarily wisdom.* Wisdom comes *through the revelation of truth,* and on that we can walk confidently.

On Day 1, we saw that "the Word [Jesus] became flesh and lived among us." "Word" here is logos, *meaning "person." Read Romans 10:17 and write it below. Then try to put it to memory.*

"Word" is also used in John 1 but with a different meaning. The word used here is *rama,* which means "revelation." Now rewrite the verse using the word *revelation.*

The most you will gain from this study course is information. The same is true of any Bible study, book, or sermon. No one can be profound enough, articulate enough, or forceful enough to change a heart. Only revelation from God can do that. Pause and ask God to turn this information into revelation for you personally.

DAY 11

JESUS CALLS HIS FIRST DISCIPLES AND BEGINS HIS MINISTRY.

READ: John 1:29–51

Two men named John and Andrew are standing with their mentor, John the Baptist. John fully realizes that his role has dramatically changed. Rather than be on center stage with the Jews, he has now become a *catalyst*, taking a backseat as Jesus begins his public ministry.

Just then, Jesus walks by in the distance, and John points Him out to the two men and says, "There walks the man who will take away the sins of the world." That's quite an introduction! Intrigued by what their mentor has said, Andrew and John immediately follow Jesus. Hearing them approaching, He stops, turns, and asks them a simple, but profound question: "What do you want?" Think of the question not as an abrupt response to an interrupted evening stroll but as a sincere desire by Jesus for these men to express what they were really after in life. Were they just curious about Him? Was their interest just a fad that would soon disappear, or were they so stirred in their spirits that they somehow sensed Jesus represented what could be a defining moment in their lives?

What do *you* want? What do you *really* want? Don't write down the nice, proper, politically correct answer. What are you really looking for? Is it success, financial security, personal fulfillment, a house in the Bahamas? Did you know that God is more interested in your wants than in your needs. This is not a prosperity statement! Your needs are *guaranteed* if you trust Him (Phil. 4:19). But what you want in your heart of hearts is what reveals your true character. If you are unwilling to acknowledge what you really want and give a cliché answer,

> If someone is honest enough to say what they really want in life, they will give you an intimate window into who they really are. What you want is what will reveal your character.

41

God will have to wait until you get real. There is no way to trick Him. So, what do you really want? *Take a minute to think about it before you answer.*

♦ **John and Andrew Answer Jesus with a Question of Their Own.**

The Jewish perspective is critical here; otherwise, it sounds like these two guys ignored Jesus' question. In Jewish culture their question was very direct. Where are you staying, when asked of a rabbi, was a way of saying, "We want to be your students; where can we find you?" This is what they really wanted. Jesus must have been overjoyed at their sincerity.

♦ **Andrew Brings His Brother, Peter. Jesus Meets Philip the Next Day (1:41–42).**

♦ **Jesus Has a Fascinating Encounter with Nathanael (1:44–51).**

Fig trees are symbolic of the nation of Israel. Serious Jews regularly studied and meditated under fig trees.

Philip excitedly searches for his friend Nathanael and finds him reading intently underneath a fig tree. He can barely contain his excitement that he has found this One about whom Moses and the prophets wrote, Jesus of Nazareth. Rather than sharing his friend's enthusiasm, Nathanael is repulsed when he hears the word *Nazareth*. He was from Judea and felt vastly superior to Galileans, especially Nazarenes.

Philip asks Nathanael to at least "check Him out," and Nathanael reluctantly agrees. Upon meeting Jesus, he is startled by His greeting. Write verse 47:

Nazarenes were despised by Judeans. They were thought to be self-absorbed and only interested in money. Nathanael suffered from deep prejudice that he would later have to yield to the Savior.

Guile means craftiness, or deceit or someone with a hidden agenda. By saying that Nathanael is a man with no guile, Jesus is giving him a great compliment. He is saying, here is a "what you see is what you get" type of guy.

Nathanael asks how Jesus knows him. Jesus' answer astounds him. Jesus says that He saw him under the fig tree before Philip ever came to get him.

When you think of someone in the Old Testament who was crafty, deceitful, and full of guile, who do you think of? _____ *(Hint for one example: He tricked his brother and stole his birthright.)*

✡ Any Jew would immediately have associated the word *guile* with this crafty Old Testament character in the above example. So Jesus was saying to Nathanael, "Here is a straight-up guy who is completely unlike crafty old Jacob, the schemer."

Nathanael's immediate response is _____

Why would Jesus say something like that out of the blue, and why did Nathanael's demeanor turn from skepticism to honor in a split second? Jesus tells Nathanael that if he thinks His seeing him under the fig tree is something, just wait until he sees the heavens open and the angels of God ascend and descend on the Son of Man. In other words, "Nate, this is just a preview of things to come."

💡 Read Genesis 28:12. Do you see anything similar to what Jesus said in John 1:51? Jesus uses the example of Jacob being unlike Nathanael because He knew that Nathanael was sitting under the fig tree reading the story of Jacob in the book of Genesis. Talk about being blown away!

DAY 12

JESUS' FIRST MIRACLE

READ: John 2:1–11

📷 Jesus and His small cadre of new disciples are invited to a wedding in the little village of Cana. Jesus' mother is there, indicating that she may have been a friend of the family and therefore was helping with the festivities. Weddings were events of great magnitude that lasted up to a week. A family's entire savings could often be spent on these lavish affairs. Aged wine was served initially and as the guests got a little "under the weather" and were less discerning, the cheap stuff was brought out.

That Jesus "saw" him under the fig tree meditating immediately convinced Nathanael that he was not dealing with an ordinary man. But even more amazing was the fact that Jesus knew the exact scripture on which Nathanael was meditating. As soon as Jesus spoke of angels ascending and descending, Nathanael knew who Jesus was. "You are the Son of God! You are the King of Israel!"

Jesus granted His mother's request, but did not violate His mandate to perform His first public miracle in Jerusalem at the Passover. The miracle of the water into wine was a private, not a public, miracle. Only Jesus' mother, the servants, and a few disciples were aware of it.

Wine was a symbol of joy among Jews. A common saying was "Where there is no wine, there is no joy." To run out of wine at a celebration such as this was seen as a critical social blunder and would be a source of great humiliation to the host. There are even records of lawsuits brought by the parents of the bride to sue the parents of the groom because of such an oversight.

There have been various ancient books claiming that Jesus did miracles as a young boy. John tells us here, very clearly, that the changing of the water into wine was Jesus' first miracle, invalidating the claims of other writings.

◆ **Jesus' Mother Appeals to Him to Solve the Problem (v. 3).**

◆ **Jesus Responds That His Hour Has Not Yet Come (v. 4).**

Jesus' first public miracle was to be performed in Jerusalem at the Passover. But, He wants to honor His mother's wishes and has no desire to see the host family shamed. He has the servants take six twenty-to-thirty-gallon clay pots, which were used mostly for foot washing, and fill them with water. (This water would have been unsuitable for drinking.)

A great passage that speaks to the idea of "finishing well" is found in Genesis 25:8 and is worth putting to memory: "Abraham breathed his last and died in a ripe old age, an old man and satisfied with life."

(How many people can you say that about?)

BE THE SERVANTS: You would, no doubt, swallow hard, look at each other in dismay, and consider your jobs as history when Jesus tells you to take a glass of this nasty, brackish water to your boss to be approved for the guests. Imagine the absurdity of it all from the perspective of the poor servants, who are just trying to make a few extra bucks on the weekend. Imagine how you would hold your breath and brace yourself for that moment when he tastes this putrid stuff and spews it out on the ground. Only, it never happens. A smile comes over the wine steward's face, and he compliments the groom on continuing to serve high-quality wine even toward the end of the party. The following Monday morning, imagine trying to respond to the question "Well, Sam, how was your weekend?"

There are many applications that can be made from this familiar story. Even at the end of the party, in our last days on this earth, the joy is meant to come with great intensity. But what happens when the wine runs out? What does a person do when their joy runs dry and their passion for life slows to a trickle? Aside from the clichés and five-step plans to restore your joy, what do you say to someone when the wine has run out in their life? What do you say to yourself? *Write your thoughts and discuss.*

Jesus Cleanses the Temple in Jerusalem.

READ: John 2:13–22

It's Passover time, and pilgrims have journeyed from distant villages and cities with their families at great expense and sacrifice to be at this most sacred of Jewish holy festivals. It is the retelling of the great story of how God redeemed His people from slavery in Egypt. God had told the people to sacrifice a lamb and smear the blood on the doorposts of their houses as a sign of faith. As the Lord passed over the houses, those with the lamb's blood on the doorposts had their firstborn males spared, while all other Egyptian male babies were killed. You can read about it in Exodus 12:12–14. Good Friday was the day of the Passover celebration and the day that the Passover lamb was to be sacrificed. For the previous twelve hundred years, the priest blew the *shophar* (ram's horn) at 3:00 p.m. The moment the lamb was sacrificed, all the people paused to contemplate the sacrifice for sins on behalf of the people of Israel. On Good Friday at 3:00 p.m., when Jesus was being crucified, He said, "It is finished." At that moment the Passover lamb was sacrificed, and the *shophar* was blown from the temple. The sacrifice of the Lamb of God was fulfilled at the exact hour that the symbolic animal sacrifice usually took place.

◆ Jesus Is Angered by the Abuse of His Father's House.

Why did the temple need cleansing? A man named Annas had been appointed high priest by Quirinius, governor of Syria in AD 7. He was deposed in AD 15. Ten years later in AD 25, Annas's son-in-law Caiaphas was appointed by the Romans as high priest. Though still recognized as high priest by the Jews, Annas gave his attention to a very lucrative moneymaking scam within the temple. The pilgrims were required to bring an animal to be sacrificed. The animal had to be an unblemished male. Most families raised a lamb from birth for the purpose of presenting it at the temple courtyard. However, Annas and his fellow priests seldom accepted the animal brought by the pilgrims. They often found some blemish that made it unacceptable for sacrifice. This problem, however, could be quickly remedied. Out back, temple sheep were kept, available for purchase at an outrageous fee. However, only Jewish coinage was accepted as payment. Moneychangers stood nearby, always happy to exchange the pilgrims' Roman coinage for a "nominal fee." In addition, a temple tax had to be paid.

45

This is why Jesus was angry. The bartering and selling was in the outer courtyard, not inside the temple, yet the priests had turned this sacred place into a haven of opportunity to swindle the people, a "den of thieves."

If Jesus walked into your community of faith, what tables would He likely over-turn? Give some thought to this and discuss if in a small group.

Why do you think Jesus intended to pass the disciples by?

With whom is Jesus angry? _____

Could He have handled the situation in a different way?

What would you have done?

Does this justify violence on our part when our values are violated? Explain.

In John 2:24–25, we see that there is a difference between being a critical person and a critical thinker. Write the difference below.

♦ **The Jewish Leaders Misunderstand Jesus' Statement in Verse 19.**

Herod the Great had begun to refurbish the temple in 20 BC, and the project was still in progress. The Jewish leaders thought Jesus' statement meant that He was would demolish that which had taken forty-six years to rebuild.

♦ **From This Moment on, the Jewish Leaders Seek to Kill Jesus.**

The response of the multitudes was quite different than their leaders' (John 2:23). However, John makes a fascinating statement about Jesus' perspective concerning His instant popularity among the people. *Summarize verses 24–25 in your own words.*

What is meant by the phrase "Jesus knew all men"? What did He know?

46

DAY 13

A LEARNED LAW PROFESSOR SEEKS JESUS BY NIGHT.

READ: John 3:1–21

Quite a buzz was circulating throughout the crowds and among the Jewish leaders about the episode in the temple. Apparently, those attending the festival had observed much more in terms of His teaching and miracles (John 2:23) than is recorded here. A highly respected Pharisee and member of the Sanhedrin is fascinated with this new rabbi who had come onto the scene. He is anxious to have a private conversation with Him. Though he does not understand it, this Jewish leader intuitively knows that God has to be behind Jesus' miracles (v. 2).

As we study, keep in mind that this cleansing of the temple was much more than an "incident." It would prove to be a major contributing factor to Jesus' ultimate death.

◆ **Nicodemus Comes to See Jesus Under Cover of Darkness.**

Why do you think Nicodemus would be secretive about his desire to speak with Jesus?

◆ **Jesus Tells This Learned Teacher of the Law That He Must Be "Born Again" in Order to Enter the Kingdom of God (v. 3).**

Nicodemus's confusion when Jesus says he must be " born again" takes on new significance when we see it from a Hebrew perspective. The phrase "born again" was a very common Jewish idiom. There were at least six different avenues through which a person could be "born again":

Whether then or now, men often have a difficult time coming to Jesus openly. Sometimes they will only come, in a sense, "by night," under cover of darkness. For a grown man, successful in his vocation, to come to Jesus, he will be admitting that all of his prior years on the planet have been lived in error.

1. When a Gentile converts to Judaism (and becomes a proselyte).
2. When a man becomes king (not of the tribe of Judah or house of David).
3. When a male is circumcised at age thirteen (Nick was way past that age).
4. Between ages eighteen and about twenty-five, a Jewish man would marry a Jewish woman and it was said of him: "he has been born again."
5. When a man becomes a rabbi around age thirty. (See 3:1, as a "spiritual ruler," Nick was already a rabbi.)
6. When he became a leading teacher in a rabbinical school around age fifty.

Nicodemus asks, "How can a man be born again when he is _____?"

Nicodemus is mentioned in rabbinic writings. His Hebrew name was actually Nakdimon Ben Bonai. He was one of the wealthiest men in Jerusalem and sometime after he became a believer in Jesus, he somehow lost his wealth. After that, he made a living as a well digger in Jerusalem.

This tells us that he had exhausted every avenue in his understanding through which this might be possible. Examine the list again. Can you picture this learned rabbi mentally checking off each of these as Jesus spoke? Finally, he comes to the end, realizing that he has qualified at every level under Jewish definition and that the only remaining option is almost too ridiculous to even mention. *Surely Jesus could not possibly mean the absurd notion of reentering his mother's womb, could He?*

Nicodemus had always believed that his Jewish heritage alone was enough to guarantee him free passage to heaven. Though the conversation continues, Nicodemus cannot understand, but he is clear about the essence of what Jesus says. No matter what his traditions and teachings, unless his spirit is renewed by the Spirit of God, he will have lived his entire life in error and never see heaven, regardless of his being a "child of Abraham."

John Is Arrested, and Jesus Leaves Judea for Galilee by Way of Samaria.

READ: Matt. 4:12; John 3:22–36; 4:1–4; Mark 1:14; Luke 3:19–20

John is baptizing people in great numbers, and now Jesus and His disciples come into the region of Judea. They minister widely among the multitudes and are also baptizing (John 3:23), although Jesus Himself was not baptizing (John 4:2). Some of John's disciples are concerned that Jesus is becoming more prominent that John. The rugged prophet's response reveals his heart.

Look at the following verses, and write in your own words four things John says to them in response:

• *Verse 27* _____

• *Verse 28* _____

- *Verse 30* _____

- *Verse 34* _____

John the Baptist is a man of great courage, called by God for a special mission. He is single minded in his focus, and yet he never forgets that he is a prophet and must speak the truth regardless of the consequences. In doing so, he is arrested by Herod Antipas and thrown into prison. Soon after John's arrest, Jesus leaves Judea and travels north toward Galilee. The Pharisees are now aware of what He is doing and that He is becoming a threat to their authority with the multitudes. He doesn't want them too close to Him at this point, so He leaves the area. As He and His disciples travel toward Galilee, they have a decision to make.

Why was John in prison? Herod Antipas had a brother named Herod Phillip. He divorced his wife, Herodius, and Herod Antipas married her. Leviticus 20:20 says that a man may not marry his brother's wife while he is still alive. John, not known for his reluctance to speak the truth, confronts Herod about his sin with all of the subtlety of a meat cleaver and is promptly thrown in jail for his trouble.

John Wesley said that a leader is not fond of his power. Such is the case with John. He knows his role and realizes that he must fade into the background, though his followers find this difficult to accept. John has great humility, something seldom seen in our present-day leadership, spiritual or otherwise. It has become the forgotten virtue, yet we will observe this great emphasis on humility throughout the Gospels.

DAY 14

JESUS TRAVELS THROUGH SAMARIA.

READ: John 4:5–31

Jesus must make a decision that all Jews had to make when traveling between Judea and Galilee. The most direct route would force them to go through Samaria. The alternate route would take them more than two days longer through an area called the *Decapolis*. This cluster of ten towns was mostly Gentile and extremely pagan. They had to pass by pagan statuaries and monuments that were very offensive to any Jew. However, to go through Samaria was also deeply offensive because of over seven hundred years of alienation.

Samaritans believed in the
law but not the prophets.
They also refused to
worship at the temple in
Jerusalem or attend the
sacred festivals held there.
They worshipped in a
temple they had erected at
the base of Mount Gerizim
at Sychar. They even
scratched through refer-
ences to Jerusalem in the
sacred writings and wrote
"Mt. Gerizim" in its place.

It began in 722 BC. The Assyrians, under the leadership of a general named Sargon II conquered the northern kingdom and its capital, Samaria. They took Jewish captives back to Assyria, with the exception of some who hid in the mountains nearby. These stragglers stayed in Samaria and eventually intermarried with non-Jews who traveled through the area. Children were born as a result of those unions and eventually, a half-breed race developed. True Jews considered any marriage outside their race a sacrilege and would do anything to avoid contact with a Samaritan half-breed. Samaritans would not worship in Jerusalem and had set up their own temple on Mount Gerizim, the place where Moses had given a blessing to Israel as they came out of Egypt. They believed in the law, but only the first five books of the Torah (also called the Tanakh). They did not believe in the prophets.

What does Jesus' decision to go through Samaria tell you about Him?

♦ **Jesus Stops by a Well in a Small City Named Sychar Near the Base of Mount Gerizim (vv. 5–6).**

Notice that when the Samaritan woman shows up to draw water, the disciples had gone into town to buy food. This is a good thing, because the bad blood between Jews and Samaritans was so intense that they would not even acknowledge each other. They would not even handle a cup or utensil that had been touched by a Samaritan. In addition, she was a woman; all the more reason to avoid any communication.

Having been trained in pharisaic Judaism, what do you imagine the disciples would have done if they had stayed with Jesus rather than going for lunch?

♦ **Jesus Asks for a Drink, and a Conversation Ensues (v. 7).**

Jesus speaks to the woman about water that will quench her thirst forever. This thought appealed to her. For one thing, she would never again have to make this journey to the well for her daily needs. It was not an issue of convenience as much as it was avoiding humiliation at the hands of the other women.

STEP INTO THE WOMAN'S SANDALS: You are coming to get water at noon rather than in the early morning or end of the day when all of the other women come. You have been unsuccessful in marriage five times. Wild rumors have circulated about the failed marriages, but only you know the reasons why. You are currently unmarried and living with a man. The gossip around town is unbearable, and you are shunned by the women. As this woman, would you not come at an hour when no other women would be at the well? Would you not be interested if someone told you He knows of a way you would never have to come back to this well again and feel the stares of the others critically boring into on you? Though Jesus speaks of a "water that can refresh your soul forever," you are only capable at this point of thinking on a physical level.

Why do you think the woman continues talking to Jesus?

♦ **Jesus Asks Her to Do Something That Is Impossible for Her (v. 16).**

✡ Jewish tradition stated that a woman may be divorced a maximum of three times. Understanding the Jewish perspective is critical. Divorce was only the prerogative of the man, therefore we know that if a divorce occurred, it was initiated by her husband. However, we can't necessarily assume that she was a terrible wife. The school of Shammai stated that divorce was legitimate only in cases of unfaithfulness. The more liberal school of Hallel said that a man could divorce a woman for almost any reason, from burning his breakfast to seeing another woman at the market whom he thought was more attractive than his wife. She could well have been the victim of some egotistical morons who divorced her for selfish reasons. Also, the inability of the woman to bear children was the most frequent cause of divorce in antiquity; the woman was often considered to be paying the price for her past sins. Again, we see this cause-and-effect thinking as we saw on Day 2 with Elizabeth and Zacharias. This could well have been the reason for one or more of her divorces. But, what about the other husbands? For all we know, they may have died (without even asking her permission). We don't know the answer to any of these things, but we do know that she was now living with a man to whom she was not married. Keep in mind that the penalty for adultery was stoning, so had she been known as a promiscuous woman, as most people assume, she would have been executed long ago. Jesus was probably the only one who knew.

Though Jesus does not condone the fact that the woman is living with her boyfriend, He sees much deeper into the pain that drove her there. To understand and to empathize is not necessarily to condone. When hope is lost, people tend to seek any avenue of retreat to assuage the pain. Jesus does not lecture her about her sin, He simply reveals Himself to her and everything changes.

ASSUMPTIONS! When we label someone, we put the person in a box from which it can be impossible to escape. It takes the potential of forgiveness and redemption out of the equation. This woman had undoubtedly made some critical mistakes, but have we assumed more negatives about her than the evidence supports? Jesus did not see a promiscuous woman. He saw a woman battered and scarred by her past, a woman who had lost hope. He longed to help her rather than write her off and label her as unfit for the kingdom.

Have you ever had a personal experience like this or known someone who has been labeled or defined a certain way without people knowing the whole story?

Many things can be learned from this encounter. Hopefully we will not miss the fact that Jesus neither condoned the woman's current indiscretion nor did He make her behavior the focal point of the problem. Unhealthy relationships are symptomatic of heart issues. Too often we define people by their behavior. This story screams out to us: "Deal with the person, not with what the person has done!"

◆ **Jesus Begins to Introduce Her to His Heavenly Father.**

The woman tries to divert the conversation to safer topics. She thinks Jesus is a prophet, but not *the* Prophet (Messiah) spoken of in Deuteronomy 18:18 and the One all Jews and Samaritans knew about. She wants to talk about the differences in Jewish and Samaritan worship. Jesus tells her that the day is coming when none of this will matter; she will worship in "spirit and in truth" (4:24). As Jesus reveals Himself to her, she becomes so excited that she runs back to tell the men in the city. They ask Jesus to stay two days longer.

Other than the woman running to tell the townspeople what happened to her, how do we know that something radical happened to the woman? Verse 28 says, "She left _____." What does this indicate to us?

PART IV: JESUS' GALILEAN MINISTRY

Jesus will go throughout the districts of Galilee preaching repentance and the arrival of the kingdom of God. He will be accepted initially by the Jewish multitudes because of His astonishing miracles, but He will also be rejected in Nazareth, where He was raised (Luke 4; Matt. 4). Completing His selection of His twelve disciples, He will give the greatest sermon ever preached (Matt. 5—7). He will perform the first of three miracles that the Jews had long ago set as the criterion for the Messiah when He came (Matt. 8; Mark 1; Luke 5). Still they will not believe Him and will even commit blasphemy in the process (Matt. 12). The Jewish leaders will soon determine that Jesus is a direct threat to their authority with the people, and the confrontations will begin. It was truly the best of times and it was the worst of times depending on who you were and where you stood.

DAY 15

JESUS ARRIVES IN GALILEE AND BEGINS TEACHING.

READ: John 4:43–45

Jesus is welcomed in Galilee, but what appears to be acceptance of Him and His messiahship is really a rejection. They flock to Him for one reason: His miracles—what He can do for them physically. How would they know He was the Messiah that had been prophesied for generations? How would they know that this was not just a charismatic rabbi with unique gifts? We must see this through Jewish eyes.

The prophets had stated clearly that the long-awaited Messiah would come to the Jews with a specific mission and ministry. Jewish tradition added the belief that the Jews would know the Messiah by three unique miracles that only He would be able to perform. It is critical to our full understanding to keep this in mind as we study the Gospels.

53

These would be the three signs that the Messiah was on the earth and should cause every Jew on the planet to fall down and worship Him.

Put these three messianic miracles to memory because they will play a very critical part in understanding the attitudes and responses of the Jews as we continue our study.

> **Miracle #1:** *The Messiah would heal a Jewish leper.* The Old Testament records the healing of Naaman the leper, but he was a Gentile. There was no record of any Jew ever being healed.
>
> **Miracle #2:** *The Messiah would heal a demon-possessed man who also was dumb* (could not speak). There were exorcists in that day as there are today. However the demon would also be communicated with through the voice of the one who was possessed.
>
> **Miracle #3:** *The Messiah would heal a man born blind from birth.*

JESUS TEACHES THAT THE LONG-AWAITED KINGDOM IS AT HAND.

READ: Matt. 4:17; Mark 1:14–15; Luke 4:14–15

Children would huddle around their grandparents and listen to the stories of God's faithfulness to His people for thousands of years. The Jewish feast days all pointed to some specific event in the future that God's special people could look forward to. The prophets had promised a coming kingdom, and now Jesus Himself will teach about it.

Luke 4:15 tells us what three things about Jesus' teaching?

1. _____
2. _____
3. _____

THE HEALING OF A NOBLEMAN'S SON AT CANA

"Now faith is the assurance of things hoped for, the conviction of things not seen" (Heb. 11:1).

READ: John 4:46–54

Teaching daily in the synagogues throughout the region, Jesus travels to Cana where he had previously turned water into wine. An official who was employed by Herod Antipas and a resident of Capernaum has a son who is desperately ill, at the point of death. The official leaves his son and journeys to Cana in one last attempt to save the boy's life. He finds Jesus and is told to return home; his son will live.

BE THE ROYAL OFFICIAL: Once again, this story will have great meaning to you if you study it empathetically or autobiographically by putting yourself in the scene. Just the small amount of information that has been mentioned is enough to understand and feel the drama of what this man and his wife must have been experiencing. Your son has become increasingly ill and no remedies are available. You are an official who works for one of the most powerful men on earth. You would have access to the best medical care, but nothing is working. You and your wife stay up night after night trying to bring the fever down. There is no ice, so cool water from a well is all you have. You cat nap while your wife watches him. She, in turn, does the same so you can rest. You must be at your job each day, but you can't concentrate. Your wife is becoming emotional, and as the fever climbs she cries, *"Do something!"*

Herod and his top officials are aware of a Nazarene named Jesus and have been monitoring His movements. The Rabbi has miraculously cured people of many illnesses and He is now in Cana, some seventeen miles away. With the dual emotions of fear of never seeing your son again and the hope of a miracle, you set out on your journey. A good day's travel in antiquity was about seventeen miles, but this is your son's life that quivers in the balance. You keep a breakneck pace, slowing down only to catch your breath and drink some water. Time is critical; your son may not have a day left. You reach Cana and ask where you might find Jesus. "Look for the crowds," they say. You come with desperate boldness as you burst to the front of the crowd that surrounds Him. You entreat Him to come to Capernaum and heal your son. You have memorized your speech for seventeen miles, but no convincing is necessary. He speaks to the crowds about needing a miracle in order to believe, then looks in your eyes and with no drama or emotion and calmly says, "Go, your son lives." He has no questions about the illness and there is no hesitation, only a firmness and confidence in His voice and compassion in His eyes. It was not what you expected. Would He not need to personally go to your home and touch the boy? You believe Him, but aren't sure why. It was some indefinable quality that you can't quite put your finger on. You can't explain it, but you walk away with complete assurance that your son will be okay.

You can't see it, but you know that in an instant, this royal official faces the classic dilemma; *should he trust God or wait and trust visible, proven results?* No cell

Project yourself into this story. Read it empathetically. What would you be feeling if it were your son? What does his wife feel? Imagine the tug of emotion as he must choose to leave his son's side in what may be his last good-bye. Think of the adrenaline rush of fear mixed with guarded hope as he hastily journeys to find Jesus, 17 miles away in Cana.

Be the man! Become the woman! They are real people with emotions and dreams just like yours. It will make the story come alive.

If you are studying this with a group, discuss the following:

Is pragmatism compatible with real faith? Can I be a pragmatic thinker and still trust God in everything?

phone or fax machines were around to verify what Jesus had said. Faith was the only option.

Could you have trusted Jesus that much or would you have had to first see the results? Why or why not?

◆ **The Following Day the Royal Official's Servants Validate the Miracle Along the Way (vv. 51–54).**

On the long journey home, the official's servants meet him along the road having no idea that Jesus had performed the miracle or that their boss knew about it. He asked them what time the boy's fever broke and it was the exact time that he had spoken to Jesus. The rest of the story is fascinating. One word in the story gives amazing flavor to what is happening and illustrates a level of faith that few of us have ever known.

In verse 52, what day did the healing occur? _____

"Because you have seen Me, have you believed? Blessed are they who did not see, and yet believed" (John 20:29).

The royal official met with Jesus at the seventh hour (1:00 p.m.) *the day before* he met the servants on the road. Where did the royal official go from 1:00 p.m. until the following day?

Step back into his sandals for a moment: You have had little sleep in weeks. Because of the urgency of the situation, you have traveled seventeen miles in record time. You have survived on pure adrenaline and the love for your child. Jesus tells you he is healed. You believe it! But would you not rush back so you could throw your arms around that little boy as fast as you could, worn out or not? Instead, an afternoon and a night pass. The next morning he begins his journey. It is very likely that the royal official, assured that his son was well, went off completely at peace and got a good night's sleep before starting for home the next morning. Amazing confidence in Jesus!

Can you believe God enough that you do not need to immediately see the results of that which you have prayed for, but simply know that God has answered? How sad that we often determine how God has blessed a gathering or event by how many people showed up. How unfortunate that, like Thomas, we *will not* believe unless we see.

DAY 16

REJECTED IN NAZARETH, JESUS GOES TO CAPERNAUM.

READ: Luke 4:16–31; Matt. 4:13–16

Jesus travels to Nazareth where He grew up. Upon His arrival on the Sabbath, He goes directly to the synagogue. He is handed a scroll of Isaiah and begins to read. This will be Jesus' *inaugural address* (4:18–19). He closes the book, hands it back to the attendant, and sits down. With every eye searing in upon Him, He drops a bombshell from which they would never recover. He says that this prophesy, written by Isaiah hundreds of years prior, is being fulfilled right before their eyes (4:21). He was the very One Isaiah wrote about. He forces them to make a decision about who He is. Those in the synagogue found it difficult to believe that this son of a local carpenter, whom they had watched grow up could possibly be the Messiah. Jesus then gives two illustrations indicating that the Gentiles will soon accept what the Jews reject. The people become furious, chase him out of the city, and try to throw Him from a cliff, but he calmly walks through the angry mob … unharmed.

How do you account for the fact that the angry mob did not throw Jesus off the cliff?

♦ **Jesus Makes Capernaum His Headquarters (Matt. 4:13–16).**

♦ **Jesus Heals a Demoniac on the Sabbath (Mark 1:21–28; Luke 4:31–37).**

The people are astounded by the authority with which Jesus teaches in the synagogue. He is unlike the Pharisees, who would continually quote other rabbis to validate their teachings. Jesus quotes no one except the Father

Imagine being a Jew, listening to Jesus say that the passage he read in Isaiah, written hundreds of years prior, is speaking of Him. They are astounded until He basically tells them that they will actually reject the Messiah they have long awaited. Who will accept Him? The hated Gentiles!

Blasphemy was considered a capital offense to the Jews and was punishable by stoning. What Jesus had just said in the synagogue would be considered blasphemy of the first order. The intent here would have been to throw Jesus off the precipice. If the fall does not kill Him, large rocks would be hurled down on Him until He was dead.

and teaches as if words from heaven are actually being whispered in His ear. The demons even recognize His authority.

◆ **Peter's Mother-in-Law Is Healed (Matt. 8:14–17; Mark 1:29–34; Luke 5:12–16).**

The mother of Peter's wife was sick with a high fever. Jesus goes to her home and heals her. Who could argue with that? The Pharisees could, and did. They charge Jesus with breaking the law. Whose law? There is nothing in Scripture against doing acts of mercy on the Sabbath. So what law were they referring to? The *oral law*, often referred to in the Gospels as *the traditions of the elders.*

Contained within the oral laws (the Mishnah) are at least 1,500 laws alone regarding the Sabbath. These laws were not commanded by God but were added by the Pharisees with the initial intent of protecting the Mosaic law. Instead, they thrust a great burden on the Jewish people, creating enormous guilt and frustration demanding what they had no ability to give.

The origin of the Jewish oral laws is not only revealing, but accounts for much of the alienation between Jesus and the Pharisees. The Jews are taken into captivity by the Babylonians beginning in 606 BC. They remained there until the Persians overthrew the Babylonians in 536 BC. King Cyrus released them to return to their homeland and rebuild the temple in Jerusalem that King Nebuchadnezzar had burned to the ground during the siege in 586 BC. Over the years, the Jews pondered what had happened to them. They were God's people. He had married the nation of Israel at Mount Sinai in Exodus 19—24. How could God have allowed His bride to be enslaved in a pagan land for seventy years? They reasoned that it was because of the lack of holiness on the part of the people. God's laws must be strengthened and protected, they reasoned. Oral laws, which the Jews claim were given by God through Moses and Joshua, were slowly compiled into what later became known as the *Mishnah* around AD 200. The original intent was to create a *fence* or *hedge* around the Mosaic law to protect it. In fact, they were often called "hedge laws." A school called the Tannaheim was developed and stated that the oral laws were in every way equal in authority to the Mosaic (written) law. Another school of thought called the Sophreim later emerged gave more weight to the oral laws than to God's written law if the two ever conflicted. During Jesus' time, most Jews had no idea what was God's law and what were these concocted laws created by the Jewish leaders. Thousands of these laws put a horrible burden on the people's backs. They could hardly move without violating one of them. Jesus will purposely break every oral law he can as a protest against their blatant attempt to try to improve upon God's truth.

Summarize in your own words a definition of the oral laws.

◆ **Many Are Brought to Jesus to Be Healed That Evening (Mark 1:29).**

The Sabbath begins with the first three stars that are visible in the heavens on Friday evening.

What phrase in Mark 1:32 confirms that the healing of Peter's mother-in-law was on the Sabbath? _____ . *As the people brought the sick to Jesus, what does verse 32 tell us about the way they had been taught to handle these situations?*

Notice how inconsistent the people's thinking was: They marveled at the authority with which Jesus spoke. They knew He had the power to heal and perform great miracles, and He did what no one else had ever done, but they were unprepared to accept that He was the Messiah.

DAY 17

JESUS' FIRST TOUR OF GALILEE: JESUS CALLS PETER, ANDREW, JAMES, AND JOHN A SECOND TIME.

READ: Mark 1:35–39; Luke 4:42–44

Jesus arises early in the morning while His disciples sleep and goes off to a lonely place to pray. His disciples awake and search for Him. They tell Him the crowds are looking everywhere for Him. His response must have surprised them. *Write His response (Mark 1:38):*

Jesus calls Peter, Andrew, and John for the second time and also calls James, John's brother to follow Him (Mark 1:16–20; Luke 5:1–11). Standing by Lake Gennesaret (Sea of Galilee) with a large crowd pressing in on Him, He gets in one of the fishermen's boats who had returned from their work and were cleaning their nets. Jesus teaches the crowds from the boat. As He concludes His teaching, He tells Peter, who is also in the boat along with the others, to push out into deep water and drop his nets there for a catch. Fishermen were very proud people who knew their trade well. They also knew the waters in which they fished. In this case, Peter and his friends had fished all night and had caught nothing. Now a former carpenter turned rabbi, who knows little about fishing, tells them to do it His way.

When Peter saw Jesus for who He was, Peter saw Peter for who he was (Luke 5:7–8).

DECISION: Does Peter trust his own professional expertise or does he trust and obey the command of Jesus? That is always the issue. "I know my business," one man says. "I can handle it," or "I wasn't given a brain and talents for nothing," says another. "I can do this!" is a typical response of proactive, capable men and women. The question is, *Will you trust your experience and expertise or will you trust God?* This was Peter's decision.

Have you ever struggled with relying solely on God versus your expertise?

If you are in a small group, discuss this question: Is there a difference between the "Christian mind" and the "mind of Christ"?

Against his better judgment and to his credit, Peter does as Jesus commands, and you won't believe what a "lucky guess" Jesus made.

God's thinking is different than anything we observe daily, including much of what is done within the church. God thinks in opposites! In His kingdom, up is down, and down is up. Consider a few of the many differences in man's mind and God's mind.

You might want to begin your own list as you become aware of the "opposites of God" in the Scripture and in your daily life.

MAN'S THINKING	GOD'S THINKING	
Self-preservation	Lose your life	Matt. 16:25
Appear wise and astute	Be willing to appear a fool	1 Cor. 3:18
Aspire to leadership	Become a servant	Mark 10:44
Seek to be exalted	Humble yourself	Luke 14:11
Always be first	Serve downward	Mark 9:35
Desire great prosperity	Be an extravagant giver	Luke 6:33
Seek revenge and "payback"	Forgive	Col. 3:13
Cover your sins	Confess your sins	Prov. 18:33
Desire to be free	Become a slave of Christ	Matt. 20:26–27
Seek recognition	Value anonymity	Matt. 6:1–4
Dream of being great	Willing to be the least	Mark 10:43

Jesus Heals a Leper and Sends Him to the High Priest.

READ: Matt. 8:2–4; Mark 1:40–45; Luke 5:12–16

Jesus has been rejected in His hometown, has incurred the wrath of the Pharisees for cleansing the temple in Jerusalem, and has violated their oral laws regarding the Sabbath. He has healed many and is the new *matinee idol* of the multitudes because of the miracles He has performed. His ministry will now take a hard right turn. He will do something unprecedented in Jewish history. By performing a certain miracle, He will nonverbally, but unequivocally, announce that He is *the* Prophet of Deuteronomy 18:18 (the Messiah).

◆ **Jesus Heals a Jewish Man's Leprosy in Its Advanced Stages.**

Leprosy was a dreaded disease and thought to be highly contagious. Lepers could not socialize with uninfected people and were banned from the synagogue. Considered unclean both physically and spiritually, they were forced to live outside the cities and beg for money to stay alive. As we saw on Day 2, because the Jews were *cause-and-effect* thinkers, they considered leprosy a punishment from God. The priests did not even bother to pray for their salvation or for their healing. Leprosy was called "the finger of God." It was God's curse on them for something in their past or the sin of their parents before they reached the age of accountability.

> Knowing that the healing of a Jewish leper could only be done by the Messiah, why did the multitudes not believe? Discuss.

What is significant about this particular leper? (Refer to Day 10.)

◆ **The Leper Would Have Known One Critical Thing About Jesus.**

He would have had to believe that Jesus was the Messiah (Luke 5:12) because only the Messiah could heal him.

◆ **Jesus Sends the Leper to the High Priest (Luke 5:14).**

The leper was to tell _____.

In rabbinical school, when the instructor came to the lecture concerning the purification of lepers in Leviticus 14, all of the students probably said what we all said in school about some of our classes: "I'll never have to use this."

Moses had commanded this as a _____ *to them.*

This is the first of three messianic signs by which Jesus would validate Himself as the Messiah. Who better than the high priest to examine this man who was in the advanced stages of leprosy and have to testify that the leper was indeed clean and fully cured? In doing so he would be indirectly saying that Jesus was truly the prophet of Deuteronomy 18:18.

There was one problem. No priest had ever performed this cleansing because no Jewish lepers had ever been healed. Turn to Leviticus 14 and you will read about the eight-day, step-by-step procedure required in the law to be performed by the priest. The humor in this is that the priest would have no idea how to perform the cleansing. Can you imagine the panic in his face and the scrambling he would have done to look up the procedure in Leviticus as if cramming for a test?

DAY 18

JESUS HEALS A PARALYTIC LOWERED THROUGH THE ROOF OF A HOME IN CAPERNAUM.

READ: Matt. 9:1–9; Mark 2:1–12; Luke 5:17–26

The Pharisees and Jewish leaders are now hot on Jesus' trail since the unprecedented healing of the leper. Now, Jesus is teaching in a home and these Jewish leaders, despite their hatred for Galileans, have come to hear Him as part of their stepped-up investigation. As He is teaching inside the house, there is a distracting noise on the roof. Pieces of clay tiles are being removed from the roof and a light residue sprinkles the crowd below until a shaft of light appears, and the faces of four men are peering down at the stunned guests in the house. To everyone's amazement, a makeshift stretcher is suddenly maneuvered through the hole and is being lowered downward in front of Jesus. On it is a paralyzed man. The scribes and Pharisees would have most likely been horrified and deeply offended at this abrupt interruption of a rabbi's teaching. Jesus, however, is intrigued and encouraged by the level of commitment of the four men to go to this extreme to get their friend to Jesus without regard for their personal image or for the reaction of the gathered crowd.

Share the most compassionate thing you have seen or heard of someone doing in order to help bring a person into the presence of Jesus.

These four men are just average Jews who live in Galilee. They like Jesus for His miracles, and because of His recent healing of a leper, may, like others, feel there is a chance that He could be the Messiah. These men are probably thinking on purely a physical level. They want their friend to be healed. However, Jesus saw a deeper problem, not visible to the human eye. The man had a hole in his heart and desperately needed to be made new.

◆ **Jesus Forgives the Man for His Sins and the Pharisees and Scribes Grumble within Themselves (Mark 2:6).**

Why did the Jewish leaders grumble to themselves and not debate with Jesus? They considered what He said to the man to be blasphemy, the most severe sin a man could commit. Remember, they are still under the instruction of the Sanhedrin to observe Jesus, but not to speak.

◆ **Reading Their Thoughts, Jesus Asks Them a Penetrating Question (Mark 2:9).**

Most of us assume that Jesus simply utilizes His supernatural power to know the thoughts of these Jewish leaders. However, if we understand the mentality of these men as Jesus did, predicting the thoughts behind their sour expressions would have been very easy. Jesus knows exactly what their reaction will be when He tells the paralyzed man that his sins are forgiven. Miracles are not always performed by Jesus simply for the benefit of the recipient. At times it is to train the disciples and almost always to proclaim Jesus' identity as Messiah. In this case, it is probably to force the scribes and Pharisees to *get off the fence* and decide if He is who He claims to be. Forgiving sins is the exclusive prerogative of God; therefore, the leaders will be forced to decide.

One of the most common Bible study methods is to hear the leader of a small group say, "Lets all share what this passage means to each of us." This is the worst possible way to study the Scripture. The truth is, what you and I think about a passage is irrelevant. The purpose of Bible study is to determine the intent of the author. He meant one thing, not several conflicting things that ebb and flow with the times. There may be several applications, but only one meaning. Responsibly getting at that one intent of the author is our goal. In addition, a passage must always be studied in context. Who is speaking and being spoken to? What are the circumstances, etc.? More than anything, is the principle we read reflected in the rest of Scripture? Paul said, "I have not shunned to declare unto you the full counsel of God" (Acts 20:27 KJV). In other words, we can't create a principle from a passage of Scripture in isolation. It must be passed through the prism of 66 Books. God does not contradict Himself. If a principle is true in one passage, it will be true throughout the rest of Scripture.

Is it easier for Jesus to say, "Your sins are forgiven" or, "Take up your pallet and walk"?

One miracle is visible and one is invisible; one is observable and one is not. The multitudes would be more excited about visible results, and normally so would the Pharisees. However, forgiving sins can be accomplished only by God. They know forgiveness was far more difficult, but if they say it, they will be affirming Jesus' messianic claim.

Remember: The invisible is always better because the observable, like the healing of the paralytic, will only last until he dies.

How would you answer this question of Jesus in Mark 2:8–9, and why?

Although healing the leper was the criterion the Pharisees had long ago determined for recognizing the Messiah, Jesus simply did not fit the profile they had fixed in their minds. He was too plain, too ordinary, too much a man of the people. Besides, they think He was born in Nazareth.

Is it possible to miss seeing the biblical Jesus and settle for a cultural facsimile simply because the real Jesus does not fit the profile we have been raised to believe? We will discover that the Pharisees believed wealth was a sign of God's blessing, but they also believed that on the flip side, those without wealth were under the wrath of God. If you were poor, you had a spiritual problem. If you were rich, God had blessed you. But, who of us does not know people who are filthy rich, but got that way by manipulation, dishonesty, or by ignoring their families? Conversely, there are amazingly godly, faithful people across the globe who don't know where breakfast is coming from. It is easy to rationalize possessions by calling them a blessing from God. Maybe a better way to think is that the blessing is that you now are honored to be entrusted as a steward and have the opportunity to extravagantly give as you have received (Luke 6:36).

Write down at least one example of how your view of Jesus and His thinking may have been clouded by the thinking you have been exposed to. If you are in a small group, this would be a great discussion. (Look back at yesterday's study about **God's thinking** *to get you started.)*

DAY 19

MATTHEW'S CALL AND A RECEPTION TO HONOR JESUS

READ: Matt. 9:9–13; Mark 2:18–22; Luke 5:17–26

Jesus has performed the first of three messianic miracles and now, before anyone can catch their breath, He forgives a man's sins. This constituted blasphemy, the most scandalous sin a Jew could commit. Now he is going to invite a tax collector, called a "publican," one of the most despised people in Jewish culture, to be His disciple and to walk with Him.

- ◆ **Matthew Immediately Responds to Jesus' Invitation (Matt. 9:9).**

There were two kinds of publicans: tax collectors and customs agents. Matthew was the latter. These jobs were secured through the Roman government, basically by bidding or by payment of a bribe. Publicans had no respect from the Romans and were considered "turncoats" by the Jews. They made their money by adding their desired commission to the taxes they collected.

Being a customs agent was a very lucrative occupation, which is why Matthew bought the position or bribed the Romans officials to get it in the first place. It certainly wouldn't have been a prudent move if the goal was to make friends or meet Jewish women. The question to consider is what made Matthew abruptly leave his high-paying job and follow Jesus? Was he getting tired of the abuse from his fellow Jews? Was he fed up with who he had become? Or did he see something in Jesus eyes that drew him in? *What do you think?*

The Jewish leaders now have begun the second phase of their investigation of Jesus by asking specific questions.

- ◆ **Matthew Invites Jesus and the Disciples to a Party in His Home.**

Who was in attendance?

The most hated people in Jewish society were tax collectors and prostitutes (called sinners). The Pharisees taught that both of the groups were beyond redemption. No respectable Jew would be seen in their presence and certainly would never enter into one of their homes, much less eat a meal with them. It would have meant defilement. They could not serve as judges or even as a witness in court, and were expelled from the synagogues. This is why the only people who would came to celebrate Matthew's conversion were other tax collectors and prostitutes, and of course, Jesus.

◆ **The Pharisees Stand Outside and Ask the Disciples Why Jesus Would Eat a Meal with Such People (Matt. 9:11).**

◆ **Jesus Overhears Them and Declares That Only the Sick Need a Doctor.**

Is Jesus saying that only hookers and tax collectors are sick and have a need? Are the Pharisees spiritually unhealthy even though they are extremely religious? What is Jesus saying? Explain and discuss.

"For I delight in loyalty rather than sacrifice, and in the knowledge of God rather than burnt offerings" (Hos. 6:6).

◆ **Jesus Tells Them What He Desires from His Followers (Matt. 9:13).**

Jesus makes a statement that is the cornerstone of His life. He says that what He desires of people who follow Him is not *sacrifice*, but *compassion* because He came not to call the righteous, but sinners. But aren't we supposed to live sacrificial lives, giving and loving sacrificially? Remember Jesus is speaking to the Pharisees, who put the spotlight on external righteousness. They were sacrificial people trying to obey the letter of the law, but had no compassion for people. They should have loved the socks off these tax collectors and prostitutes. Instead, they inflicted every ounce of restriction and hatred they could muster. The word *righteous* is being said tongue in cheek by Jesus here because the Pharisees were in His mind, *pretenders of righteousness*. True righteousness reflects compassion, not sacrifice. Sacrifice can be self-generated, but true compassion comes from God. Think of it this way: Jesus went to the cross for us, making the ultimate sacrifice of His life. Do you honestly believe that as He went to the cross He was thinking of what a great sacrifice He was making? Was it not compassion and love for us that sustained Him during those dark hours? We see it as sacrifice, but for Him it all flowed from compassion for us. What if a murderer broke into your home and held a gun on your family? Just as he starts to pull the trigger, you instinctively dive in front of those you love and take the bullet yourself. Tomorrow's paper will say "LOCAL RESIDENT SACRIFICES LIFE TO SAVE LOVED ONES." People will call it sacrifice, but your motive was instinctive. Your action was driven by compassion and love.

KEY VERSE: "I desire compassion, and not sacrifice, for I did not come to call the righteous, but sinners" (Matt. 9:13).

A sacrificial approach to life can look very impressive, which is why the Pharisees chose it. Image was everything and substance was of little consequence. The people admired and respected the Pharisees, but behind closed doors, in their secret heart of hearts, they were hypocrites. Sacrificial people are weary, guilt-ridden people. Why? Because those who live that way never know if they have sacrificed enough. Every day is a grind and everyone is watching. The mask must be kept on at all times for fear of being exposed, and when you lie in you bed at night, you wonder if you are really fooling anyone. When you know who your are in Christ, everything you do is motivated not by obligation and sacrifice, but by gratitude and compassion. This is the difference between *law* and *grace*.

Take a minute to examine your approach to life. Why do you go to church, Bible studies, or a small group? Is it sacrifice? Is it to appear spiritual, or is it out of a real desire to grow and deepen as a person? **Pen your thoughts.**

Authentic sacrifice is never perceived as sacrifice by the one who performs it. It is an unconscious act that is seen as sacrifice only by those who observe it. A true sacrificial act is done with no hidden motives, no hope for recognition, and is generated purely by compassion and love.

DAY 20

THREE PARABLES THAT EXPLAIN WHY JESUS' DISCIPLES FEAST RATHER THAN FAST

READ: Matt. 9:14–17; Mark 2:18–22; Luke 5:33–39

The development of the oral laws was initially intended to protect or put a "hedge" around the Mosaic law. However, these oral laws put the Jews in bondage. There were thousands of oral laws added to the Mosaic law, and the Pharisees' love for these laws began to outweigh their love for God. This is vital to understanding their constant criticism of Jesus.

◆ **The Pharisees Question Jesus on the Issue of Fasting (Luke 5:33).**

In Matthew's account we read that even John's former disciples ask Jesus why everyone else fasts except His disciples. Had Jesus not taught them properly? Had they been out sick the day He covered the discipline of fasting?

What happens to truth when it is not reinforced within the core of believers? _____ *(Hint: What happens when a bucket of water is left out in the blazing sun day after day?)*

◆ **Jesus Answers with Three Pointed Illustrations.**

1. "When you're celebrating a wedding, you don't skimp on the cake and wine. You feast. Later you may need to pull in your belt, but not now. No one throws cold water on a friendly bonfire" (Matt. 9:15 MSG).

What is Jesus saying about Himself?

2. Why would you put a new patch of new cloth on an old garment? The new cloth will shrink and the threads will pull apart.

3. Why would someone pour new wine in old wineskins when he knows it will burst them open as the gases expand during fermentation and the old skins have no more ability to stretch?

There can never be common ground between truth and error. They are completely incompatible. Jesus came *as the Truth and to bring the truth.* The Pharisees were teaching error and leading the people down a dead-end road. By trying to merge God's law with their oral laws, they had created a form of Judaism that was like a torn garment that needed mending. Jesus says that His message of grace and liberty can never coexist with the man-made traditions of the Pharisees. There can never be an understanding of Jesus' message until men and women have new hearts.

Jesus Heals a Lame Man on the Sabbath and Explains His Actions to the Hostile Pharisees.

READ: John 5:1–47

Once again Jesus offends the Pharisees, first by having a meal in a tax collector's home, and then to make matters worse He uses biting illustrations about the incompatibility of His truth with their error. Now Jesus and His disciples are at a feast, possibly Passover. They are walking together and pass by a pool at the sheep gate, which in Hebrew is *Bethesda*. Lying beside this pool were many blind, lame, and broken people. Jewish tradition stated that if an angel stirred the water, the first to get in the pool would be healed. Jesus comes upon a man who has been there for thirty-eight years.

STAND IN THE MAN'S SANDALS: Again we must study this story empathetically to feel the impact. Imagine spending thirty-eight years hoping and praying that this would be the day of your healing. Imagine being completely dependent on others to get you down to the pool and to see to your needs. Imagine basing your hope on a religious tradition that had never delivered. In all probability you have lost hope and no longer really expect to be healed.

♦ **Jesus Asks the Man a Strange but Insightful Question (v. 6).**

Why would Jesus ask a man who had been lame most of his life if he wants to be healed? It seems like a no-brainer until you consider who is asking the question. Jesus obviously understands what happens to a man who pins his hope on that which cannot deliver. He also knows that the man realizes that he would lose an easy and consistent income through begging if he were healed. He would have to take responsibility for himself, get a job, and become a productive member of society. Maybe Jesus saw that the man had simply lost the will to care, and sickness had become a comfortable place to be.

Define hope:

Think of the hordes of people in this country who hope against hope that they will hit it big in the Publisher's Clearinghouse sweepstakes or the state lottery. They throw away their food and rent money dreaming of that one big payday. The truth is, the check is not in the mail! Biblical hope is built on certainty, not luck.

Even a pin carried in the hem of a garment was considered work, and therefore, a violation of the Sabbath.

What are three false hopes in which people often place their trust?

1.

2.

3.

♦ **Jesus Heals the Man, and Again, the Pharisees Miss the Point.**

Why are the Pharisees upset?

Jewish theology teaches that Israel was created for the purpose of honoring the Sabbath. The Mishnah records over fifteen hundred laws regarding the proper honoring of the Sabbath. The Pharisees were obsessed with policing this issue among the people. They had completely lost perspective on a law that was originally given by God as a gift to protect the people and to give them a time of rest from their labors.

Jesus said His works were the works of His Father. Traditionally, a Jewish boy would always copy the mannerisms of his dad. His familiarity and intimacy with God was something they just couldn't handle.

Notice that in verse 17 Jesus refers to God as "Father." In Jewish thinking, the firstborn male is considered equal to his father. Therefore when Jesus uses this relational term, He is claiming equality with God.

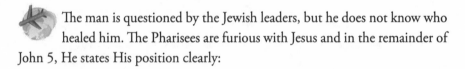

The man is questioned by the Jewish leaders, but he does not know who healed him. The Pharisees are furious with Jesus and in the remainder of John 5, He states His position clearly:

- His works are the Father's works (vv. 19–20).
- He has authority to give life to whom He wishes (v. 21).
- The Father has given all judgment to the Son (v. 22).
- He is the source of resurrection and of judgment (vv. 24–29).

DAY 21

CONTROVERSY AGAIN ARISES, THIS TIME OVER THE DISCIPLES EATING GRAIN.

READ: Matt. 12:1–8; Mark 2:23–28; Luke 6:1–5

It is again the Sabbath and the disciples walk through a grain field eating the heads of grain as they go. Naturally, the Pharisees are watching nearby and confront Jesus about His protégés' violation of the law. Jesus derails their argument, citing King David's eating of the consecrated bread on the Sabbath (1 Sam. 21:1–6). He also points to the fact that certain works by priests are permitted and that acts of mercy have always been lawful on the Sabbath (see Hos. 6:6). He concludes by saying that they have misunderstood the purpose of the Sabbath. It was made to *help* people, not to restrict them.

> *"The Sabbath was made for _____ and not man for the _____."*

Think of the restrictive measures we often place on one another that are not necessarily violations of God's commands, but simply violate our cultural bias. What comes to mind?

While walking through a grain field, if a disciple accidentally dislodged a grain of wheat from its stalk, it was considered work by the Pharisees and therefore a violation of the Sabbath.

◆ **The Third Sabbath Controversy Involves a Man with a Withered Hand (Matt. 1:9–14; Mark 3:1–6; Luke 6:1–5).**

In the local synagogue, Jesus encounters a man with a withered hand, while the Pharisees lie in wait to see if He will heal him. Knowing their agenda, Jesus asks them if it is lawful to do good or harm on the Sabbath. They won't answer. Jesus heals the man, forcing the issue that *acts of mercy* done on any day of the week violate neither God's laws nor their oral laws.

This healing is significant because the Jewish leaders had been uncertain as to their course of action until after this healing, but now, it is no longer an issue.

They even team up with the Herodians, whom they hated, in order to plan Jesus' death (Mark 3:6).

Jesus continues healing people as He travels in the area of Tyre and Sidon near the Sea of Galilee. As people come from everywhere, Jesus casts out evil spirits and curiously ... *they always know who He is* (Matt. 12:15–21; Luke 6:12–16).

For three-and-a-half years, the central issue among the multitudes, the Jewish leaders, the disciples, and even the Gentiles was this: *Who is this Man? What is His true identity? Could He really be who He says He is?* In every town He entered, the inhabitants discuss and debate the issue, but the demons are *certain* of His identify. This is the central issue today. Everything of any eternal consequence circles around the question of who Jesus is. If He is really God in the flesh, He cannot be dismissed with a yawn, a shrug of the shoulders, or a pat on the head. His life and His words can no longer be *interesting, inspiring, or thought provoking.* If Jesus is God, then He is also *Life* and *Truth.* Anything less than absolute allegiance to Him is insanity.

> *How would you explain the irony of the Jewish religious elite not recognizing Jesus' identity and the demons always knowing who He is?*

The Herodians were very much in favor of Roman rule. They were always at odds with the Pharisees, who deeply resented it. Here, however, they join forces based on their mutual hatred of Jesus.

JESUS SELECTS THE TWELVE DISCIPLES AFTER PRAYING ALL NIGHT.

READ: Mark 3:13–19; Luke 6:12–16

The disciples whom Jesus had called to follow Him had seen a little snapshot of what lay ahead of them, but their understanding of Jesus' identity was in its infant stages. Jesus had to make a final decision as to the twelve men into whom He would pour His life. Like everything He did, His dependence would be completely on His Father for wisdom and discernment. He prays all during the night and then selects His men. From the standpoint of reputation, expertise, leadership experience, and education, no one in their right mind would have picked this bunch. They were common, ordinary men, uneducated, and with limited social skills (Acts 4:13), yet Jesus saw in them something no one else was able to see. It may have been a teachable spirit, their unbridled enthusiasm, and in some it may have simply been their raw thirst for adventure and willingness to risk everything. Whatever their underlying potential was, the right choice was made, including Judas, whose actions were used to accomplish God's purpose.

Without looking at the text, how many apostles can you name? Write below.

Jesus chose the Twelve to be _____ *Him (Mark 3:14).*

People generally believe that discipling someone requires fairly broad theological knowledge. They assume that discipleship is basically passing this knowledge on to their protégé. However, when these men were chosen by Jesus, they knew next to nothing other than the traditions taught them by the Pharisees. Jesus knew that if they would simply be *with* Him they would never recover from that kind of exposure. Probably 90 to 95 percent of discipling another is being *with them* and 5 to 10 percent is information—just the opposite of what most of us think.

Few people, especially men, understand the value of simply being with others without a specific agenda. Kids get it; they call it *hanging out.* Women get it! They call a friend for lunch and she responds, *"What time?"* When a man calls a friend for lunch, he *wonders what is wrong.* Jesus had three years to equip these men with the truth, yet they never saw discipleship notebooks and color-coded strategy charts on how to win the world. Jesus knew how to *hang out* creatively so they could see and feel every emotion. Being *with* someone without a planned agenda is the surest path to the heart.

There is a good probability that some of the disciples could neither read nor write. Their average age when they began to follow Jesus was probably around 22.

DAY 22

THE SERMON ON THE MOUNT

READ: Matt. 5—7; Luke 6:17–49

The Sermon on the Mount is the purest expression of God's law. It was never intended to be the standard for a Christian lifestyle.

Immediately after Jesus chooses His twelve companions, He takes them to an area that was actually a level plain (Luke 6:17), probably near the base of a mountain in Galilee. His recent series of conflicts with the Pharisees concerning their oral traditions had in all probability confused His disciples because of these Jewish leaders' lifelong influence in their lives. Jesus takes them off to teach them on a deeper level. In the next five days, we will look at an aerial view of the sermon, diving in for a closer look at some passages.

> NOTE: Before we look at this amazing teaching, it is critical to understand what the sermon is and what it is not. The Sermon on the Mount is a picture of the type of righteousness God required in the Mosaic law in order for a person to enter the kingdom of God. It is a practical snapshot of what life was intended to look like if it was lived in perfect obedience to God's standards. The problem is that only one person has ever accomplished that kind of perfection, Jesus Christ (Gal. 4:4; 2 Cor. 5:21; Matt. 5:17). The sermon is not what most people think it is. Most of us have been taught that the Sermon on the Mount is a creed or set of moral standards that should govern our lifestyle. You will often hear someone say, "I live my life by the Sermon on the Mount." A reasonable response to that statement might be, "How's it going?" The last verse in Matthew 5 should answer that for you: "Be perfect, just as your Father in heaven is perfect" (5:48 NKJV). It is not a standard we could ever attain, and God does not intend for us to attain it or even try to get close. If this sounds strange, just hang in there for a minute.

Trying to adjust my lifestyle to the standard of the Sermon on the Mount is to throw the spotlight on my external behavior rather than on the change of heart God requires. This was the crux of Jesus' long-running debate with the Pharisees. Their focus was on external performance, while His emphasis was always on a new heart.

THE LAW: The first five books of the Bible (the Torah, or Pentateuch) contain 613 laws, which God gave Moses. However, most of the time when we speak of God's law we are speaking of the Ten Commandments. What is the purpose of these laws? "For us to obey," we all say as one. But if that was the expectation of God, He would be like the proverbial "Little League" dad who demanded a home run from his son every time he comes to bat. Would a loving father or a loving heavenly Father set his child up for failure unless it was to convince him of a better way? Is it impossible to obey God's laws completely? No! So why would God give them to us? So that we would attempt to obey them and fail? The law is like a brick wall that we crash against trying to conquer. Finally after many migraines and repeated failures we fall to our knees in frustration and despair and say, "God, this is impossible; I can't live up to this!" And God's response is *"Thank you. I know you can't; that's why you need a Savior."*

The same is true of the great sermon we will briefly look at. Sure, some of us will do better than others if we all try diligently to conquer these passages. But if you and I and a couple of other friends take an exam in school and you get a 55, Jenny over there achieves a 50, I get a 45, and Chuck gets a 40, we all fail the exam. You may have bragging rights to a higher F than the rest of us, but we're all in trouble. The truth is, none of us is capable of passing this exam. Jesus lived the law perfectly. If He is in you and you will yield to Him, He will live God's commands out in your life.

"The letter [of the law] kills, but the Spirit gives life" (2 Cor. 3:6).

Read these passages carefully and briefly summarize in your own words:

"No man can justify himself before God by a perfect performance of the Law's demands—indeed, it is the straight-edge of the Law that shows us how crooked we are" (Rom. 3:20 PH).

Think of it this way; we have two choices: 1. Try to live out the requirements of God's law by our own tenacity and self-discipline or 2. Give up and yield to the Spirit of God in us, allowing Him to be our righteousness. If you opt for the first, you must live the law perfectly every moment of your life until you die.

"The Ten Commandments were given so that all could see the extent of their failure to obey God's laws. But the more we see our sinfulness, the more we see God's abounding grace forgiving us" (Rom. 5:20 TLB).

"Law is not made for a righteous person, but for those who are lawless and rebellious, for the ungodly and sinners" (1 Tim. 1:9).

Don't misunderstand. I am not advocating a passive or sedentary life where we just sit and watch *Oprah*. This study was not written by hoping God would magically write it. Long hours of study and research went into it. Jesus said His works were done not by Him, but by His Father. Does that mean Jesus was passive and lazy? When God says start a school, then start one. But if you plow ahead in your own strength and energy, you'll fail. Yield everything to God and He will accomplish it through you.

"The Law has become our tutor to lead us to Christ" (Gal. 3:24).

Where does that leave us? We can't live out God's requirements (the law) and Jesus is the only one who ever did or could. The exciting paradox is that we don't have to live them out. If we have received Him by faith, He resides in us and will live out these requirements of God through us without our determination or self-effort. To the degree that we step back and yield to His life within us, we then allow Jesus to simply be Himself in us. Then, by His strength and ability, we will be able to meet God's expectations because it is done by Him through us.

Though the Sermon was taught to His disciples, the Pharisees were lurking in the crowd, listening intently. Over time, their allegiance had moved from God to religious observances and traditions. Their oral laws served to create great burdens on the people. When we impose impossible standards on ourselves that only produce guilt and hopelessness, we create intolerable burdens. If we could obey the Sermon on the Mount, we wouldn't need Jesus. The liberating truth of the Gospels is that God is not demanding that we do what He knows we are incapable of doing. Instead, He opens to us the possibility of allowing His Spirit to live out God's holy requirements from within our lives with only our willingness and availability. All God needs from us in facing daily issues of life is to yield to His life within us, and He will live out His commands in us while we are in a posture of rest.

If we fail to study the Sermon on the Mount from this perspective of grace, we will unconsciously put ourselves and anyone we may teach under law. We will also ensure for ourselves and our hearers a built-in guarantee to fail.

Before we look at this great teaching, briefly summarize what you have just read. Doing so is critical for understanding this teaching.

DAY 23

THE BEATITUDES

READ: Matt. 5:3–16

The law of God must always be passed through the prism of love and grace before it is applied to people.

The Beatitudes are simply the kind of perspective Jesus wants to produce in those who walk with Him. Each of these "attitudes" begins with the word *blessed*, probably best translated as "happy." You might say that these attitudes are a condition within a person that engenders calmness of spirit and peace with God and with oneself. There are nine of these "blessed attitudes" that give us a picture of the character God wants to develops in us. The blessed attitudes are the foundation on which the rest of the sermon is built. We are not capable of creating these attitudes in our own lives, but if we yield to Christ in us, he will make the following four things happen: We will be ...

- Verse 13 _____
- Verse 14 _____
- Verse 14 _____
- Verse 15 _____

◆ **"Blessed are the poor in spirit, for theirs is the kingdom of heaven."**

Who are the poor in spirit? Look up the following Old Testament passages and write words that are common to all three:

• *Isaiah 57:15*   • *Isaiah 66:2*   • *Psalm 51:17*

According to these verses, the poor in spirit are people who

_____ .

These are people who hate sin and are crushed with sorrow for their own arrogance in attempting to do what only God can do. These people understand that their only hope is the grace of God.

◆ **"Blessed are those who mourn, for they shall be comforted."**

Mourn? Mourn what? Be sad and pathetic-looking all the time? Look up the verses below and summarize what they collectively say:

• *Isaiah 51:3,12,19*   • *Isaiah 54:11*   • *Isaiah 61:2*   • *Isaiah 66:13*

The pain associated with loss rearranges all of our priorities. Hurricane Katrina devastated the Gulf Coast. Many fled; others refused to leave their homes. In the aftermath, those who survived told moving stories of overwhelming gratitude for their lives being spared. Those who had fled and returned seemed more focused on the extent of their loss. Same storm, two different perspectives. Somehow, in the midst of mourning and pain, those who stayed in the storm experienced supernatural comfort. Coming to the end of yourself and hitting the wall seems to release a blanket of well-being and comfort that self-protection and avoidance of pain can never know.

◆ **"Blessed are the meek, for they shall inherit the earth."**

Many years ago a great young man named Jon Coe died of cancer at age 27. At the memorial service, one person after another came up to an open mike and told stories of Jon's impact on their lives and his great love for and faith in Jesus. A huge gathering of mourners filled with pain and suffering was slowly transformed into the most magnificent expression of joy, thanksgiving, and comfort I have ever experienced. This goes right to the heart of what I believe Jesus is saying.

Read Psalm 37:9–11. What is the essence that the psalmist expresses?

When a Hebrew heard "The meek shall inherit the earth," he would have immediately thought of Psalm 3. The entire psalm is about those who refuse to compromise God's principles and who allow the righteousness produced in them to be expressed toward others. Meekness is power under control. A wild stallion that is broken so it can be ridden is no less powerful than before, but the energy is now diffused and usable. "Inherit the earth" was a phrase commonly used by the rabbis as a state of blessedness of the righteous after the resurrection.

- **"Blessed are those who hunger and thirst for righteousness, for they shall be satisfied."**

  Look up the following Old Testament passages and summarize in a phrase.

  - *Isaiah 55:1; 65:13* • *Psalm 22:26; 37:17*

If a believer is spiritually hungry and thirsty, that hunger and thirst will be satisfied. He will be made whole. We will see this more clearly later when Jesus teaches at the Feast of Tabernacles in John 7.

- **"Blessed are the merciful, for they shall receive mercy."**

Just as loving God and one another are inexorably linked, so is expecting forgiveness from God and being willing to forgive others.

  Being unmerciful in marriage can result in _____
  (1 Peter 3:7).

- **"Blessed are the pure in heart, for they shall see God."**

What does it mean to be *pure in heart?* Do you know anyone with an absolutely pure heart? We may know people are *good hearted, honest, and*

Keep in mind that getting through these beatitudes is not a goal that will help to enrich your life. Take time to reflect and meditate on each of them. Discuss them with trusted friends and allow God to teach you. Don't be in a hurry!

compassionate, but who has a truly *pure heart*, free from personal agendas and whose only desires are God's honor and the absolute best for others? First of all, who of us has ever looked at another person's heart or interior motives? We may see the reflection of a good heart in their character, but only God can know the heart.

So, what is a pure heart? Look up Psalm 24:3–4 and summarize.

Consider this: Those who are pure in heart are never infatuated with the things that eventually become gods to many people. They are not enamored with those things others deem to be of ultimate value and around which they plan their time and priorities. These individuals are not false in any of their dealings with God or with people.

Remember the purpose of the law? The Sermon on the Mount is the purest expression of the law that we have. Who can be pure in heart? Who never gets carried away by the exciting false gods of this world (money, cars, lake houses, power)? Who is never false in any of his or her dealing with the Father or with people? Only Jesus. As He is in you and you yield to His life, He who is pure in heart will begin the process of creating that same heart in you so that you will become pure in heart.

DAY 24
THE SERMON CONTINUES.

◆ **"Blessed are the peacemakers, for they shall be called sons of God."**

Consider a true peacemaker as being one who seeks to introduce others to a kind of peace that comes only from God Himself … a peace that is not temporary and does not depend on favorable circumstances. As we saw on Day 5, peace has much to do with understanding and believing our identity before God. It means rejecting the definitions given to us by a world that knows nothing of peace and contentment.

Sons of God will naturally reproduce, because God is a Father who desires more children.

What is the difference between a peacemaker and a peacekeeper?

- "Blessed are those who have been persecuted for the sake of righteousness, for theirs is the kingdom of heaven" (also vv. 11–12).

What words come to your mind as you read this verse?

And all of this time we were thinking that following Jesus was about living a life of joy and bliss, free from worry and strife. Actually, the passage is not about *martyrdom*. Jesus is not telling the Twelve to go out and be so spiritually obnoxious that people will hate them and thereby prove their piousness.

Read Isaiah 51:1: "You who _____ righteousness."

The Hebrew word here is *radaf,* which means "to run after." Jesus was not encouraging His disciples to go looking for ways to spiritually irritate the world (v. 11 says "because of Me"). It is not some pious act on their part for which they are blessed, but simply because of their identification and companionship with Jesus. He is speaking of a perspective or an attitude that the believer must possess as he or she pursues a deeper and more intimate relationship with the Father. The world is running after a different set of values, and the contrast between their goals and ours will cause people to think we are nuts and often cause alienation.

Notice what Jesus says to the contrary in Luke 6:26. (Write it out:)

Blessed (happy) are those who remember what those who have gone before had to endure, even Jesus Himself. We're in good company.

SUMMARY: We can now begin to see why this teaching of Jesus must be studied and understood through the perspective of grace and not laws to be tenaciously obeyed by self discipline and determination. Not only will we become depressed, guilt ridden, and frustrated by failing constantly, but there are no parameters to tell us how much is enough. How pure in heart must I be in order to see God? How merciful or poor in spirit? To what degree do I need to be a peacemaker? How will I know when I'm there? I can't! The Sermon on the Mount is not our gold ring. Knowing Jesus is the gold ring. He, then, is free to live through us and produce mercy, peace, and other "blessed attitudes" in our lives.

Jesus Tells the Disciples Who They Are.

READ: Matt. 5:13–16

♦ **We Are Salt.**

One of the chambers of the temple compound was called *the Salt Chamber*. The salt stored there came from the Dead Sea and was called the "salt of Sodom." It is a salt that does not lose its salty taste. If it ever did, its usefulness would be limited to sprinkling the granules below the altar to be trodden underfoot by the priests so they would not slip on the sacrificial blood. According to Leviticus 2:13, no sacrifice could be offered without salt.

In addition to salt's usefulness as a flavoring agent in food, and the above mentioned use in the temple, salt is also a preservative. The lack of refrigeration made it necessary to pack meat in salt to prevent spoilage. In other words, it kept meat in its *original state*. Consider the fact that Jesus did not come to start a new religion called Christianity or even to operate outside the parameters of Judaism. Jesus was the promised Messiah of the Jews. When a Jew decides to follow Him, he does not become a Christian, but a *completed* or messianic Jew. When you accept Jesus, you become a *true Jew*. Jesus wants His disciples to preserve the message of the kingdom in its *intended state*. In the following verses, we will see that Jesus came to *fulfill* or *complete* the law

Keep in mind that these statements of Jesus are the identity of the believer from the moment he receives Jesus in his life. We don't try to be salt and light. We are salt and light, even when we don't feel like it. The Pharisees tried to be light by shining on the outside, but their hearts were dark. If the heart is right, the whole vessel will be illuminated.

81

not to abolish it. When the church ceases to preserve God's intended message, the world will trample it underfoot and its effectiveness will cease.

◆ We Are Light.

Religion is salvation by self-discipline or, as my friend Bob Warren puts it, "salvation without God."

Jesus' expression "a city set on a hill" is related directly to light. Rosh ha Shannah 2:2 says, "Formerly fires were lighted on the tops of mountains for the purpose of announcing the full moon." Obviously, the fires had to be set on hilltops in order to be seen. Therefore, believers were to be like those lights on the mountaintops so that others would see those characteristics in their lives that reflect God's glory.

To abolish or destroy the law meant that someone was misinterpreting it. To fulfill the law meant to properly interpret it. No Jew would ever consider abolishing or destroying the law and yet, the Pharisees had slowly perverted it with their add-on laws.

Jesus teaches His disciples that His purpose for coming was not to start a rival religion or to destroy the sacred laws of Judaism. God's laws are still valid, but are impossible for the believer to live out in his own strength. Even the thought of abolishing the law would be unthinkable to a Jew. A quote from Jewish literature says, "The one who destroys even the smallest letter of the Law, the sin is so great, that if it could be done, the whole world would be destroyed."

In contrast to this, the Pharisees were destroying the original intent of the law by trying to make it compatible with their oral traditions. What was the original intent of the law? It was to frustrate our efforts to be righteous, showing us our need for a Savior. The Pharisees taught that man could obtain righteousness by obeying the Mosaic and oral laws.

DAY 25

JESUS SIGNS HIS OWN DEATH WARRANT (MATT. 5:20).

Had you been a Pharisee, how would you interpret what Jesus says in verse 20?

The original definition of righteousness (*tzedakah* in Hebrew) was salvation or deliverance. By the time of Jesus, righteousness had been reduced to three fundamental things: prayer, fasting, and the giving of alms. Jesus tells them that if they have reduced righteousness to those three spiritual disciplines, they could kiss the kingdom of heaven good-bye. Can you imagine their anger as Jesus systematically dismantles their theology?

Look carefully at verses 33, 38, and 43, and notice the similarity. What is Jesus referring to when He prefaces His teaching with these words?

JESUS DISCUSSES PERSONAL RELATIONSHIPS.

In the remaining verses in the chapter (21–48), Jesus addresses personal relationships. Most of these principles would have been completely new thoughts to the disciples. He first deals with anger and lust, equating anger with murder, and lust with adultery. Jesus wants His disciples to understand that the *brain* is the most powerful organ in the human body. How they *think* determines how they will *act*. He goes on to explain to them that trying to maintain a relationship with God while being alienated from a brother is a colossal waste of time and energy. If your brother has something against you, get off your knees, close your Bible, and go to him. Deal with the problem, then come back to your quiet time. Otherwise, you make a mockery out of your relationship with God.

The word *racah*, which Jesus warns against our using, means empty-headed or incompetent.

Verses 29–30 are almost impossible to understand except through Hebrew eyes. Jesus uses a common Jewish teaching method of His day called *kal va homer*. It means "light and heavy." He is saying that if you cut sin off at the knees, while it is in its *infant* or light stages, you will prevent it from growing into a monster that will destroy you. It has nothing to do with actually cutting off hands or plucking out eyes.

Amazing how many people write off faith in Jesus, pointing to verses that talk about "plucking out eyes" and "cutting off hands." This was simply a method of Jewish teaching that Jesus used to say, "Nip sin in the bud, before it eats you alive!"

Jesus deals briefly with divorce (we will cover this more fully later when He teaches on the subject). He then speaks about making vows. Again He contrasts what they have been taught in the past with what He will teach them now. People made vows for many reasons and would swear by almost anything dear to them. Jesus is teaching the Twelve to give a simple *yes* or *no*. If they make a promise to someone, always keep the promise. If they fail to do so, they are to go and explain their failure, asking forgiveness. Verses 38–39 are the keys to understanding the passages that follow. Jesus is quoting a well-known Old Testament principle (see Ps. 24:19; 37:1, 8). He is *not* teaching that we should throw up our hands and be door mats for the evil intent of others. Rather, He is teaching that we should give up any thoughts or plans for retribution or payback toward a brother who has his nose out of joint. Jesus is expressing a believer's basic relational posture toward his neighbors. We do not simply *tolerate* evil, but our response to the angry neighbor or someone with *road rage* should be different than those around us.

If we respond differently to an angry person meaning us harm, what will be the result of that attitude? *(Look up and summarize in a sentence 1 Thess. 5:15; 1 Peter 3:9; Rom. 12:14, 17–19.)*

If a Roman, who could by law, demanded that a Jew carry his burden for 1 mile, he is in control of that Jew. If the Jew voluntarily decides to serve the Roman and take the burden a second mile, who is in control during mile 2?

Your boss or mother-in-law manipulates and takes continual advantage of you. Rather than lie in bed each night seething, you drop to your knees and pray for him or her and their family. Where does the control lie?

 The following verses (40–47) are essentially accenting the same issue of dealing with someone who is unkind or hateful. Jesus is saying that our response should be reflective of who we are, not simply a reaction that mirrors our natural emotions. Voluntarily carrying the load a second mile for an oppressive Roman who has demanded compliance for the first mile, giving to the needy, turning the other cheek, and praying for your enemies speaks more convincingly of authentic faith than a thousand Bible studies or sermons.

How are you doing so far? Can you muster up enough self-discipline and determination to let this great teaching be the sacred creed that you hope to one day conquer? If so, read verse 48 and write it below.

TRUE RIGHTEOUSNESS AND THE VALUE OF ANONYMITY

READ: Matt. 6:1–21

Though the teaching in the Sermon on the Mount is intended for the disciples, Jesus indirectly chastises the Pharisees right from the beginning of Matthew 6. He teaches the Twelve by using the three most important acts of righteousness to a Jew: alms giving (vv. 2–4), prayer (vv. 5–15), and fasting (vv. 16–18). He teaches them that acts of righteousness such as these should not be done in order to impress others. God's knowledge of it is all that matters.

Be honest. When you say a prayer over your Caesar salad in a restaurant, is it always *because of a sense of gratefulness to God, or is it to appear thankful to someone who might be there from your church? Are you thanking God or impressing people? Can you think of other ways that can be unconscious attempts to put our spirituality on display?*

Ancient Jews were taught that the three virtues of prayer, charity, and repentance (shown by fasting) were the evidence of a heart which had turned from sin.

♦ **Giving with the Right Spirit (vv. 2–4)**

Jesus warns the Pharisees about "sounding the trumpet" when giving their alms. The word *alms* was synonymous with charity to the poor during the first century. In the women's court of the temple were thirteen oddly shaped collection boxes for alms that made a unique sound as the coins were deposited. These containers were wide at the bottom and narrow at the top, resembling a trumpet. Often the Pharisees who wanted their charity to be noticed would drop a large number of coins in at one time, a practice that was called "sounding the trumpet." Jesus opposed their desire to let everyone know how much they were giving.

Is the primary intent of giving to those in need to help them or to help the giver? Read Acts 20:35. For whom is the real blessing intended? Why?

♦ **Praying with Meaning and Substance (vv. 5–13)**

In verses 5–8, Jesus contrasts two attitudes of prayer. What are they?

Does this mean that we should never pray publicly?_____ If not, why would Jesus make such an issue of it to the Twelve?

85

In the original language, praying in a *private room* meant praying in a room with no windows. When Jesus mentions the "vain repetitions" of the Pharisees' prayers, he is referring to the fact that they memorized or read their prayers ... the more elaborate and flowery, the better. The original Hebrew thought was that the type of prayers that last into eternity were prayers of thanksgiving, and that the highest form of prayer was silence; because only then could you listen and allow God to speak to you.

◆ **Jesus Teaches the Twelve How to Pray (vv. 9–15).**

After teaching the disciples how *not* to pray, Jesus gives them a model prayer intended to instruct them in the basic elements of talking with the Father. He had just instructed them not to use vain repetitions as if repeating a mantra. It is interesting that the very things He tells the disciples *not* to do, we do today with the Lord's Prayer. We repeat it in most of our churches each Sunday morning, we say it in locker rooms after the ball game, and we teach our children to say it every night. Is that necessarily wrong? No, but it was not Jesus' intent in giving it to us. Notice that in verse 9, Jesus says, "Pray, then, *in this way.*" In other words, pray like this, in this manner. It does not say, *pray this prayer every time you gather.* This prayer, actually *the disciples' prayer,* contains all the elements prayer should contain, such as praise, thanksgiving, petition, and confession.

"Do not prattle in the assembly of elders, nor repeat yourselves in your prayers" (Ecclesiasticus, Sirach 7:14).

DAY 26

FASTING WITH A TRUE SENSE OF HUMILITY (MATT. 6:16–18)

Why do people fast today?

To a Jew, *repentance* was the reason for fasting. If you had no need to repent of anything, you did not need to fast. Fasting is also for the purpose of *inner reflection,* which would draw a person toward a place of repentance. Fasting today for many believers is for the purpose of getting something. It is a way to show God your sincerity for something you have asked of Him. Jews fasted only during daylight hours, from morning until evening. By Jesus' time, the Pharisees were demanding that all Jews fast at least twice a week, on the second and fifth days. They turned a *volitional act* of devotion into a *mandatory observance* that had become burdensome and was viewed as a tradition.

It didn't bother Jesus when the Pharisees wanted to obey these practices, but when they began to teach that God expected the people to systematically keep them, He challenged this. Here in the sermon Jesus rebuked three aspects of their fasting:

1. He told them to be cheerful, not sad-looking, haggard, and pitiful (v. 16).
2. Those fasting were not to have a self-righteous attitude and must fast secretly rather than drawing attention to themselves (vv. 16, 18).
3. He refused to let the Pharisees force their rules on others. It was a personal decision (v. 18).

♦ **Jesus Briefly Addresses Investing.**

In verses 19–21 Jesus makes a simple but profound statement concerning investing your assets. How do you "store up for yourselves treasure in heaven"? People store up treasure for themselves every day via mutual funds, real estate, etc. How does this apply to heaven, where you will spend eternity? There seems to be only one real way. Invest in that which is going there. *People!* Where you invest is in direct proportion to where the true intent your heart really lies (v. 21).

How can you invest your treasure in people?

♦ **Having a "Clear Eye" (6:22–23)**

These two verses make little sense unless seen from the Jewish perspective. Take your best guess at what the basic idea expressed by Jesus is in these verses, before reading the thoughts below.

These two verses are notoriously misinterpreted. Most sermons you hear and many commentaries will generally relate these verses to lust or sexual immorality. This is because we see a Jewish text through Gentile eyes. A "clear eye" can also be translated, "single eye" or "good eye." The Mishnah Terumouth 4:3 says, *"The person with a good eye gave the fortieth part of the first fruit of the heave offering for the maintaining of the priests, while the person with the evil eye gave only a sixtieth."* A Jew thought of someone with a "single eye" as a *generous giver,* while one with a bad or evil eye was stingy and self-absorbed. Jesus had just spoken of storing up treasure in heaven, and now He follows by saying that a generous giver is one whose attitude will affect his whole body in a positive manner.

List three positive ways you are emotionally and physically affected because of your generosity.

1.

2.

3.

Money is a means, a medium of exchange, not an end in itself. The love of it will dominate your thoughts and drive your actions. It will captivate your allegiance and steal your time. Jesus speaks much about it because it can become a major obstacle in a healthy, loving relationship with God and one another.

Before teaching on worry and anxiety, Jesus deals with an issue critical to these disciples in their developing leadership role in building the church. He warns them about trying to live on both sides of the fence, seeking prominence in the world and the kingdom. They can't be in love with money and God at the same time.

Why can a person not love both God and money? Does this mean some-one who acquires wealth is opposing God?

♦ **Jesus Addresses Worry and Anxiety (vv. 25–34).**

These are very familiar verses, even to the occasional reader of the Scriptures. Though speaking primarily to the Twelve, Jesus' words strike at the heart of the twenty-first-century stress that lurks in every dark corner waiting to ambush us. **BE THE DISCIPLES:** You will be living in an increasingly hostile environment, preaching an unpopular message to a largely disinterested world. With no visible means of financial support, you will have to trust God for

Trying to flourish in an atmosphere of criticism is like an alcoholic trying to get sober in a bar.

every need. The potential for anxiety and stress will be a constant threat. Your tendency will be to try to control and manipulate your circumstances, a fruitless endeavor, and a perfect recipe for *angst* and *worry*. Jesus is reminding you that the Father cares for you just as He cares for the lilies of the field and the birds of the air who sweat and obsess over nothing. Why? They are not responsible for their own nourishment and energy. He is patiently teaching you and your companions that your focus must be on *embracing* and *enjoying* the Father and His righteousness, and the issues of life that can cause stress will lose their power and intensity.

◆ Jesus Addresses Judging Others (Matt. 7:1–6; Luke 6:37–42).

Would you believe that Matthew 7:1 has now surpassed John 3:16 as the single most quoted verse in the Bible? Judging what? That's the question. What Jesus is *not* saying here is as important as what He *is* saying. He is *not* saying that we have no right to call sin what it is, or that every moral or social offense is none of our business. Never to express absolutes in a relativistic society is *not* in line with the rest of Scripture. Jesus is saying that we have no right or authority to judge the *heart* of another. No one can see into your heart except God. When you hear this verse quoted, it is often by someone who feels that his behavior, regardless of how inappropriate, has no effect on anyone else. Someone driving like a maniac has a direct effect on others who are on the highway. I have a right to call his driving into question, but not his character. For all I know he may have received a desperate call that his wife is in the emergency room at the hospital. Therefore, judge not *the heart of another*, lest he and others do the same to you.

"She can say whatever she wants, but I know what she's thinking." Or, *"He claims it was just an oversight, but I know he did it on purpose!"* Ever said anything similar to that? You are questioning a person's intent. You have never seen an intent or a motive and you never will. We all think we know the secret agenda behind those things that displease us, but we can only speculate. When we use energy to speculate, a "house of bitterness" toward another is built on a foundation of which we can never be certain. The actions may be discernable, but the motive of the heart is not.

In verses 3–5, Jesus is addressing the Pharisees (indirectly) through teaching the Twelve. They had put heavy burdens of legalism on themselves and others, then condemned all who could not comply. Jesus is telling them to back off and examine the issues in their own lives.

Possibly the reason Matthew 7:1 is so often quoted is that in a world void of absolutes, our morality tends to dictate our theology.

If there is any inward sense of satisfaction or joy in confronting the destructive behavior of another, we are out of line. Jesus took no pleasure in addressing the error of the Jewish leaders. His love for them was great, but He knew that by their misleading of the people, an entire generation would suffer.

Look up the following verses and notice that making a judgment can *be an act of love:*

- 1 Cor. 5:1–5—Paul admonishes the church for immorality.
- 2 Cor. 2:5–10—Motive: Is judging sin an expression of vindictiveness or is it an act of love?
- Gal. 2:11–12—If truth is a revelation from God rather than man's attempts to control another, then we must "speak the truth in love." Love means to will the best for another.
- 1 Cor. 6:1–5—The saints of God will one day judge the world.

DAY 27

PRAYER, THE GOLDEN RULE, THE NARROW WAY, AND FALSE PROPHETS

READ: Matt. 7:7–23

Jesus concludes His great sermon with both a *challenge* and a *warning* to the Twelve. One who is a beloved child of his father does not have to be concerned about receiving anything but positive gifts from him. Those who have had a painful relationship with an earthly father may have a difficult time believing in the extravagant love of a heavenly Father. However, we must separate the two and not judge God on the basis of a dad who was abusive, inattentive, or just not there. We need only ask, and the Father, whose nature exudes the joy of giving, will *run with great joy* to answer our requests.

◆ Two Roads: The Narrow Way and the Wide Way (vv. 13–14)

Jesus then addresses two roads one can choose in life: the *wide way* and the *narrow way*. Religion is often defined as a system of ethics, a code of conduct, an ideology, or a creed. To a Hebrew it is none of these. A Hebrew understood his daily life of faith in terms of a journey or a pilgrimage. His faith was synonymous with the way he chose to live his life. If a person knows God, he walks in intimate fellowship with Him down the road of life. He makes every part of his life available for God's use. Over time, ceremonialism and ritualism may creep in, and in Jesus' day, they had taken over. But to a true Jew, real faith is walking with God in wisdom and righteousness, and serving others.

In this great sermon, Jesus uses familiar Hebraic imagery to teach about the two potential ways one can *walk*. This passage is a great example of why we must know to whom Jesus was speaking and what they had formally been taught. Contrary to the way many of us have been taught, it is *not* the wide way that is easy and the narrow way that is difficult. That would certainly be logical to the Gentile mind, but it's a matter of perspective. Jesus wants the Pharisees and all who are under their teaching to know that the *narrow way* is really the easy way because a disciple *lives by* and *draws from* God's very life, not by his own efforts. The wide way of pharisaic teaching was to circumvent redemption through God's Messiah and to attempt to achieve it on their own merits. It was not only difficult, but *impossible*. If the narrow way seemed hard, it was because those who had been taught external righteousness by obeying the law would find it difficult to accept that their performance had nothing to do with their own attempts at a righteous life.

Truth is the narrow way because it can only be realized by complete reliance on Jesus. The wide way is humanity's attempt to produce in our own lives the righteousness only God is capable of producing.

◆ **Beware of False Prophets.**

Jesus concludes His teaching with a warning to beware of false prophets and a challenge to build on a solid foundation. When the cold, north wind blows and truth is challenged by the world, we can stand firm, knowing what we believe, and walk in the light of that truth by His strength and energy.

The question for the disciples, and for us, is **what will we now do with the knowledge we have?** *Look back over this study of the sermon we have covered, and write down three things God has impressed on you that might change your perspective in the future.*

1.

2.

3.

Jesus Heals a Roman Centurion's Servant.

READ: Matt. 8:5–13; Luke 7:1–17

Jesus and *the Twelve* have now left the hill region of Galilee and journeyed to Capernaum, a sizable city in Jesus' day (Luke 7:1). Peter's home there had become their base of operations. There is a very unusual Roman officer in this town, a centurion with one hundred soldiers under his authority. Think of him as the chief of police, whose job it was to keep the Jews in line. Rather than being antagonistic toward these Jews, whom the Romans felt were inferior, he has great compassion and love for them. In fact, he loves them so much that when they need a synagogue in which to worship, he builds it for them with his own money. His servant, whom he also loves, is very ill and he hears that Jesus is in town (v. 2) and sends some Jewish elders to ask Jesus to please come and heal the man (v. 3). Jesus, obviously intrigued at hearing of this centurion's uncommon affection for the Jews, comes to grant his request (v. 6). A short distance from the centurion's house, Jesus is met by some friends who have been sent to tell Him that He does not need to come personally. The centurion feels unworthy both to come before Jesus and for Him to come in his home. He simply requested that Jesus say the words and his servant would be healed. The friends continue to relay the message from the centurion, saying that he understands Jesus' source of authority for he also is a man under authority. He commands his soldiers and they act by his command (vv. 7–8). He obviously believes with all his heart that Jesus has authority over illness. Jesus marveled (was astonished, amazed) at the man's insight and faith, saying that He had never seen faith such as this, even among the Jewish people (v. 9). The friends return to the house and find that the servant has been healed (v. 10).

A REMINDER:

Always read the parallel passages each day before you begin the study. You may sometimes be tempted to skip them, but the purpose of this study is for you to learn to draw truth from the Scriptures for yourself, not to simply complete the study.

This is an incredible episode in Jesus' ministry that has numerous implications. The word for *unworthy* or *unfit* used by the centurion (Luke 7:7) is, interestingly, the same word used by John the Baptist when he said he was *not fit* to untie Jesus' shoe laces. What was the man saying? He realizes that he, as a Gentile, is not part of the reason for Jesus' coming. He graciously defers to Jesus, not wanting to impede His focus.

By studying the historical setting, we know that Jesus came to bring the good news to the Jewish nation. Paul even says in Romans 1:16, *"to the Jew first, and also to the Greek."* Did He not care about the Gentiles? Yes! The perfect plan had been to reveal the truth to the Jews, who would accept the Messiah, and in turn introduce Him to the Gentiles. We later find that the Gentiles will accept the Messiah the Jews rejected. In addition, if you read the Matthew and Luke accounts, they appear to disagree on how Jesus is asked to come and heal the servant. Matthew says the *centurion "came"* and Luke says that *"he sent"* the Jewish elders to Jesus. Through Hebrew eyes this is the same thing. To send the elders means that they were sent *in his authority* (like a power of attorney), as his personal representatives. It was viewed as the centurion having gone to Jesus personally.

Let's consider several possible applications that could make a difference in our lives. First of all, think about this unusual man. Describe what you can see in this man's character.

I see a man who ...

Think about it: Have you ever put your reputation and possibly your job on the line to stand beside a person or group of people who were disliked and resented by your friends and colleagues—even your church?

Where do you imagine a Roman soldier from a pagan culture, living among friends and colleagues who hated Jews and their religious beliefs, could obtain such a level of faith that even Jesus marveled?

Consider the matter of authority. The centurion says that he understands Jesus' authority because he "too" (like Jesus) is a man under authority. How was Jesus under authority? (See John 14:10.)

In modern-day Jerusalem, there is, outside of the Holocaust Museum, an area where the Jews have planted trees as a memorial to certain Gentiles. It is called the Trees of the Righteous Gentiles. Each of these trees bears an inscription to honor Gentiles who helped the Jews escape Nazi extermination during WWII. Among those names is Corrie ten Boom, who saved many lives from Hitler's death squads by hiding Jewish families.

What amazed Jesus was that the centurion knew that having authority comes from being under authority. Define the difference between authority and power.

POWER:

AUTHORITY:

DAY 28

LINGERING IN PRISON, JOHN THE BAPTIST WONDERS IF HE "TAPPED" THE RIGHT MESSIAH.

READ: Luke 7:11–17; Matt. 11:2–19; Luke 7:18–25

◆ **Jesus Heals a Widow's Son at Nain.**

Followed by a large crowd, Jesus and the Twelve encounter a funeral procession in the little town of Nain. A widow's only son was being carried along in a coffin. Moved with compassion, Jesus tells the woman not to weep. He walks up to the coffin, touches it, and tells the dead son to "arise." The boy sits up. Imagine seeing this if you were in the funeral procession or among the crowd following Jesus.

One of the great benefits of learning to study the Scriptures for yourself is that you are no longer at the mercy of whoever steps to the podium or writes the next best seller. The Jews had relied so heavily on their leaders to tell them what to believe that when Jesus spoke the words of eternal life, they waited for a "thumbs up" from the Pharisees, which, unfortunately they never got. So, utilize the pastors, teachers, and mentors God has placed in your life, but don't rely solely on their counsel. Study for yourself and "own" what you believe.

Notice the response of the people; they were "gripped with fear" and said, "A prophet has arisen among us." Wonder why they didn't say *the Prophet is here*? The reason may well lie somewhere within their dependence on *their leaders' opinion* to guide and direct their thinking. We will begin to see that the downfall of this generation of Jews was in their inability to think for themselves and come to their own conclusions about Jesus based on the evidence they saw. *Sadly, their reliance on their leaders to tell them what to believe was their undoing.*

This miracle has a special significance to the people in this area. Nearby is the town of Zarephath. To a Jew it was famous because the prophet Elijah had restored another widow's son to life there many years prior (1 Kings 17:17–24). Jesus is therefore identifying Himself with the Old Testament prophets and underlining the historical significance of the event.

FOR THOUGHT AND DISCUSSION: *Where does your spiritual perspective come from? Do you have to go to your pastor, Bible teacher, or some best seller for the standard upon which personal beliefs are built, or are your beliefs built on personal study of God's Word?*

◆ **John the Baptist Struggles with Doubt (Matt. 11:2–9; Luke 7:18–28).**

BE JOHN: You have prepared your entire life to do *one thing*. You think you have done it, but suddenly you find yourself rotting away in a nasty prison surrounded by thieves, murderers, and rapists, all of whom deserve to be there. You, on the other hand, are there simply because you did what you were supposed to do. You are a prophet, a man whose role is to speak for God to the people and to the king. Herod Antipas married his brother's wife, and you confronted him with the truth in Leviticus, which forbids it. As a way of thanking you for your honesty, he throws you into prison, and there you sit waiting to hear any bit of news about the movements of the Messiah, whom you had introduced to the world. Word has trickled back about His miracles and the multitude's positive reaction to Him. But you are also aware that the Jewish leaders were rejecting Him. *This isn't the way it is supposed to happen,* you reason. *Is He really the One? Have I made a colossal mistake? Why am I stuck here missing out on all of the action? How can this be God's will? I was given one role in life: to prepare the way for the Messiah. Could I have blown it? Could I have tapped the wrong man?* Day after day these disturbing questions become more pronounced until doubt and uncertainty have slithered their way into your mind. You send word to some of your former disciples whom you had gladly given to Jesus when He began His public ministry. They come to visit you in prison, and you ask them the burning question: *"Go back and ask Jesus if He is truly the Messiah."*

◆ **Jesus Responds to John's Question.**

Jesus does not answer "yes" or "no" as we might expect. Instead He tells the disciples to report to John the following (Luke 7:22). List the six things Jesus says:

1. _____

2. _____

3. _____

4. _____

5. _____

6. _____

✡ Is this a fair answer to the question that is tormenting John? If you think like a Gentile, the answer would be "no." If you see it from a Jewish perspective, it is an answer John would certainly have understood immediately. (We have already seen the first of three messianic miracles that the Jews said would identify the Messiah when He came.)

Ancient Jewish scholars and rabbis encountered a problem when studying about the coming Messiah. They read passages like Ps. 2; Zech. 14; Isa. 63—65; and Jer. 25 about a Conquering King who would establish a reign of peace on earth from His throne in Jerusalem. However, they also studied about a Suffering Servant who would come in humility, be despised and rejected by His people, die for men's sin, and be resurrected (Isa. 40—53; Ps. 22; Dan. 9). They were deeply conflicted over this. Most opted to believe that the Messiah would be more like King David than a Suffering Servant. That God would submit Himself to be abused by mortal man was unthinkable. Many Jews of the 1st century even thought there would be two Messiahs.

Jesus uses this "code word" or phrase in His answer to John that would have left no doubt in John's mind that he had tapped the right man. (Look back at Day 17 along with these verses in Luke 7:22–23.)

What is this code phrase? _____ *How would that satisfy John's question?*

◆ **Rather Than Criticize John About His Doubt, Jesus Speaks of His Greatness (vv. 24–35).**

Write the things Jesus says about John.

7:24 _____

7:25 _____

7:26–27 _____

7:28 _____

Jesus finishes by saying that as great as John is, the very least within the family of faith is greater than John. If the *greatest man ever born of woman* can have doubts, isn't it okay for us to have doubts from time to time? *Write down any doubts you tend to struggle with from time to time, whether they are about God, the Scriptures, or how you fit into the whole picture. Then ask God to reveal the answer to you.*

DAY 29

JESUS WARNS THREE CITIES ABOUT THEIR APATHY, THEN TEACHES ABOUT HIS FATHER.

READ: Matt. 11:20–30

Jesus rails at the cities of Chorazin, Bethsaida, and Capernaum, where He had performed most of His miracles. Why? Because even after His miraculous signs, they were apathetic toward Him. They saw His miracles and heard the truth, but refused to repent. Sound familiar? He even compares them to Tyre and Sidon, two cities on the Phoenician coast that were notoriously pagan. He says it will be more tolerable for these cities at the judgment than for them. Then changing pace, He thanks the Father for hiding the simple truth from those who consider themselves worldly-wise. Truth is revealed to the humble.

If you ever get the idea that genuine humility is optional, read the Gospels.

Why do the humble hear the truth and the worldly-wise scoff at it?

◆ **Jesus Offers Rest for Two Categories of People: The Weary and the Heavy Laden (vv. 28–30).**

The obvious questions are: Weary *from* what? Heavy laden *with* what? Jesus is speaking to a problem of the people that He has just mentioned. He is also speaking of the Jewish leaders and the multitudes that follow Him around. Remember that the Pharisees had put a great burden on the shoulders of the Jews by introducing thousands of oral laws that they said were equal to and even greater than the Mosaic law. The people were watched by these "morality police" and were crumbling under constant failure to live up to its standards. No matter how hard they tried, they failed, day after day. Wouldn't you be weary? Wouldn't you feel the weight of this burden of trying to obey laws that were impossible for any man or woman to obey? Wouldn't you be tired of never feeling that you were pleasing God? These people were spiritually exhausted!

This passage in Matthew 11 is a great example of interpreting a passage within the flow of its context. How many sermons or Bible studies have you heard where the phrase "weary and heavy laden" has been related to all kinds of problems? The burden referred to here is the intolerable demand of trying to be righteous through your own strength by obeying laws that are impossible to obey. It was like trying to kill an elephant with a pea shooter. They were weary of constant guilt and failure and heavy laden with unreachable spiritual goals.

Can you identify? Have you ever felt exhausted trying to work for God and please Him with your performance? You've been to the Bible studies, worked at the pancake breakfasts, served on the committees, attended the retreats, read the books, and taken a leadership role in your church. Still, in your heart of hearts, you know it just isn't working. You are empty, spiritually and emotionally worn out, guilt ridden, and frustrated!

*On a scale of 1 to 10 (10 being highest) how spiritually tired are you right now?*_____ *Have you ever heard the phrase* **Sabbath rest**? *No,*

God will not change that which you and I are not willing to acknowledge.

I'm not talking about a nap after church or no golf or movies on Sunday. Look up Hebrews 4:9. Write it out and put it to memory.

What day is the Sabbath? Unless you're a Jew or a Seventh Day Adventist, it's Sunday. For a New Testament believer, however, every day of your life is the Sabbath. We don't live under the law, where we get really spiritual and pious on Sunday and loosen up the rest of the week, then put our game face back on again next Sunday. *Look up 1 Corinthians 10:31 and write it out:*

On a personal note: I first learned about Sabbath rest from a great Bible teacher and dear friend in Kentucky named Bob Warren, whom I mentioned in the preface. It is one of the most freeing truths I have ever encountered, and it has altered my approach to life and work.

Every day is a day to worship and honor Jesus Christ. Sunday is a great day to worship and sing praises together as a body of believers, but *every day* is the Sabbath. Everything we do, even something as mundane as eating, drinking, shopping, or washing the car we do with the intent of putting God's glory on display in our lives. If every day is the Sabbath, then when do you take your Sabbath rest? EVERY DAY! Then who works for God? Have you ever considered the fact that, contrary to what many believe, God doesn't want or need you to work for Him. *"He wants you to enjoy Him as He works through your life while you are in a state of rest"* (Bob Warren). The yoke will never be easy, nor will the burden be light as long as you and I carry it. It only becomes easy and light when Jesus carries it. This *doesn't* mean we are to be passive or lazy. We are available to Him always, but we are at rest knowing that anything that is accomplished is done *by* Him and *through* Him. An African friend once made a statement I will never forget but did not understand until years later. He said, "I have learned the secret of *working rested*."

Have you learned the secret of "working rested"?

The Pharisees were sad-eyed, weary people, and those whom they taught were sad-eyed and weary people because they knew nothing of the Sabbath rest Jesus came to offer.

♦ **A Sinful Woman Anoints Jesus' Feet in the Home of Simon, a Pharisee.**

READ: Luke 7:36–50

A Pharisee named Simon invites Jesus to dinner hoping to find fault with Him. As they are having dinner, a prostitute, having learned where Jesus was, quietly but boldly enters the room. Without comment or waiting for approval, she begins pouring oil on Jesus' feet and wiping them with her hair. Simon is outraged for a couple of reasons. First, a Pharisee believed that the presence of a prostitute in a Jewish home meant *contamination*. Second, he assumes that because Jesus allows the woman to anoint Him, He cannot be a prophet. Otherwise, He would have known who she was and disallowed it (v. 39). Jesus reads Simon's thoughts and shows him that He knows all about this woman as He tells a pointed story.

Summarize briefly, in your own words, the point of Jesus' parable:

Jesus shows that the prostitute is light years ahead of the Pharisee because she understood her need. Jesus again reveals His identity by forgiving the woman and He turns up the heat on the Pharisees by contrasting the love, compassion, and hospitality of a common prostitute with the prideful, judgmental, and arrogant attitudes of these men who considered themselves above reproach. Again, He is saying to them, *"Stop dangling in the wind, make up your minds and get off the fence!"*

Pharisees believed prostitutes and tax collectors were beyond redemption and would never see the kingdom of heaven.

◆ **Jesus' Second Tour of Galilee (Luke 8:1–3)**

Jesus will now make His second tour of Galilee. The first time, He had gone alone, but now He travels from city to city with the Twelve and others who follow as well. A small cluster of women were among the crowd that followed, but these women were different than the rest: *They took responsibility for His financial needs* (Luke 8:1–3).

In these short few verses we see a principle that is critical for all, but understood by few. Jesus will soon feed five thousand in Matthew 14, four thousand in chapter 15, and tells Peter to look in a fish's mouth for a coin to pay their taxes. Why did He not also supply His own financial needs instead of letting these women provide it? Think back to the Sermon on the Mount and what we saw concerning the purpose of giving. (See Day 26.)

DAY 30

THE JEWISH LEADERS MAKE A FALSE AND UNFORGIVABLE ACCUSATION ABOUT JESUS, AND HIS MINISTRY TAKES A PIVOTAL TURN.

READ: Matt. 12:22–37; Mark 3:20–30

This is a fascinating and critical juncture in Jesus' life and ministry. It is not an overstatement to say that what happens in Matthew 12 is the *most critical and explosive* event in Jesus' life until the cross. The event is paradoxical in that Jesus will perform the second messianic miracle—healing a demon-possessed man—only to have the Pharisees challenge the origin of His power to do it. Even many of His friends will believe the Jewish leaders and *disregard* the wonders they have seen. They will be persuaded that Jesus is a gifted, well-meaning soul who has unfortunately lost touch with reality.

Jesus' response to the accusations of the Jewish leaders not only results in His changing the direction of His ministry, but will eventually result in the devastation of an entire generation of Jews.

◆ **Jesus Heals a Demon-Possessed Man (Matt. 12:22).**

Jesus had healed many demon-possessed people, but this one was different. How was he different?

Why is that significant? (See Day 15.)

How does the crowd respond?

How do the Pharisees respond?

Can you hear what these Jewish leaders are saying? They are claiming that Jesus is actually possessed by Satan and that He is able to perform such an unprecedented miracle *only* because He receives His power from the "Ruler of Darkness," not from God the Father. Why would they have such a violent and radical response to this particular miracle? It was His second messianic miracle. The first, healing a Jewish leper, forced them to take Him seriously. Now, He performs a miracle that would either force them to concur that He *has to be the promised Messiah* or to dismiss it to the multitudes by crediting His works to the Devil.

There were exorcists in Jesus' day just as there are today. The demon was entreated to identify itself through the voice of the person who was possessed. It had been witnessed many times. The Jewish leaders had long ago agreed that *only* the Messiah could exorcise a demon from a man who could not speak (no voice box). This is what prompts their outlandish charge.

In verses 25–29 Jesus responds to their absurd accusations with a reasonable and rational illustration. If someone is possessed by Satan, why would he cast out Satan? Why would evil cast out evil? It would be like trying to fill a clay pot by smashing it! Jesus continues by asking them that if He casts out demons by Satan's power, then by whose power do other Jewish exorcists cast them out? How could a house stand when its structural supports are cut in half? His reasoning does not faze the Pharisees, whose minds are already made up.

Logic and reasoning had no impact on the Jewish leaders. Fear of losing their power coupled with sheer adrenaline and emotion caused them to take the posture of "don't bother us with the facts, our minds are made up!"

◆ **Jesus Makes a Charge That Will Curse a Generation of Jews (30–32).**

Many have struggled with the notion that at some point in their past, they have said or done something that they fear is the *"unpardonable sin."* There are tearful admissions from people that range from cursing at God in a fit of rage to sneaking into a church one night and having sex with someone on a church pew. None of these acts are unforgivable sins. Jesus is speaking here of a *national sin, a generational sin,* by the Jewish leaders. They commit blasphemy of the highest order by claiming that Jesus performed His miracles by Satan's

Notice the term, "this generation" in vv. 41–42, and 45. This blasphemy and the price that would be paid was not meant for all Jews. It was a national sin affecting that generation only.

God has patiently endured the abuse and accusations that humankind has thrown His way for thousands of years. But, can you think of anything more offensive and devastating than for the Son of God to be told that His power is derived from the Prince of Darkness himself. No wonder this blasphemous statement was a sin of such gravity that it would impact an entire generation.

It is important to understand that the "curse" on that generation of Jews was not some angry knee-jerk reaction by Jesus. His love for them was beyond measure, but their refusal to see the truth time and again caused Him to turn His energy and focus toward those who would listen: His disciples and the Gentiles. Choices have consequences and that generation chose to believe their jealous and threatened leaders rather than the Author of truth. Jesus gave up on that particular generation, not on Jews for all time!

power. Think about it. What can you imagine that would be more heretical and offensive to God than that?

How does Jesus vividly describe these leaders in verses 33–35?

Again, in verses 36–37, just as on the matter of blasphemy, many have lived under the guilt of these verses as saying that *any careless word* they have ever said will be accounted for in the day of judgment. Can you imagine the length of our lists if that were so? Once again, Jesus is referring to the words that the leaders have said about Him. So relax, *"Therefore there is now no condemnation for those who are in Christ"* (Rom. 8:1).

The Jewish leaders ask Jesus for a *sign*, to which He responds that no more *signs* will be given except the "sign of Jonah." He had just validated his messiahship for the second time by the Jews own criteria and now they ask for a sign. What they wanted was for Him to give further evidence that He was the Messiah. This is where Jesus' ministry takes a major detour. To this point, every miracle was done to show the people who He was. Now, because of their leaders' blasphemous accusations, Jesus will make no further public efforts to show the people who He is, with one exception. He will perform what He calls the "sign of Jonah," meaning the *sign of resurrection*. (Jonah was in the belly of the fish three days and three nights just as Jesus would be in the belly of the earth for the same time.) A resurrection preceding His own would be the raising of *Lazarus* in John 11.

◆ **Jesus Basically Writes Off an Entire Generation of Jews.**

The leaders have caused this generation to be placed under a curse. Why not just the leaders? They told the people what to believe about Jesus. Is that fair for all to be punished? You bet! They had the truth in front of them: They saw Jesus' miracles and heard His teaching, but they made the *choice* to listen to their leaders rather than believe the truth. The fruition of this curse comes forty years after Jesus is crucified in AD 70. A Roman general named Titus will annihilate the city of Jerusalem and 1.1 million Jews will lose their lives, and 97,000 will be taken captive (some of them are standing in the crowd at that moment).

This half of a chapter is packed full of critical building blocks upon which the remaining years of Jesus ministry will be built. Try to summarize in a short paragraph what has been happening here to solidify it in your understanding.

You'll notice as you study the Gospels that when Jesus heals a Jew, He will command them not to reveal it to anyone. However when He heals a Gentile, He will tell them to go make it known everywhere what God has done.

DAY 31

JESUS BEGINS SPEAKING IN PARABLES.

READ: Matt. 13:1–35; Mark 4:1–34; Luke 8:4–18

The word *parable* means "a placing beside." Therefore it is usually an illustration or a comparison that Jesus will *place beside* a principle of truth. Jesus gives five of these "coded" illustrations in rapid succession. We will give a brief *aerial view* of the last four, then take a closer look at the parable of the sower.

Jesus leaves the house where He is staying and walks down by the sea and takes a seat (the typical position of a rabbi when he teaches). Crowds surround Him, so He gets into a fishing boat and begins to teach.

In these parables, notice that Mark and Luke will refer to the "kingdom of God" while Matthew says the "kingdom of heaven" (same term). Matthew is a Jew writing to Jews. Luke and Mark are writing to Gentiles. Matthew knows Jews will be offended at the use of God's name, so he says, "kingdom of heaven."

The parable of the seed growing by itself (Mark 4:26–29) is a picture of how the gospel message has the power to bear fruit of its own accord.

The parable of the tares (Matt. 13:24–30, 37–43) relates the fact that in the future as the church develops, error (tares) will be sown (taught) along with the truth of the gospel. The tares will attempt to look like wheat. (Error disguises itself as truth.) At the end of the age, both tares and wheat will be harvested. The followers of truth, bearing good fruit, will be ushered into the kingdom, while the followers of error will not.

The parable of the mustard seed (Matt. 13:33–35; Mark 4:30–32) points to the manner in which the gospel will spread during the age of the New Testament church. However, false doctrine will also be taught and will steal the truth from many, like birds stealing away the seed.

The parable of the leaven (Matt. 13:33–35; Mark 4:33–34) is spring loaded and directly aimed at the Pharisees. Leaven in the Scriptures is a symbol for error (Matt. 16:5–12; 1 Cor. 5:6–8). The parable points to the false doctrine that will be mixed with truth as the church grows.

The parable of the sower (Matt. 13:3–23) is one of Jesus' best-known parables.

> ***Under each of the four results of the seed being sown write a short application. (See vv. 18–23.) How does this happen to people?***

- Some seed (truth) falls by the road and is eaten by the birds (v. 4).

- Some seed falls among the rocks and springs up but is scorched by the sun because there is no depth of root (vv. 5–6).

- Some seed falls among thorns and is choked out (v. 7).

- Some seed falls on good, fertile soil and yields abundantly (v. 8).

JESUS' MOTHER AND BROTHERS COME TO TAKE HIM HOME.

READ: Matt. 12:46–50; Mark 3:31–35; Luke 8:19–21

Jesus goes inside a home (probably that of Peter and Andrew) and delivers more parables, but first there is an interesting encounter with Jesus' mother and brothers. They are worried about Him and are aware of what the Jewish leaders have been saying. Think back to the first week of our study when Gabriel spoke to Mary and she spent three months with her cousin, Elizabeth. She appears to understand, but now, some thirty years later, she seems somewhat confused about her Son's identity. We know she understands to some degree, but read Mark 3:21 and decide for yourself. It appears that she and Jesus' brothers think He means well, but has lost His way and is confused. They have come to take Him home to Nazareth, about thirty miles from Capernaum. When told they are outside waiting for Him (Mark 3:35), He appears to be abrupt, but it was simply His way of saying it is now time for Him to subordinate His earthly ties and focus on the spiritual task set before Him.

Why do you suppose Jesus' family is so worried about Him?

Be careful not to get an *attitude* about Mary, Jesus' mother. It's true that after thirty-plus years she should be convinced about her Son's identity, but step in her sandals for a moment. She is listening to scuttlebutt in the streets and at the synagogue. Every day she hears from the learned rabbis and scribes that her Son, though He may be well intentioned, has unknowingly fallen prey to the Evil One. She hears from people she has always respected that her Son derives His miraculous power to heal from the Devil. She knows better, but still, she may feel that He has strayed a bit off course and lost His bearings. She knows that He is in grave danger because He is no longer an inconvenience to the Jewish leaders, but a serious threat that must be eliminated. What would be more natural than for the motherly instinct to then overrule what she knows to be true? She must get Him out of there, take Him home, and nurse Him back to *emotional health*.

Have you ever noticed that dissenting voices can sometimes echo so loudly that they can pull your focus from that which you have always believed? Respected and devout people whom Mary had known for years were saying that her Son had lost His mind and needed help. How many of us would have wavered in her circumstances?

DAY 32

AFTER GIVING MORE PARABLES, JESUS CALMS A STORM ON THE SEA OF GALILEE.

READ: Matt. 13:36–53; 8:18, 23–27; Mark 4:35–41; Luke 8:22–25

Before leaving Capernaum, Jesus explains a parable He had previously given to the multitudes as well as several more He gives inside the house to His disciples. The *parable of the hidden treasure* and *the parable of the pearl of great price* teach basically the same truth, that the value of the kingdom of God is worth everything you have.

Through Jewish eyes we will see these two parables a little differently. What if Jesus was the man who found the treasure? In this case the treasure is Israel (Ex. 19:5; Ps. 135:4, God calls Israel His "own possession." Jesus gives His own life, and purchases that treasure with His own blood. My friend Bob Warren poses the question, What if the *pearl of great price* points to the Gentiles in the same way the *hidden treasure* points to the Jews? Then Jesus (the merchant who sold all he had) will give His very life to purchase this pearl, meaning the salvation of many Gentiles during the church age to come. This is how a believing Jew might have understood these parables as they related to his present situation.

The parable of the net: There is a "sea" full of Gentiles. These Gentiles will be gathered into the net and separated one day. Those who have received Jesus by faith will be ushered into the kingdom. Those who have rejected Him will be judged (Matt. 25:36–41) and cast in the furnace of fire.

JESUS CALMS THE STORM (MARK 4:35–41).

By now you should be gaining some feel for how confused and bewildered the Jews who followed Jesus must have been. He had been speaking plainly for a year since beginning His public ministry. After the Jewish leaders accuse Him of gaining His power from Satan, everything changes. Now He speaks in a *coded language* that they cannot decipher. The disciples, on the other hand, are being taught and trained by these parables as Jesus explains everything to them. The Twelve board a boat with Jesus and row to the other side of the Sea of Galilee. They had learned much as they walked with Jesus and their lives were taking on new dimensions, but as we will see, there was still something they did not know. They had no real understanding of *who* was in the boat with them.

Before we look at the story, don't miss something important that is happening as the disciples make the transition from hearing and being given understanding concerning the parables and what happens on the lake. Often when God reveals to us a principle of life, our tendency is to write it down in a notebook or journal and tuck it away and forget it. We may share the thought in a small group or with a friend, but it often remains as only a "profound truth" that never really penetrates the heart. This is apparently what happened to the Twelve. Even after witnessing this astounding miracle of the loaves and fish, they filed it away as a *great event* and missed its significance within the whirling vortex of their everyday lives.

Notice that upon learning new truth, adversity strikes! God gives the disciples an opportunity to see firsthand that His principles are not given to simply jot down and tuck away. They are the *bone marrow* of life. God doesn't reveal truth to us for intellectual stimulation or to supplement this week's Sunday school lesson. However, the truth He gives remains only an intellectual whet stone on which we sharpen our wits until adversity comes. This is when we find out if all this stuff is more than just spiritual *pixie dust*. If you run from or resist adversity, the truth remains only *information*. It becomes *revelation* only after it crashes into the circumstances of your life.

Has there been a time in your life when God revealed the truth to you and on the heels of that revelation a major storm came and made it real? Take some time to really think about this. Don't just write something to fill up space. Come back to it later if you need to.

When Truth Became Revelation to Me:

Through the avenue of adversity, we come to know much more than the truth. We come to know the One who speaks the truth. The goal is not to know truth as an end in itself, but for truth to be the vehicle through which we come to know the truth as a Person.

Romans 10:17 tells us that "Faith comes from hearing, and hearing by the word of Christ."

We saw on Day 1 of our study in John 1 that the "Word" (Logos) is a person. In this passage, "word" is not capitalized. The Greek rendering here is *Rama,* which means revelation. So here, Paul is saying that faith comes to us when we hear the truth, and hearing comes by God revealing it to us. In other words, information that we hear will not produce an ability to trust God. Only when God turns that information into revelation will it change our lives.

Storms often arise abruptly during certain times of year, seemingly out of nowhere. Being in a small boat can be treacherous during these storms on the Sea of Galilee.

◆ A Raging Storm Shakes the Disciples' Boat and Their Faith (vv. 36–37).

Jesus is emotionally and physically exhausted. He falls into a deep sleep in the back of the boat. Sometimes, in our attempt to accentuate Jesus' deity, we tend to lose sight of His humanity. His feet got sore, He had bad breath when He woke up in the morning, He felt sadness, He laughed, and now He is tapped out both emotionally and physically. Remember the rejection He has endured. The reality has hit home, the dream of redeeming His beloved Israel will, at least for now, remain only a dream. God forces no one to love Him, but in Jesus' humanity, the absence of love being returned must have been devastating.

◆ Jesus Rebukes the Storm and the Disciples (vv. 39–40).

The Sea of Galilee It is really not a sea at all, but a freshwater lake that is only 160 feet deep at its deepest point. It lies about 1,500 feet below the Mediterranean Sea, which is only 30 miles away. It is situated in a kind of bowl that is surrounded by mountains and a ravine on the west side, which channels cool breezes that meet the warm air from the valley lake. This can cause violent storms in the blink of an eye that can easily capsize a fishing boat.

As the waves pound the boat, the disciples' fear overshadows all they have seen and heard. Jesus had performed miraculous healings and had just raised a widow's son from death at Nain. After seeing that, you would think a mere storm, even a hurricane, would be *peanuts* for God to handle. The problem is, that information had still not become revelation and they still don't know that He is God (Matt. 8:27)! They wake Jesus, He calms the storm, then challenges them concerning their failure to trust in Him.

What do we do with this in terms of right now? There are a couple of glaring applications. First, before we can stand in awe, convinced of God's power and might, we must first realize our inability to calm the storms in our lives. The disciples struggled with the storm before coming to Jesus. Several of these guys were fishermen and were used to rough seas. This is where our gifts can become liabilities. We have expertise in an area and think that because of our proven proficiency, we can handle the storms in our own strength.

What is a gift you possess that has or could become a liability?

A second lesson we all must learn is to trust God by *remembering His track record*. Why does the psalmist praise God so much? Is praise a "woman thing" and for men who are the "touchy-feely" type? No! Praising God for who He is and for what He has done not only honors Him, but reminds us of His power and might, and His faithfulness in the past. It forms in us an attitude of confidence in Him and therefore an ability to trust Him rather than to try to take matters into our own hands.

Spend a few moments thinking about the character of God. Write these attributes down in the following space as fast as they come to you. Then ask God to build confidence in you in terms of your willingness to rely on His integrity to be those things in your life amid the storms that come. Visit this list from time to time, but use it regularly as an act of praise and a way to remind yourself of His faithful history in your life.

These two simple exercises are not magic, but given time, will nurture you into a way of thinking about God's character and ability. It can help enlarge your faith to allow Him to deal with the small storms as well as the hurricanes in life.

- • • •

- • • •

- • • •

Write some specific ways that God has been faithful to you.

DAY 33

JESUS HEALS EXTREME DEMON POSSESSION IN THE COUNTRY OF THE GADARENES.

READ: Matt. 8:28–34; Mark 4:35–41; Luke 8:22–25

After Jesus calms the storm, His disciples are, no doubt, licking their wounds and struggling with various emotions when He chides them for their lack of faith.

BE THE DISCIPLES: *Write down your emotions after what you have just experienced as you row to the other side of the lake:*

I would feel …

I would probably wonder ...

They reach the other side and pull the boat ashore. They are now in Gentile territory, a very uncomfortable place for a Jew. Furthermore, as their eyes nervously scan the hill region around the lake just outside the city of Gadera, they see a steep cliff about forty yards from shore, its bottom jutting into the water. In the distance they notice at least five things that probably would have caused them to not even want to get out of the boat:

The abyss is a holding place for demons, evil spirits, and for Satan (Rev. 9:1).

1. *They were in Gentile territory.*
2. *They saw at least two naked men running around.*
3. *They saw a herd of pigs.*
4. *They saw tombs marking grave sites.*
5. *They realized that demon possession was present.*

Any and all of these things spelled *defilement* to a Jew. Again, they must trust Jesus, not by seeing visible results or by using their own gifts and abilities, but by trusting Him over their culture, their background, and their religious training and traditions. Have you given this much thought in your own life? Can you trust Jesus Christ even if it conflicts with what you have been taught by people you love and respect?

FOR EXAMPLE: OUR CULTURE TEACHES US TO BE RUGGED INDIVIDUALS
AND THAT WE CAN PULL OURSELVES UP BY OUR BOOTSTRAPS

The Scripture teaches no such "bootstrap" principle but rather interdependence with one another ... that we need each other desperately.

Our culture teaches us to always compete with one another.
The Scripture teaches us to cooperate with one another.

Our culture teaches that Jesus was the founder of a new religion called "Christianity," which He wanted to establish in the world.
The Scripture teaches that Jesus came to present Himself to a hurting world, never to start a new religion. He never once used the terms "Christian" or "Christianity."

Every place in the Gospels the issue is always Jesus' identity: "Who is this man?" The demons always knew Him. Notice that this man immediately refers to Him as "Son of the Most High God."

◆ **Jesus and the Twelve Are Immediately Met by a Man Possessed by Demons (Luke 8:26–27).**

What do we know about this man from the three parallel accounts?

Luke 8:27:

Mark 5:3–4:

Mark 5:5:

◆ **The Demoniac Cries Out and Bows Down at Jesus' Feet (Luke 8:28).**

What does the man already know about Jesus?

◆ **Jesus Casts Out the Demons.**

This *demoniac* had obviously been bound in chains by the local inhabitants for their protection. Jesus asks the man his name, but it is the demons who reply. This lets us know that the demons are in complete control of him. His name is Legion, meaning many demons had entered him. (A legion is three to six thousand.) The demons beg to be cast in the pigs. Jesus does so and the pigs commit suicide by running over the cliff into the water and drowning. (Suicide may sound strange, but the fact is pigs are good swimmers … they obviously chose not to survive rather than to live with the alternative.)

We will find that the man's hometown is the Decapolis, a group of 10 small towns, mostly Gentile. We will hear of this man again and see that his healing resulted in many becoming believers in the 10 towns.

◆ **The Local Herdsmen Tell Those in the City of Gadera and Outside the Country What Has Happened (v. 34).**

◆ **The Man Wants to Join the Twelve, but Jesus Sends Him Back to His Hometown to Tell of What God Has Done (v. 39).**

Jesus makes no effort to stop the herdsmen from telling everyone what they had seen and Jesus tells the demoniac to tell everyone. Why this contrast from His previous healing when Jesus said "tell no one"? (See Day 30.)

DAY 34

Jesus Heals Both the Obscure and the Prominent.

Have you noticed that Jesus never seems to be in a hurry? Did you ever notice that He wore sandals, not Nikes? I live in New York City, where everybody is in a hurry and most aren't sure why. Jairus is in a hurry to have Jesus save his daughter, but Jesus is perfectly calm. John Wesley said, "Though always in haste, I am never in a hurry, because I never undertake more work than I can go through with calmness of spirit."

READ: Matt. 9:18–26; Mark 5:21–43; Luke 8:40–56

Jesus and the Twelve now row back across the Sea of Galilee, probably to Capernaum. This is back into Jewish territory, which is important to know. Upon their arrival, they are met by a large crowd and a synagogue official named Jairus, who is probably a layman with administrative responsibilities. He falls at Jesus' feet and implores Him to come lay hands on his daughter who is near death. Followed by a large crowd, Jesus and the Twelve follow Jairus through the streets toward his home.

The first issue we see in the story is that _____ is critical.

> Answer
> on next page

What words would best describe Jairus's emotional condition?

- ◆ **A Woman with a Hemorrhage Slips Through the Crowd and Touches Jesus' Robe (Matt. 9:20).**

  What do the gospel accounts tell us about this woman?

  Matt. 9:20:

  Matt. 9:21:

Mark 5:26:

BE THE WOMAN: What is your emotional state? What are you feeling?

Answer
from previous page

"Time" is critical.

♦ **Jesus Feels the Power Leave Him and Asks, "Who Touched Me?"**

♦ **The Woman Confesses and Jesus Says Her Faith Has Healed Her.**

BE JAIRUS: As your eyes dart anxiously between Jesus speaking to the woman and the road leading to your dying child, describe your feelings.

I am feeling …

I am wondering …

I wish …

The question, "Who touched My robe?" seems as ludicrous to us as it did to the Twelve. Jesus is being jostled and touched from every side in a large crowd. But in this we observe something of the nature of Jesus, the man. Then, as now, He can always tell the humble, expectant touch of faith of one small hand from the indiscriminate push of the turbulent crowd.

As Jesus talks to the woman, word comes that the little girl has died. Jesus overhears the message and tells Jairus to no longer be afraid, but continue to believe. Jairus had believed in Jesus' ability to heal his daughter initially or he would never have come. Jesus is saying, *keep believing just as you did when you first took the risk to ask Me.*

We have seen that *faith* must surface and take priority over our *gifts and abilities* in the storm on the Sea of Galilee. We have also seen that *faith* must go beyond *visible evidence* as seen in the healing of the nobleman's son at Cana (Day 15). We saw the decision Peter had to make (Day 17) at the Sea of Galilee when Jesus told him where to cast his net: Will he trust Jesus or his professional experience? During the encounter with the Gaderene demoniac (Day

33), the disciples learned that *faith* must stand firm amid *contradictions to our religious and cultural bias.* Now we see in Jairus, who may well be a secret believer, that we must trust Jesus in the midst of impossible circumstances. His daughter is dead! Could you keep on believing as you did when you first came to Jesus? What is the first critical issue in the story? *Time!* Jairus's daughter is near death. Jesus never hurries. He never has to. He is Lord over *time.* He had taken water and made the *best* wine, which only becomes the *best* over *time. We are always in a rush;* Jesus never is. He wears sandals, not Nikes. The fact that time had run out on the little girl's life is an issue of finality to everyone in the story *except* Jesus. He is not bound by time. He is seldom early, but never late!

◆ **Jesus Goes to Jairus's Daughter at His Home and Gives Her Life (Mark 5:41).**

The atmosphere when He arrived was one of _____.

It was customary to hire professional mourners to come in at the point of death. Apparently the little girl's death was so imminent that Jairus's wife had made those arrangements while Jesus was in route.

Who goes in the house with Jesus?

Why only these five?

When Jesus arrives at the house the weeping and wailing was probably deafening and certainly obnoxious. When He assures them that the little girl is only asleep, the mourners stop crying and start laughing at Him. He kicks them all out of the house for a couple of reasons. This is a Jewish home and He will only do miracles privately and when approached on the basis of personal need. (as Jairus did). Additionally, there would have been anything but an atmosphere of faith in that home among these professional mourners.

Why does Jesus command the family **not** *to tell what has happened?*

The idea of hiring professional mourners seems absurd to us, but the act of mourning the dead was serious business in ancient Israel. The idea was to assist the family in the process of grief. In addition to the wailing and crying, Matthew mentions that flute players (9:23) were present. You can imagine the scene as Jesus approaches. Keep in mind also the contrast between Jairus's faith and that of his wife. He sought out Jesus, still hopeful. She, on the other hand, had already hired the mourners to come in, obviously having given up on the possibility of her daughter being healed.

Did anyone find out (Matt. 9:26)? _____

The last part of verse 43 tells us something additional about Jesus. He has given the little girl life, but now tells her parents to give her something to eat. Why would both Mark and Luke mention what seems irrelevant to the point of the story?

DAY 35

JESUS HEALS THE BLIND AND DUMB, THEN IS AGAIN REJECTED IN HIS HOMETOWN OF NAZARETH.

READ: Matt. 9:27–34; 13:54–58; Mark 6:1–6

Two blind men approach Jesus begging for mercy. They refer to Him as "Son of David," a popular Jewish title for the coming Messiah. Before Matthew 12, this greeting would have pleased Jesus, but notice how He continues into the house, not responding to them. (Review Day 30.) Only after He asks them if they *personally believe* He can heal them and they say yes does He perform the miracle. He warns them to tell no one, therefore *we know they are Jews.* Naturally, they tell everyone (v. 31).

Jesus and the Twelve return to Nazareth, where He grew up. He teaches in the synagogue and the people are amazed, but they cannot reconcile Jesus' ordinary upbringing, which they had witnessed, with His claim to be the Messiah. *He was the carpenter's kid, an ordinary laborer just like them, a great kid, but surely not messianic material.* Jesus is wounded by their unbelief and lack of faith. He can do no miracles in Nazareth.

Why would Jesus subject Himself to the pain of being rejected again in His hometown? They had run Him out of town once before (Day 16). Surely He doesn't think things have changed. Why go back? Because ...

a. He thought the sentiment may have changed toward Him?

115

b. He refused to give up on His hometown?
c. He wanted to use this to train the Twelve?
d. He loved a challenge?

Obviously, it was part of the training of the Twelve. He wants them to see that taking *His Name* into a hostile world after He is gone will involve rejection and ridicule. They need to be aware of the cost.

In his book published many years ago *Dedication and Leadership*, Douglas Hyde (a former Communist) describes the rigorous training involved in becoming a Communist Party member. Bright-eyed, confident young men and women were sent out with no training, to hand out *The Daily Worker* on street corners in the cities. They were cursed, spat upon, and sometimes physically assaulted. They limp back, mortified and discouraged, only to realize that this is part of the intended motivation to be trained. Now they are ready to learn, because they know what they are up against. To train a disciple of Jesus Christ is a process of helping a man or woman learn to deal with failure and pain. One who follows Jesus does not win all the time. Sometimes we fail. The question is, can we regain our composure, become more teachable, and be able to stand against the north wind? This is what Jesus is willing to do to help the Twelve regardless of the sorrow He felt.

What personal experience have you had with rejection? Was it redemptive?

JESUS SENDS THE TWELVE OUT IN TWOS, THEN DETOURS TO GALILEE FOR THE THIRD TIME.

READ: Matt. 9:35—11:1; Mark 6:6–13; Luke 9:1–6

Having been rejected for the second time in His hometown, Jesus steps up His training of the Twelve. He knows that real disciples are not made in a classroom, and He wants them to get their feet wet and see how they deal with adversity. He wants them to feel the compassion for people that He feels and not be fooled by people's polished exterior or apparent confidence. He wants His disciples to understand the condition of people's hearts.

♦ **Jesus Is Moved with Compassion as He Teaches and Heals.**

The people recognize Jesus as He passes from village to village. Like a wave on the ocean, the crowd builds and builds. When He and the Twelve arrive at their destination, a gigantic crowd had gathered. People tend to look at crowds in different ways. A politician sees votes, an entrepreneur sees opportunity and money, but Jesus looks at the crowd and feels compassion because they are like *"sheep without a shepherd."* Compassion comes from perception. How do you see the masses of people at a concert, a ball game, or as you navigate through traffic? There are thieves, pathological liars, and adulterers, just as in the multitudes that Jesus saw.

Who had always been their shepherd? The Jewish leaders. They demanded perfection in obedience to the law. They had little interest in the deepest yearnings of the heart. Jesus knew the multitudes were spiritually starved, wandering aimlessly through life, looking for leadership. They were seeing Jesus as their *potential* Shepherd and were drawn to Him. However, their former shepherds had told them Jesus was demon-possessed and was not who He claimed to be. They were stuck, wavering between the two, *like sheep without a shepherd.*

♦ **Jesus Explains That the Harvest Is Plentiful, but the Laborers Are Few (Matt. 9:37).**

Notice that Jesus' compassion for people prompts Him to say the exact opposite of what we might have thought. We might suppose that because of His compassion He would instruct His disciples to rush out, recruit leaders, and put together a mass evangelistic campaign. On the contrary, He does not say, "Go," nor does He say, "Recruit and deploy."

How does He tell them to use their energies? _____ *(v. 38)*

What is the difference between your pick of a laborer and God's pick?

The reason cults are able to recruit so successively is because people yearn so deeply for leadership. When genuine leadership fails to surface, anyone who steps to the microphone becomes a candidate. The pharisaic platform had always led the people because it was powerful and intimidating, and it was the only game in town. They are intrigued and drawn toward Jesus, but can't seem to make a decision, so they dangle, stuck in the middle.

◆ **Jesus Sends Them Out to Test Their Wings, but First Gives Them Authority and Specific Instructions (Matt. 10:1).**

___ Go with a giving spirit: *Have the heart of a learner (10:8).*

___ Go without your security blanket (money). *He wanted them to leave themselves no avenue to potentially bail out (10:9–10).*

___ Trust God to supply your needs by allowing people to give back to you. *It is more blessed to give, but it's harder to receive.*

___ Don't waste time trying to argue people into the kingdom. *We need only lift up Christ and He will draw people to himself (10:11–15).*

___ Go out as sheep among wolves. *Focus on being a sheep; follow the Shepherd and He will deal with the wolves (10:16–20).*

___ Don't be afraid of your enemies. *They can kill you, but they can't eat you (10:21–28).*

___ Remember you are of great value to God (10:29–33).

___ The cost of discipleship is heavy, but those who persevere will reap great rewards (10:34–39).

To the left of each of the admonitions, rate where you think you are on a scale of 1–10 (1=low, 10=high) if you were in the disciples' sandals.

Of these eight admonitions given by Jesus, write down the two with which you struggle the most. Discuss if in a group.

1.

2.

HEROD EXECUTES JOHN THE BAPTIST BUT HARBORS DEEP FEARS.

READ: Matt. 14:1–12; Mark 6:14–29; Luke 9:7–9

 It's Herod's birthday and he is thoroughly enjoying all of the attention. His wife, Herodias, had formerly been married to his brother, Philip,

We learn from John 6:4 that it is Passover time. This means that it is one year before Jesus will be arrested, tried, and crucified.

until Herod persuaded her to abandon the marriage and marry him. John had previously confronted him because his actions violated the Mosaic law. Not being a man who appreciated accountability, Herod Antipas threw John into prison. As the birthday celebration wears on into the night. Herodias's daughter, Salome, performs a provocative dance in her stepfather's honor. Herod was so pleased and aroused that he makes an absurd promise to give her anything she wants up to half of his kingdom. Prompted by her mother, she asks for the head of John the Baptist on a platter. Herod had been intrigued by John, but was also afraid of him and of the multitudes of Jews that followed him. Now, he has no choice. Afraid of losing face, He orders John's execution. The disciples come and take his body away for burial.

Why was Herod so fearful after he beheaded John the Baptist (Mark 6:16)?

PART V: THE TRAINING OF THE TWELVE DISCIPLES

After John's death, it is obvious to Jesus that the Jewish leaders will step up their attempts to remove Him from the scene. His focus in training the twelve disciples is so that they will be able to stand in the face of a landslide of opposition after He is gone. Even the miracles He performs are for the primary purpose of training His men. He will instruct them about His death, but they will not understand. They will still believe that He has come to overthrow the Roman government and set up a new political kingdom ruled by the Jews. He will focus much on the cost of discipleship and three of the twelve will even have the opportunity to see His glory, which had been veiled since His coming to earth.

DAY 36

JESUS HEARS ABOUT JOHN'S DEATH AND WITHDRAWS TO A SECLUDED PLACE WITH THE TWELVE.

READ: Matt. 14:13–21; Mark 6:30–44; Luke 9:10–17; John 6:1–13

As we observe Jesus' training of the Twelve, it is unmistakable that His focus is on formation, not information. You can't change people's perception of reality simply by word, no matter how articulate and powerful. They must go into the marketplace and get their feet wet.

We can only imagine the grief and sorrow Jesus felt upon hearing the news that His friend had been executed. He first goes off by Himself, obviously to grieve and to process what had taken place. The crowds follow Him. Even in the midst of His personal pain, He compassionately heals those who are brought to Him (Matt. 14:13–14). In the evening, the disciples join Him. They have just returned from a successful but stressful mission and need some rest (Mark 6:31). The crowds are relentless, nightfall is near, and the disciples want to send the people away into the nearby cities to get food. However, the size of the crowd makes that impossible. Jesus tells the Twelve to provide food themselves for the hungry multitudes.

Why would Jesus ask His disciples to deal with the problem themselves?

♦ **Jesus Takes Physical Food and Makes a Spiritual Point (Mark 6:42).**

120

💡 The purpose of this miracle is not to prove that Jesus is the Messiah. Remember, He said in Matthew 12 that He would no longer perform *signs* for the Jews to believe. First of all, this miracle is *not* public, but *private* even though there were five thousand men present plus women and children. Consider the fact that the people were put in groups along the hillside. As the huge crowd settles in, a little boy with the loaves and fishes stands in front with Jesus and the Twelve. It was late in the evening (Mark 6:35) and would have been difficult to see. The people were unaware that a miracle had taken place. All they knew was that they were amply fed. Second, the miracle was done primarily to *train* the disciples. Jesus takes five loaves and two fish and feeds thousands. What does that say about our assumption that we always need *more* faith? It is important that the disciples understand that *amount* is never the issue; it's always about where our faith is directed. Minimal faith will yield great abundance if Jesus is its object. Thirdly, Jesus wants the Twelve to realize that they are going to be responsible for the spiritual feeding of many people in the years to come. The key word in these passages is *satisfied.* If they are to shepherd the New Testament church, they must learn to feed the sheep under their care until they are spiritually full or satisfied.

What does it mean to satisfy someone spiritually?

The 12 baskets of fish and bread left over could well have been the 12 disciples' personal wicker-type lunch baskets that were usually carried by those who traveled on long journeys from place to place.

JESUS RETIRES TO THE MOUNTAIN TO PRAY, WHILE THE TWELVE FACE A TREACHEROUS STORM AT SEA.

READ: Matt. 14:22–33; Mark 6:45–52; John 6:14–21

Jesus sends the crowds away and tells the Twelve to take the boat and go on ahead of Him to Bethsaida. He wants time alone with His Father. The crowds see how Jesus has met their physical needs and now want to actually take Him by force and make Him king (John 6:14–15).

Even if you didn't know the story about the storm at sea, based on Jesus normal pattern of training the Twelve, what can we expect following His visual illustration of faith in the episode of the loaves and fishes?

Remember: Always read each rendering of the story. Don't cheat yourself.

121

♦ Later, Jesus Sees the Twelve Straining at the Oars in the Midst of a Great Storm (Mark 6:47–48).

✡ The story comes even more alive if we understand the Jewish reckoning of time. Evening was the period of time between 6:00 and 9:00 p.m. We know that Jesus fed the crowds *when it was evening*, probably between 6:00 and 8:00. At Jesus' instruction, the Twelve leave Him, take the boat, and row out to sea. Mark tells us that Jesus sees them struggling against the seas "at about the fourth watch of the night." The fourth watch is between 3:00 and 6:00 a.m. It is conceivable that the disciples had actually been struggling in this violent storm from seven to nine hours when Jesus came to them on the water.

Mark 6:52 is a very telling passage; it says of the disciples: "they had not gained any insight from the incident of the loaves, but their heart was hardened."

♦ Walking on the Sea, Jesus Intended to Pass Them By (v. 48).

Why do you think Jesus intended to pass the disciples by?

It seems that sometimes God does things that may at first appear that He doesn't love us in order to prove the depth of His love for us. A perceptive and loving parent will not always bail out a child who is caught in the middle of a turbulent situation. Sometimes it may be best for the child if we "walk by." However, notice that Jesus does intervene at the right time, at the intersection between a valuable lesson learned and keeping them out of harm's way.

♦ The Disciples Think They Are Seeing a Ghost and Are Terrified (vv. 49–50).

✡ There was a superstition among Jews that when one saw a *spirit* at night it meant imminent disaster. The disciples' terror was probably prompted by what they assumed was a *water spirit*.

♦ Jesus Tells Peter to Come to Him in Response to Peter's Question (Matt. 14:28–31).

What distracted Peter as he began to walk toward Jesus?

The disciples have no idea what a real, *internal storm* is and they won't know until Jesus is arrested. If you have a fear of something, how do you overcome that fear? Certainly not by avoidance. You learn to overcome your fear by facing it head on. You stay in the storm until you become accustomed to it, and eventually the fear will pass. Jesus is not being unkind. This is part of their *training*. He knows that they will never survive what they will face in the book of Acts unless He prepares them. Have you considered the fact that storms of adversity are the only things that bring you to a place of maturity? God causes you to thrive in the midst of it so that you can learn to enjoy being still and help others down the road. In *Penses,* Blaise Pascal said that man's greatest problem is his inability to sit still in a room amid the silence of four walls (paraphrased).

What would you say is your biggest distraction in terms of trusting Jesus?

NOTE: Only Matthew records the incident of Peter's attempt to walk to Jesus on the water.

Is there a storm in your life that you have been trying to row out of rather than allowing God to use it to deepen you and conquer your fear? The first step toward change is acknowledgment.

Consider the storm as the vehicle rather than the problem. The storm is the avenue through which we mature and grow.

DAY 37

JESUS CHALLENGES THE CROWDS WITH THE COST OF BEING HIS DISCIPLE.

READ: Matt. 14:34–36; Mark 6:53–56; John 6:22–71

After their harrowing ordeal, the Twelve worship Jesus saying, *"You are certainly God's Son!"* (Matt. 14:33). So what? It was a great profession, but they understood nothing about applying what they knew, even after what they had seen in the last twenty-four hours. They believed intellectually but had no notion of how to trust Jesus moment by moment.

Exhausted and probably embarrassed, they row to the other side of the lake. Knowing their desperate need for rest, Jesus probably took them to a secluded spot to sleep in preparation for the following day. They will come to an area called Gennesaret, which is on the west side of the Sea of Galilee, where throngs of people are waiting. Jesus is now recognized wherever

The disciples are worn out. They returned from a long and stressful training trip going two by two (Day 35). They got little rest on the mountain, and they had the long and harrowing bout rowing in a storm. Jesus knew they were tired, but that was part of the training. They have to learn to think and make good decisions when they are tired. My college football coach, Bear Bryant, used to say "Fatigue makes cowards of us all." He was right. The last thing Jesus wanted was cowards leading the New Testament church.

He goes. He has lost any anonymity He might have had early on, as word of His miracles and teaching spread across the land like a forest fire. From Gennesaret, the little band travels back to Capernaum, which had become their home turf.

Keep in mind that many of those among the thousands Jesus had fed followed Him across the Sea of Galilee to Gennesaret and on to Capernaum. They see Him as *someone* who can meet their physical needs (Mark 6:24–25). This is the reason that the *prosperity gospel* has gained great popularity in America. It's all about *what Jesus will do for* me!

◆ **The Jews Ask How They Might Work the Work of God (John 6:28).**

Before you read the passage, how would you answer the question, What is the work of God?

To understand John 6:28, we must rethink the concept of "working for God." Frantic activity and titanic self-effort on God's behalf must be replaced by simple trust and the unhinging of our grip as we relinquish the powerful need to control the circumstances in our lives.

If you answered with works like evangelism, discipleship, caring for the poor, or working in the church, you are in good company. That is the answer that most believers would give to that question. We have all been trained to think that the word *work* means breathless activity, meticulous planning, organization, and measurable results. According to Jesus, the *work of God* is quite different. Sharing your faith, discipling another, caring for the poor, etc., are vital, but are not the *primary* work of God. The work of God, according to Jesus (v. 29) is to "believe in Him whom He has sent." Period! Nothing added. Sounds too simple, doesn't it? The fact is, trusting in God for every part of every day of your life is the most difficult work you will ever do.

- Let's say you are a parent of a child who is of driving age, and he or she is out with friends on a Friday or Saturday night. You have no control over their driving or any of the morons that peruse the city streets. There is no "work" on earth more difficult than to sit back, loosen your emotional grip, and *trust (believe)* God to protect your kids and give them wisdom in their choices.

- You are up for a significant promotion at work. There are two other candidates as well. Do you lobby and campaign behind the scenes hoping to affect the outcome, or do you exercise simple trust in God's sovereignty and leave the results to Him?

💡 *Believing and trusting Jesus Christ is* the hardest work there is. Sharing your faith with a Buddhist monk or trying to disciple an arrogant know-it-all is a *piece of cake* by comparison. If we apply that kind of total reliance on Jesus to our concern for people, then evangelism, discipleship, concern for the poor, etc. will naturally follow because all of these things and more are already on His heart; and He will put these things on our hearts as well.

After hearing Jesus' response, what do they still want?

Read vv. 31–35. The crowds love having their physical hunger met, but Jesus wants them to know that He is not simply the bread giver; He is the _____ (v. 35).

Notice that Jesus uses the same phrase six times in the following verses: 33, 38, 41, 50–51, 58. What is it?

The "work of God" is not "winning the lost" or even discipleship. If it were, Jesus would have given that answer. This may well be the primary reason that "many no longer followed Him." They wanted to make something happen; they wanted frantic activity and immediate, measurable results. How will believing in Jesus bring down the Roman Empire? But the "work" has always been to learn to trust Jesus every moment of our lives and in every situation—the hardest and most productive work ever conceived.

💡 The multitudes consume bread and fish and are *satisfied*. Now Jesus wants to take them to a deeper level of spiritual contentment. As they listen to Him, many who claimed to be disciples (not the Twelve) begin to grumble about the difficulty of the things He says. For instance, Jesus had told them that the kind of intimacy He desired with them was that they eat His flesh and drink His blood (vv. 53–58). This was a shocking image to Jewish listeners. It is a direct reference to the sacrament of the Lord's Supper, which is a covenant of intimacy with God. Just as the wedding ring is a symbol of the covenant of love and commitment of man and woman, holy Communion is a symbol of the blood covenant of our union with the Savior.

Many disciples can't handle this and depart, no longer following Him. As they leave, Jesus asks the Twelve if they also will leave. Peter speaks for the group and his response is classic. Write it out and put to memory (vv. 68–69).

Jesus indicates that there is *one* for whom Peter does not speak (vv. 70–71). This is probably the event that triggered the beginning of Judas's betrayal.

Is there anything in the Bible in terms of walking intimately with Jesus that you have ever considered as too difficult or even unfair? How have you dealt with it?

DAY 38

THE PHARISEES BECOME UPSET THAT JESUS FAILS TO HONOR THEIR HAND-WASHING TRADITIONS.

READ: Matt. 15:1–20; Mark 7:1–23; John 7:1

After John's death and the subsequent hard words Jesus had spoken in Capernaum, He will no longer walk in Judea because of the Jews' desire to kill Him (John 7:1). He will now stay in Galilee. Therefore the Pharisees and scribes from Jerusalem who are keeping tabs on Him are forced to travel great distances (Mark 7:1). Keep in mind that the most critical issue they had with Jesus was that He would not observe their oral laws and traditions. In fact, He will continue to break these man-made laws at every opportunity in order to drive home the error of their thinking and also to train His disciples.

♦ **The Pharisees Attack Jesus about His Disciples Failure to Observe the** *Traditions of the Elders* **(Mark 7:1–5).**

When the Pharisees are offended over Jesus' failure to observe the washing of hands, it's not simply because of hygiene, but because He was flagrantly violating oral tradition. As with many abuses in life, they began with a solid principle. There are extensive ceremonial laws in the Old Testament and many that are explained in Leviticus 15. Some laws concern cleanliness and others are symbols of purity. In the course of a day a Jew was thought to become ceremonially defiled and was cleansed by pouring water over the hands as a symbol of purity. As always, the Pharisees tried to improve on the law of God by adding more laws. They reasoned that if washing before meals is good, then washing after every meal is even better. The Mishnah contains pages of tedious details of how the water should be poured and how it must be allowed to run down the wrists. They even began washing hands between each course of their meals for fear that they might rub their eyes and bread crumbs might cling to their hands and cause them injury. On and on the absurdity went, and Jesus refused to tolerate it.

◆ Jesus Confronts the Hypocrisy of the Pharisees (Mark 7:6–8).

Jesus will not be intimidated by this lame attempt at superspirituality and He faces it head on. He summarizes what the Pharisees are doing so they will not miss the point: "Neglecting the commandment of God, you hold to the tradition of men." Man-made rules that masquerade as God's truth not only confuse us but are extremely dangerous.

Even mighty men of God like Dwight L. Moody, a preacher in the late nineteenth century, was not beyond confusing personal preferences with biblical injunctions. He lamented that it was a sin for men to wear ruffled shirts, which were the style of the time. At the turn of the century, evangelist Billy Sunday called it a sin for women to chew gum. There were even those who called whistling a sin. We have protected many "traditions of men" and arbitrarily *ordained* them as God's commands. Going to movies, dancing, long hair, miniskirts, body piercings, and dozens of other personal choices have been deemed as sins by well-meaning people. The issue is not that some of these things can and do affect our walk with Jesus, but that they are *not* commands of God. They are personal opinions and preferences of well-meaning people that are being interpreted as direct commands of God. For example, Paul's admonition to "flee the lusts of the flesh" is a biblical principle. To suggest practical ways one might do that can be very helpful. However, when we make those personal convictions into laws of God by saying He hates movies, dancing, and two-piece bathing suits, we create a "biblical command" out of a personal preference. This is essentially what the Pharisees were doing by creating oral laws that they believed would improve on and further define God's commands.

Does this ring a bell? Have you ever been guilty of thrusting personal preferences or standards on others and calling it what God says? How?

◆ Jesus Gives a Graphic Example of Pharisaic Hypocrisy (7:10–12).

Here Jesus uses an example that hits close to home. He tells the Pharisees that the inconsistencies in what they claim and what they have become even extends to their lack of care for their own parents. The Mosaic command to *"honor your mother and father"* had been compromised in order to serve their own selfish needs.

The word *Corban* used by Jesus in verse 11 refers to the behavior of the Pharisees. *Corban* is a transliteration of a Hebrew word meaning "offering." When *Corban* was used in a vow it was a way of formally dedicating one's income or material wealth to God. The money, however, did not necessarily have to be used for religious purposes. It often became a way by which a self-absorbed, irresponsible son could circumvent taking any financial responsibility for his elderly parents and blame it on his religious vow. An elderly parent comes to his son to ask for help with his medical expenses. As he shuffles up the front walk, the son makes a quick vow declaring his financial holdings as *Corban*. With a furrowed brow and a look of deep concern, he tells Dad that he has *unfortunately* declared his money *Corban*, and like magic, he's conveniently off the hook.

The *Corban* principle used by the Pharisees and others is a perfect example of what happens when we structure our theology to accommodate our lifestyle. For instance, if a person's life is consumed by material wealth and the possessing of beautiful things, he or she will often develop a theology that either supports gross materialism or simply ignores it as an issue. They will join a church where they are in the company of like-minded, wealthy people. Look carefully at the religious cults that Hollywood celebrities tend to embrace. Look closely at the tenets of that group and you'll find a very lax or nonexistent attitude toward sex outside of marriage, and the latitude to create their own set of values and, in effect, create their own god.

How can we turn this very prevalent tendency around in our own lives?
How can my love for Jesus guide my lifestyle?

People's morality and
lifestyle tends to dictate
their theology.

◆ **Jesus Concludes with a Parable about Eating Taboos (vv. 14–23).**

✡ Understanding Jewish teaching is helpful here. Jesus is redefining the idea of defilement, which had been a longstanding Jewish concern. They taught that one could be defiled by such things as unclean hands, touching a leper, entering a Gentile home, eating pork, and dozens of other things. Jesus is saying that God doesn't think that way. Defilement comes from an impure heart, not by all of these external taboos. Intimacy with God cannot be interrupted by improper washing, only by sin.

DAY 39

JESUS WITHDRAWS AGAIN WITH THE TWELVE, FIRST TO TYRE AND SIDON, THEN TO THE DECAPOLIS.

READ: Matt. 15:21–38; Mark 7:2—8:9

Jesus and the twelve disciples journey to the cities of Tyre and Sidon. Tyre was an ancient Phoenician seaport that was located on the Mediterranean in an area that is now modern-day Lebanon. Twenty-five miles to the north is Sidon, the oldest Phoenician city. The two cities were greatly influenced by Hellenism and thoroughly steeped in idol worship. Mark tells us that Jesus went there hoping to be anonymous, but with no success (Mark 7:24). He wanted to have an opportunity to teach His disciples alone. By now He is spending more time in Gentile areas. He realized that the influence of the Pharisees on the Jewish multitudes was so deep that they would not understand His message and follow Him.

A Syrophoenician woman pleads with Jesus to have mercy on her and heal her demon-possessed daughter. Notice that she addresses Him based on His messianic position, calling Him "Son of David" (Matt. 15:22).

129

The disciples try to have Him send her away because they are still deeply prejudiced against Gentiles. She also calls Him "Lord" indicating personal faith. He responds by using the images of "lost sheep" and "dogs."

Answers on next page

The "lost sheep of the house of Israel" were _____ .
The "dogs" refers to _____ .
Jesus came first for the _____ *and then for the* _____ .

The woman's response touches Jesus deeply and He heals her daughter. Paraphrase the woman's response (Matt. 15:27).

Homosexuality was a well-accepted pattern of behavior in Greek culture. Even the Olympic games promoted homosexuality and cultic activity. One could gain apprenticeships in homosexual philosophy at one of the classical academies, and the military utilized homosexual erotic apprenticeships to encourage the formation of close-knit teams of warriors.

Jesus and His companions journey to the Decapolis, which was a cluster of ten cities that stretched from a point northeast of the Sea of Galilee southward to Philadelphia (modern-day Amman). They were highly cultured Greek cities but were also inhabited by a significant number of Jews. There was great cultural conflict between the two, but mostly due to the Jews' opposition to the open endorsement and practice of homosexuality and pagan rituals in these cities. Jesus fearlessly walks right into the heart of this pagan Gentile territory.

In the Decapolis region, a man is brought to Jesus who is deaf and has great difficulty speaking (Mark 7:32). *Jesus heals the man, but He does what two things that tell us the man is a Jew?*

1. _____ (7:33)

2. _____ (7:34)

"A man with an experience is never at the mercy of a man with an argument."

◆ **The Unlimited Potential of Simply Telling Your Story (Matt. 29—38).**

From Jesus' next encounter we hear *the rest of the story*. It began in the country of the Gadarenes back on Day 32. Jesus healed a wild man who was living among the tombs, possessed by a legion of demons. Because the man was a Gentile, Jesus sends him to his home to tell everyone what God had done for him (Luke 8:39). Did he do it? You be the judge. When the people in this highly pagan, Gentile area become aware that this man named Jesus of Nazareth is in a mountainous area nearby, they come to Him in large numbers with the

130

sick and lame. Matthew tells us they "marveled" at His healing power and "glorified the God of Israel."

Answers
from previous page

The Jews

The Gentiles

The Jews and the
Gentiles

Why, in this pagan area, would such large numbers of people swarm around Jesus, and why do you suppose Gentiles would "Glorify the God of Israel?"

Take a few minutes and read 1 John 1:3. You might think of John's words like this: *The things that we have seen and heard, (principles that have been tried and tested in our lives) are the things we intend to tell you about. We don't want to simply parrot last week's sermon or echo what was in the latest best seller; we want to tell you about* what we know for certain *because of the change that has occurred in us.*

The power of this band of early believers was that they spoke of *what they knew for certain.* Many lack confidence in their biblical knowledge and are nervous about the questions they fear they may be unable to answer. But have you realized that you are an expert on your own life? The greatest validation of God's ability to radically change lives is in what has personally happened to you. The man who discipled me told me long ago that if you are only sure of one thing, that God loves you, tell only that to people and He will bless it beyond measure. Then He will give you something else of which you will become certain, then another, and another. Why speak of what someone else knows for sure? *Own* your own faith! If taken seriously, the following exercise could have the same potential impact that the demoniac of Gadera's story of change had on the ten towns of the Decapolis.

Write down the things you know for certain … things you know that are nonnegotiable … things that you would defend with your life. What you write down should become the basis of your message and value system.

If your list is very short, don't worry about it. Live what you know by the power of Jesus Christ and God will give you new truths in time.

For example, "I know for certain that I was created for intimacy with God rather than to do things on His behalf." That was #1 on my list of over 30 years ago and it still is.

"I know for sure that the Scripture is the unvarnished truth straight from the mind and heart of God." Don't try to mimic some church doctrine; just say what you know for certain in your own words and see the confidence and authority that will come and the lives that will be blessed.

THE THINGS I KNOW FOR CERTAIN

1.

2.

3.

4.

5.

6.

7.

8.

9.

10.

DAY 40

JESUS FEEDS FOUR THOUSAND, THEN CROSSES BACK OVER INTO JEWISH TERRITORY.

READ: Matt. 15:32–39; Mark 8:1–9

After three days of following Jesus, the multitudes had long since run out of food, and Jesus felt compassion for them. Just as in the feeding of the five thousand, the disciples' response is the same, and Jesus is obviously annoyed. After feeding four thousand, they cross to the western shore of the Sea of Galilee to go to Dalmanutha. Immediately the Pharisees come out and begin arguing with Jesus, asking for more compelling proof that He is the Messiah. He refuses, knowing that belief is a matter of the will. Their predisposition was *not* to believe. He leaves them and goes to the other side to Bethsaida. Here He rebukes them for their lack of understanding, then performs a two-stage miracle on a blind man.

Two of the amazing properties of yeast are that it is invisible once mixed with water and it will permeate the entire loaf of bread. The Pharisees could look very respectable and even helpful, while at the same time destroying the very people who admired them most.

◆ **Jesus Warns His Men to "Watch Out" for the Leaven of the Jewish Leaders (Matt. 16:5–12; Mark 8:13–26).**

The first-century ear heard something quite different than we might hear today when the word *leaven* or *yeast* is mentioned. To us, it is something you add to dough to make bread rise. To a Jew it meant *corruption* and *error*. There would have been nothing more degrading to a Pharisee than to be referred to in this manner. By saying this, Jesus is serving up the final volley against a huge political machine. He is saying that the Jewish leaders had corrupted the commandments of God by adding man's ideas and had kneaded this error into the "bread" of Jewish thinking.

Who does Jesus also include in His warning (Mark 8:15)?

The disciples had forgotten to take bread with them when they departed for Bethsaida. They think Jesus' warning to them about the "leaven" concerned physical bread.

Jesus' annoyance with them is due to what? What does their question remind you of (Matt. 15:33)?

Jesus heals a blind man in two stages. In the same way the disciples' spiritual blindness will be partially removed while they are with Him, and then completely at Pentecost. After Jesus' first touch, the man's vision remains blurred. Jesus touches him a second time and the man sees clearly.

Is this not the unbridled hope of the believer, to see all things clearly as Jesus saw? In what basic area of your life would you desire a second touch?

PETER'S GREAT CONFESSION
AT CAESAREA PHILIPPI

READ: Matt. 16:13–20; Mark 8:27–30; Luke 9:18–21

Jesus will now travel a short distance from Bethsaida to Caesarea Philippi This city was built by Philip, the brother of Herod Antipas, named after Tiberius Caesar and himself. It lies near the base of Mount Hermon, the largest mountain in Israel and is just north of the Sea of Galilee. Originally named *Paneas* for the Greek god Pan, whose shrine was located there, it is a particularly pagan area. A huge rock cliff towers over the city. A powerful stream of water flows at the base of the cliff, and thousands of small stones that have broken off the cliff line the bottom of this crystal clear stream. Keeping this image in your mind will be valuable as we look at this event.

When Jesus asks a question, it is never because He is looking for information.

♦ **As They Stand in the Shadow of the Towering Cliff, Jesus Asks the Disciples What People Are Saying about His Identity (Matt. 16:13).**

Jesus asks a question that permeates the Gospels from beginning to end. It was not an informational question because Jesus already knew what the perception of Him was. He does it for His disciples' benefit, wanting them to realize that this is *the* issue of life. They tell Him that the answers range from John the Baptist to Jeremiah to Elijah. It was like saying, "Everyone has an opinion, but nobody really has a clue!"

Would this not be a sad but fair caption to put over a portrait of Jesus in most churches? The world never has had a clue, but even in the church of Jesus Christ opinions abound. If we remove the clichés with which we have been trained to respond, the answers are mostly intellectual in nature. For example, most would say "Jesus is Lord," meaning, sovereign, owner, ruler. It means "to place oneself under the authority of someone." So? *What does it mean in terms of personal impact on a life? Explain.*

♦ **Peter's Answer Far Exceeds His Understanding (16:16).**

Have you ever given a response to a question that you knew right away was far beyond your capabilities to have said it? Peter's answer was 100 percent correct, but as we continue our study, we see that Peter had only a surface understanding of what he was saying. He may have understood it intellectually to some degree, but the implications would not be fully comprehended by any of the disciples until Pentecost in Acts 2. To assume that Peter's answer is in direct proportion to his spiritual maturity is a bad assumption. We often make the common mistake of assuming that biblical knowledge automatically means spiritual depth. To be able to articulate biblical truth with great passion and clarity is a gift, not a sign of spirituality. What a person knows is not the issue; *who* he or she knows is what matters.

◆ **Jesus Affirms That Peter's Answer Did Not Come from Peter** (v. 17).

In contemporary language, Jesus says to this impulsive and passionate disciple, "Peter, you have given an amazing answer, but you're not that smart! My Father revealed that to you. I am going to build My church upon the statement you have made and the miracle is that an ordinary man like you could be the means through which the Holy Spirit will do extraordinary things."

The Greek word *Peter* is *Petros* meaning a small detached stone or pebble (like those in the stream below the great cliff above them). However, the word *rock* in Greek is *petra*, which means "a large rocky mass." It was not Peter or *Petros* (the pebble) on whom the church would be built, but Peter's statement, *Petra* (the huge boulder)—that Jesus is the Christ, the Son of the Living God—on which the church will be built. The gates of Hades will not prevail against it because it will not be built upon man's cleverness or ability, but upon the power of God. Jesus gives Peter the keys to the kingdom, which means, among other things, that Peter would be the one that would announce to the Jews that the door to the kingdom would be unlocked and open to the Jews and later to the Gentiles.

It is interesting that Satan used Peter, the very person who would possess the keys to the kingdom, to try to get Jesus to circumvent the cross.

Hades is the Greek term used in the New Testament for *the place of the dead*. The Hebrew term for the same place is *Sheol*. This was not simply *hell*. The *place of the dead* had two sides, the side for the redeemed of God, which was called Abraham's bosom, and the side for the unredeemed, which was hell. The souls of Old Testament believers like Abraham, Moses, David, and Isaiah were sent to Abraham's bosom. There they waited until Jesus was raised from the dead and ascended into heaven. They then followed. Jesus must be the first; therefore the saints who died prior to His death waited in Abraham's bosom.

◆ **Peter Rebukes Jesus for Saying That He Must Suffer, Die, and Then Be Resurrected** (vv. 21–23).

When Jesus says to Peter, "Get behind me Satan," what was He saying and why do you think He said it?

Why is Peter's statement to Jesus in verse 22 a strong hint that he does not really understand what he was saying in verse 16?

DAY 41

JESUS EXPLAINS THE COST OF DISCIPLESHIP.

READ: Matt. 16:24–28

What better time to teach these men about *cost* than immediately after telling them the price He would be paying on the cross? These verses are among the most misunderstood in all of Scripture. (Again, I am grateful to Bob Warren for helping me gain a fuller understanding of this truth through the eyes of grace.)

Let's say a close friend or relative comes to you after reading this passage. With complete sincerity they ask you what it means to "take up your cross and follow Jesus." Based on your present understanding, write a short, concise paragraph explaining this biblical principle.

Look at your definition. Does it have a negative or positive spin?

Does your interpretation of the passage involve a sacrificial determination requiring a concerted effort?

If your answer has either a negative tone or a requires that you must simply *bow your neck* and exert a Herculean effort to *get it done*, then maybe the following will help.

Before Jesus was crucified, the cross was, to every Jew and Gentile, a symbol of a horrible, agonizing death. What does the cross now symbolize to those who believe? Incalculable love. Nothing related to crucifixion should ever be a negative for those who are "in Christ." So we know that this verse cannot mean some difficult, burdensome, and law-driven process. *"Well, we all must bear our crosses,"* says the man with sad and weary eyes. *"Yes,"* replies the woman with furrowed brow and slumped shoulders. *"I suppose these financial woes are just my cross to bear."* Sounds pretty pitiful, doesn't it? Well, it is, and it has nothing whatever to do with these verses. There has never been but one significant cross in all human history, the one in AD 30. Therefore, Jesus must be speaking of the cross *He* would endure.

What did this cross accomplish? The death of sin, the place where everything in me that was offensive to God died as well (Rom. 6:6; Gal. 2:20). It represents a new beginning, a new life! These verses say that the old me and the old you died on the cross with Jesus. I can wake up in the morning and say, "It is no longer the old me who is now living, but Christ within this physical body that I use to walk around on planet earth."

For me to "take up my cross" means that I *own* and *acknowledge* the fact that the old me (the troublemaker) is already dead, and this life that I am now living is accomplished by Christ inside of me. Taking up the cross is recognizing that life is not up to me anymore. My only job is to enjoy my friendship with Jesus and yield myself to Him as He lives His life through me. The cross *enables*; it doesn't *restrict*. The cross is not some kind of burden; it is the very thing that *frees me* to live. To deny myself is to say and believe that because the old me is dead, I will be unresponsive to the control of *anyone* other than Jesus and to *anything* other than truth.

◆ **Jesus Gives a Principle of Opposites (vv. 25–26).**

Man's predisposition has always been to protect and shield himself at all cost in order to survive. God designed life to be discovered in the process of becoming vulnerable and in giving yourself away. To release the security to which we cling so tightly is a risk, but that to which we cling can never be enjoyed until it is released and allowed to return of its own accord. (See also Day 39.)

The Transfiguration of Jesus Christ

READ: Matt. 17:1–8; Mark 9:2–8; Luke 9:28–36

Peter did not understand because he had been trained by the Pharisees, who did not teach about a suffering Savior. However, the Bible does (Gen. 3:15; Ps. 22: Isa. 53).

Jesus takes Peter, James, and John on an extended hike up a mountain, which was probably Mount Hermon. The traditional site for the Transfiguration is Mount Tabor, but the closeness of Mount Hermon to Caesarea Philippi makes it a more likely setting. The mountain is over nine thousand feet high and is the tallest in the Holy Land. It evidently takes them six days to climb it. Luke 8:28 tells us that there was an eight-day interval after Peter's confession. Luke may have included the day in Caesarea Philippi and the day of the Transfiguration in his calculations. The other nine disciples stay at the bottom of the mountain. Jesus is praying, evidently a short distance from the three disciples. The three fall asleep and awaken to see Jesus' clothes become dazzling white. Even His appearance changes, and two men—Moses and Elijah—are standing beside Him. Imagine the disciples' emotions. These two Old Testament guys had been dead for over thirteen hundred and eight hundred years respectively. Before they have time to process everything, the two appear to be leaving. Peter has a great idea. He wants to build a tabernacle for each of the three.

When Jesus was born, God put a veil or covering over His glory. For a few brief moments on this mountain, the veil is removed and Peter, James, and John had the awesome privilege of seeing what no man had ever seen.

Peter's spontaneity was not really out of line at all if we understand this action through Jewish eyes. Most commentaries assume that Peter simply wants to prolong the stay of Moses, who represents the *law*, and Elijah, who represents the *prophets*. Consider the fact that there are *seven holy seasons* in the Jewish year. Each of these seven holy feasts is a *picture* of something that will occur in history after the Messiah comes. In other words, every Jew, including Peter, had been taught that all of these sacred "holidays of worship" would one day be fulfilled by a specific event initiated by the Messiah. The following chart shows how each of these holy seasons would be fulfilled.

THE SEVEN HOLY SEASONS	POINTED TO
Feast of Passover : Lev. 23:5	Jesus' death – 1 Cor. 5:7
Feast of Unleavened BREAD: Lev. 23:6–8	Jesus' holiness – 1 Peter 1:19
Feast of First Fruits: Lev. 23:9–14	Jesus' Resurrection – 1 Cor. 15:20
Feast of Pentecost: Lev. 23:15–22	The Indwelling Holy Spirit – Acts 2
Feast of Trumpets: Lev. 23:23–25	The Rapture of the Church – 1 Thess. 4:13–18
Day of Atonement: Lev. 23:26–32	The Great Tribulation – Lev. 23: 27; Rev. 5:19
Feast of Tabernacles: Lev. 23:33–44	The Messianic Kingdom – Zech. 4:16–21; Matt. 21:8–11

Peter has just made a great profession of faith, saying that Jesus is the *Son of God* (Messiah). Now he awakes to see the Messiah standing with Moses, the *law giver*, and Elijah *the prophet*. He naturally assumes that the messianic kingdom has begun. What does the messianic kingdom fulfill? The Feast of Tabernacles! Therefore what does he want to build for each of the three men? A tabernacle! He was right, but his timing was wrong. The intent of God was that the Messiah would come and be accepted by the Jews, and they would, in turn, take the message to the Gentile world. But how can you have a messianic kingdom when the subjects of the kingdom reject the King? Because of the Jews' rejection of Jesus, the messianic kingdom will come when He returns and reigns for a thousand years. Peter was just a tad early! As Peter is speaking a cloud envelops them and they are deeply fearful. A voice says to them, *"This is My Son, My Chosen One, listen to Him!"*

The Feast of Tabernacles, also known as the Feast of Booths, celebrates the completion of the harvest and commemorates God's goodness to the Jews in their wilderness wanderings. The name "tabernacles" comes from the shelters that were built and covered with boughs and branches of trees during the 7 festival days. It was one of the 3 great pilgrimage festivals during year. Occurring in the 7th month of the year, all males were required to attend.

Was there another time when God spoke of His Son like this? (See Day 9.)

SOMETHING TO PONDER: What would you be thinking if you had seen and heard what Peter, James, and John just experienced? How can they seemingly forget all of this after Jesus is arrested? *Write any thoughts you have in the margin.*

Have you ever had a defining moment with God that was so powerful that you knew it would set the tone for the rest of your life, only to fall back in the same rut a short time after? What was that defining moment?

As Moses and Elijah speak with Jesus, they refer to His death as a "great accomplishment." Why would they use a term like this about death?

◆ **Jesus Instructs the Three Not to Tell What They Have Seen Until After the Resurrection (Mark 9:9).**

Why would He do that?

◆ **Reaching the Bottom of the Mountain, Jesus Is Immediately Tested.**

Could we not have predicted this? On the heels of one of the great events in Jesus' life, He is immediately challenged about His ability as a leader (Mark 9:17–18). Notice the key words at the end of verse 18. Summarize the event briefly. (Why had the disciples failed?)

Many believers think Muslims hate Jesus. Nothing could be further from the truth. Though they don't believe that He is God, as we do, they have great respect for Him. One cannot be considered a good Muslim without great respect for Jesus. He is mentioned some 93 times in the Koran. Their great stumbling block is the cross. They cannot conceive that God would allow Himself to be subjected to humiliation and pain by mortal men. Therefore, a Muslim spits when he sees the cross. This is the same point the Twelve are now dealing with.

The disciples were probably feeling pretty good about things after Peter's confession at Caesarea Philippi. The confusion would have begun when Jesus told them He will be killed. They, like all Jews, were waiting for a Messiah who would come and set up a political kingdom and get the oppressive Romans off their backs. The Pharisees had taught about the coming Messiah, but did not believe in a "suffering Savior" that we see in Psalm 22 and Isaiah 53. This idea of Jesus suffering and dying at the hands of mortals threw them a major curve ball. Peter, James, and John go up the mountain with Jesus and are privy to things the other nine waiting at the bottom have not seen. They had been given authority to heal when they were all sent out by Jesus, but now are unable to help a demon-possessed boy.

"After a certain point, all of our growth comes in terms of humility."
—Oswald Chambers

As we have already seen, our gifts can turn on us and become liabilities. The disciples had seen God do great things through them when they went out two by two. Riding on that success could have made them a little cocky. Suddenly, they are confronted with this demon-possessed boy and could not heal him. Why? Jesus said that their missing ingredient was *prayer*. What is prayer? It is our fundamental acknowledgment of our complete dependence on God's ability

140

and not our own. They leaned too heavily on the gifts they had been given. Have you ever become so successful at something that you began to think you could pull it off by yourself? Prayer shows utter dependence on God. Lack of prayer shows self-sufficiency and arrogance. *Humility is almost always the missing link.*

DAY 42

IN CAPERNAUM, JESUS IS CHALLENGED ABOUT PAYMENT OF THE TEMPLE TAX.

READ: Matt. 17:24–27

Once again, Jesus will speak of His death. As the little group passes through Galilee (Matt. 17:21–23; Mark 9:30–32; Luke 9:43–45), Jesus continues to train the disciples privately (Mark 9:30). They are again in Capernaum and the tax officials ask Peter if Jesus pays the two-drachma tax for the maintenance of the temple. Peter answers yes. Inside the house (presumably Peter's), Jesus asks Peter if the kings of the earth collect taxes from their sons or from strangers. Peter answers the latter, and therefore Jesus says, "The sons are exempt."

Every male twenty years of age or older was required to pay an annual tax of two drachmas (equal to half a shekel and equivalent to two days' wages) during Passover. As it is nearing the time of the Feast of Tabernacles, the tax was about six months overdue. Jesus' statement that the sons of the king were exempt from paying tax was alluding to the fact that Roman citizens were considered *sons of the king* (Caesar) and therefore did not pay taxes. Jesus was "King of the Temple." The implication is that because the disciples are in God's royal family, they are true sons of the King.

Jesus does not technically owe the tax, but keep in mind His focus since Matthew 12; He is training His disciples. As we mentioned previously, *humility* is an indispensable characteristic that a disciple must possess. Jesus tells Peter to go down to the sea, throw in a hook, and look in the mouth of the first fish he catches. With the shekel coin that Peter finds there, he is to pay the tax official, covering both Peter's and Jesus' tax. Why would Jesus not fight for His

Why did Jesus not fight for His rights concerning the paying of the temple tax? It makes little sense in a culture like ours that is consumed with the issue of rights. But Jesus models for us in this passage the highest level of spiritual maturity. His focus was the training of the Twelve. Fundamental to that training was to teach them humility. What better way than to voluntarily give up His legitimate rights for a greater purpose? Every relationship in life is doomed if both parties cling to their rights. In marriage, I have a right to privacy, but my wife has a right to know me. To the degree that we both demand our rights, compatibility takes it on the chin. Spiritual maturity is the process of giving up our rights for the good of another. Jesus was far more interested in modeling humility in training His men than in being right.

rights? Did He cave in to pressure, or was there a bigger issue at stake that He wanted to teach Peter and the others?

♦ **Jesus Teaches a Lesson in Humility.**

Immediately following the tax issue in Capernaum, the Twelve are walking with Jesus and Jesus asks them what they were discussing along the road (Matt. 18:1–5; Mark 9:33–37; Luke 9:46–48). Obviously embarrassed, they do not answer. Jesus sees a child standing in the crowd. Without a word, He brings the child before them. Those who walk with Jesus are to be like children.

Write three words that are characteristic of children:

_____, _____, *and* _____

Do Jesus' words in any way appear optional? *(Read Matt. 18:3.) Why or why not?*

Jesus had just humbly paid a tax He did not owe in order to teach His disciples humility. How could they be jockeying for position in the kingdom right on the heels of this great object lesson? In the classic *Mere Christianity*, C. S. Lewis says that *pride* is the great sin that leads to all other sins.

Humility is no small matter throughout the Scriptures. It requires brokenness. Look up Psalm 51:17 and put it to memory. In the chart below, check the boxes that are the biggest stumbling blocks for you. For most of us there will be several, but don't overwhelm yourself; just pick one for now. Would you be willing to pray a simple one-sentence prayer for one of these areas of offense for the next thirty days asking that God would remove it from your life?

Let's look at some basic differences in pride and humility as they work themselves out in our lives:

A PROUD PERSON	A HUMBLE PERSON
Has to prove he is right	Is willing to yield his right to be right
Feels confident in his knowledge	Feel overwhelmed at how much he has to learn
Desires personal success	Is motivated to be faithful and help others succeed
Focuses on the failure of others	Is overwhelmed with a sense of his own spiritual need
Wants to be recognized	Is thrilled that God would use him at all
Is quick to place blame	Accepts personal responsibility/clearly sees his own failures
Feels he has little or nothing to repent of	Possesses a continual attitude of repentance
Is self-protective of image and reputation; desperate for respect	Wants to be real, authentic; concerned with what God thinks
Is defensive when criticized	Receives criticism with a vulnerable and receptive spirit
Has the attitude of a teacher	Approaches every relationship as a learner
Seldom shares spiritual needs with others	Is willing to be transparent; anxious to be healed
Is wounded when others are honored and he is overlooked	Is eager for others to get the credit and rejoices when others are recognized

JESUS REBUKES JOHN FOR AN INAPPROPRIATE ATTITUDE.

READ: Matt. 18:6–14; Mark 9:38–50; Luke 9:49–50

Just when you were probably thinking that Peter, James, and John were getting preferential treatment from Jesus, John gets nailed for his elitist attitude toward other spiritual leaders. Were you beginning to think that Jesus would probably look the other way when the "big three" messed up? Not a chance! That Jesus allowed Peter, James, and John to see and experience more than the others is no indication that they were treated any differently. Their role in the emerging church was solely based on their gifts, their heart, and their potential. Jesus' love was no greater for them than for the others.

Go back and look at the chart contrasting the proud and the humble. Write a *J* beside those characteristics that seem to fit John, and write your initials by those that fit you.

◆ **John Reveals Spiritual Pride.**

143

John tells Jesus of his concern that a man who was not part of their group was casting out demons in His name. He had already tried to make the man stop (Mark 9:38). John is suffering from spiritual pride. He thought, like many churches, "If you're not one of us, you're not part of the real deal."

♦ Jesus Refuses to Be Sucked into Spiritual Competition.

Do you truly like everything God likes? Give some thought to this. How about those churches in your area that preach Jesus but worship differently and have slightly different theological perspectives? How about those groups who are more aggressively evangelistic than you feel comfortable with? Does God like them? If so, why don't you? Is it not true that if we love God, we will share His affections regardless of any personal bias we have been taught? If they preach Christ, why do we not embrace them?

What is the difference between liking and tolerating (coexisting)?

After rebuking John and continuing to deal with the issue of humility, Jesus speaks of those who would cause His followers to stumble. These are people who would encourage us down the wrong road. Keep in mind that it can be very easy to blame the secular world for actions that are simply the characteristics of a life apart from Jesus Christ. To expect a pornographer to view a woman with dignity and honor rather than a quick way to make a buck is ludicrous. If a man falls into Internet porn, the guy who put it on the Web site is not the stumbling block that Jesus is speaking of. We can't shift the liability for our lust to the porn people. What we see on TV and in the movies is not what is destroying our values. Movie executives aren't out to create values, they're out to make money! They give us movies that they know we will pay to see because they reflect the values we already have.

Here Jesus seems to be speaking of believers who are rebellious and disobedient and who seek to entice others to disobey God, as well. It is a serious offense to Jesus, and those who do such things will reap bitter consequences.

Jesus speaks of His great love for children and warns that no one should ever hinder them. Do children have divine protection (Heb. 1:14; Acts 12:15)?

- **Jesus finishes His Teaching by Using Salt to Illustrate How He Sees His Disciples (Mark 9:49–50).**

Salt was a very important commodity in the first century. Salt is incorruptible and imperishable. Due to the lack of refrigeration, meat was packed in salt, which acted as a preserving agent. Salt also flavors food. Additionally, salt was used in the temple (as we learned earlier). Sacrifices offered were salted, a sign of incorruptibility. When salt lost its saltiness, it was used on the temple floor to soak up the animal blood so that the priest would not slip while performing his duties (see Matt. 5:13–16).

DAY 43

DEALING WITH A CANCER IN THE BODY

READ: Matt. 18:15–35

- **Dealing with the Sin of Our Brothers and Sisters**

Dealing with sin is a matter of tremendous controversy within the church today. If you are a parent, there is nothing more pleasing to you than to see your children get along well, and as they grow up, to see them develop a warm, loving relationship with one another. Jealousy and alienation between siblings breaks the heart of any parent. This is the way God feels about His beloved offspring. When we are contentious, it hurts Him. This is why Jesus addresses the matter of church discipline in Matthew 18. We must preserve the unity within the family of Christ.

Review Day 26. We briefly addressed the idea of judging. Calling into question the destructive behavior of another is a necessary component of healthy relationships. It is when we judge a person's heart motives that we step over the line. Having to exercise church discipline is not about being cruel or condescending; it is a loving act with the goal of restoration.

Let's say you have a friend who has a serious problem with gossip. She rips people apart behind their backs and causes disparity in the way others are perceived. It has become a cancer that must stop. Do we say, "It's none of our business," and allow it to continue? Do you care enough about the person and the negative effect on the body of Christ to risk the person's displeasure and insist that they deal with their problem?

That which is kept in the dark is like bacteria that will continue to multiply until it is exposed to the light of day.

In this scenario or in any other you may have personally seen, think of some of the potential damages when the matter is not dealt with.

Disunity and alienation in the church of Jesus Christ is a serious matter to God. In Matthew 18:15–17 Jesus tells us how to approach a brother or sister who continues to sin.

STEP 1: Take the initiative. Go to the person and address the issue (v. 15).

None of this is any fun, and if it is, your offense in enjoying it may be worse than the sin of the person you are confronting. When God has to chastise His children, He never sees it as a day at the beach. It hurts Him deeply, but "He disciplines those whom He loves."

> If you feel angry and accusatory toward the offender, you should not be the one to go. Pray long and hard that God would give you a spirit of brokenness and humility. If you derive any secret pleasure or satisfaction from this confrontation, your motives are messed up.

STEP 2: If the person is defensive and will not listen, take one or two others back with you to confront him again.

> As in the initial step, the motivation of the one or two others who go to the offender should be nothing but compassion, with no hidden agendas. Remember, expressing compassion and gentleness does not mean that you are merely "winking" at the offense.

STEP 3: If the offender still will not listen, you must bring him or her before the church.

> This does not mean that we are to bring the person up front at the 11:00 a.m. service on Sunday morning. This is not the Salem witch trials A group of elders or spiritual leaders of the church in a closed meeting is sufficient. The intent is not to humiliate, but to offer a last opportunity for repentance before being forced to apply the final step.

STEP 4: The refusal to repent and seek help should result in the offender being dismissed from the church.

This is where many churches take a flyer. They feel this is cruel and unusual punishment, thus allowing the cancer to affect the body. Jesus' intent in this drastic measure is not to humiliate or be dispassionate, but that the offender be ultimately restored to fellowship with God and others.

A CAUTION: If you exercise this discipline within your church or even if you have to confront a friend or family member on a private basis, don't go unless you are willing to be there for him when the dust clears. Hit-and-run confrontation is not biblical. What you are doing is worse than what you are accusing him of doing. The poem in the sidebar addresses this.

Read an example of this action in 1 Corinthians 5:1–5. Briefly describe the situation:

Now read 2 Corinthians 2:5–8. This is the same person who had been disciplined. What happened?

 Jesus then addresses the issue of agreement (18:18–19). What this passage does not mean is almost as important as what it does mean. The context is critical here. Jesus is still speaking of discipline within the church (body of believers). He had just told us to take one or two when we go to a person about an offense. Now He follows that by saying that *where two agree on anything on earth, it will be done by the Father.* Fantastic! Let's get together and agree about that new sports car you've always wanted, or how about a beach house you can't afford? Obviously, if we read this in context, it is not a free pass to *name it and claim it.* Jesus is still speaking about *people* and *broken relationships*, not *stuff*. Agreement with one another concerns how to best be a catalyst in mending that which cripples the person and the church. Similarly, the idea of *binding* (forbidding) and *loosing* (permitting) have to do with the authority given to the church. It was not about determining guilt or innocence, but *announcing* it.

◆ **Peter Asks about Parameters on Forgiveness.**

Finally, Peter asks Jesus if he should forgive someone *seven times* if he sins against him. Jesus replies that he should forgive "seventy times seven."

147

Peter is being generous here with the number *seven*. The Pharisees taught that an offense was to be forgiven three times.

What is Jesus' point in saying that we should forgive seventy times seven?

 Believers ask many silly questions when we're trying to cut our-selves a deal. Three of the most absurd are as follows:

1. *Forgiveness:* "I just have to tell God to forgive me and not the person I wronged, correct?" The truth is, if we keep count, we often have forgiven only outwardly, not inwardly. We've only made a symbolic gesture which is not from the heart and does not involve the person we wronged.

2. *Tithing:* "Am I supposed to tithe out of my gross or my net income?" Anyone who would ask that question just doesn't get it. That turns something that was meant for your growth and maturity into a legal issue similar to the attitude with which most of us pay our taxes. (How little can I legally get away with?)

3. *Head of the house:* "Who's supposed to be the head of the house—the man or the woman?" What a stupid question! It should be a perpetual race between you and your spouse to see who can serve the most, not who gets to call the shots. When a marriage functions that way, there is no strife over headship.

DAY 44

JESUS ATTENDS THE FEAST OF TABERNACLES.

Once again, if the other apostles had thought that Jesus would play favorites with Peter, James, and John, they would probably have abandoned their call-ing after this incident.

READ: John 7:2–10

Jesus' half-brothers have no idea who Jesus is. They think in a secular manner. How does their statement to Jesus in verses 3–4 reflect this?

It's interesting that there is nothing in the Scriptures telling believers to *promote* Jesus Christ other than by the way we love Him, love one another, and live our lives. Jesus made no effort to market or advertise Himself. In fact, we have seen that when the crowds came, He often departed to another place. Now, Jesus' half-brothers want to step up the publicity and have Jesus put on a dog and pony show. They still think like the multitudes who wanted a new political regime with Jesus as King. His brothers believe this is a great marketing strategy.

On Day 17, we discussed the fact that God's thinking is 180 degrees opposite from our thoughts. Therefore, if Jesus' half-brothers think that self-promotion will help Jesus' ministry, the opposite will be closer to the actual truth. Consider the fact that Satan is a counterfeiter. His aim is to disguise error and make it appear as truth. Why is he so effective in the world? He knows that person will always bow at the thrones of expedience, convenience, and measurable results. The quickest way to become famous is extensive publicity. (Look at Paris Hilton.) It is easiest and appears logical. But, consider Satan's own strategy. He never advertises himself or seeks publicity. He is subtle, he never hurries, and he is committed to the long term. He trips us up in ways we would never expect, working behind the scenes. Very quietly, he counterfeits the truth with a lie. He is, in many ways, smarter than the children of light.

Review the ways Satan tempts Jesus on the mountain (Day 10). Every one of these is logical in asking Jesus to prove His deity. If Jesus thought like people think, even bowing down to Satan to gain the kingdoms of the world makes sense. "Give a little to gain a lot," thinks the *businessman, the politician,* or even the *minister.* "Think of all I can do if I just sell out a little here and there." It's done every day! But the truth leads to wisdom and wisdom to discernment, and discernment to freedom. Not so with human thinking.

> "The most difficult meeting to get believers to attend is one where Jesus is the only attraction."
> —Dr. Elton Trueblood

Jesus will go to the Feast of Tabernacles, but He will go _____, without fanfare or publicity (v. 10). He will travel with His disciples from Galilee through Samaria, but sends them ahead to make lodging arrangements.

Go back and reread what the Samaritans did after Jesus spoke to the woman at the well in John 4 (Day 14). What had changed on this visit?

They were on their way to the festival in Jerusalem and the Samaritans were hostile to Jews going to worship there. Where did Samaritans worship (Day 14)?

James and John (the "apostle of love") make a startling statement after they are turned away at Samaria. What do James and John want to do?

JESUS DEFINES THE COST OF BEING HIS DISCIPLE.

READ: Luke 9:57–62; John 7:10

Somewhere along the road between Samaria and Jerusalem the little band encounters a group of pilgrims who are also heading to the festival. The first one makes an unconditional pledge of commitment to Jesus that is not unlike what many of us have heard or even made in a moment of great emotion. The second two contain conditions.

◆ **"I will follow you wherever you go"** (Luke 9:57—58).

The man appears sincere, but Jesus sees something in him that prompts His answer. What do you think it is?

When Jesus speaks here of *foxes* and *birds,* His meaning to this man is much more than the obvious. The Herodians were Jews who supported Roman rule and were resented by other Jews who hated Roman oppression. *Birds,* as Jesus uses the term here, were the Romans. An eagle was the emblem on the standards carried by the soldiers. *Foxes* refers to Herod Antipas. Jesus referred to him as "that fox" (Luke 13:32). In the context of this man's seemingly bold statement to follow Jesus wherever He goes, he hesitates, putting a condition on his pledge ("But first"). Jesus sees this and says in essence, *If you follow Me, you will be a man in the middle. You will be aligning yourself with another kingdom and will not be able to vacillate between My kingdom and theirs. Are you really willing to sign up for that?*

In a very emotional and moving moment, we have all made sweeping statements that, upon sober reflection are more than we can or will deliver. This is why Jesus leans hard on the issue of cost. The gain is everything, but the cost is also everything. Jesus knew that if they didn't understand the cost, they would disappear without a trace.

♦ **"First Let Me Go Bury My Father," Says Another.**

This man was not asking to first go home to attend his dad's funeral. According to pharisaic teaching, a son could not leave home until one year after the death of his father. In the parable of the prodigal son, the son violated this. The man hesitates, putting a condition on his pledge ("But first"). Jesus' response seems harsh until we consider what the man was really saying. **What was he planning to do?**

♦ **"First Permit Me to Say Good-bye to Those at Home."**

Most Jewish parents had already rejected Jesus' messiahship. Had the young man returned home, his parents would have, in all likelihood, talked him out of following Jesus.

Based on these three encounters, define the cost of being a disciple of Jesus.

THE COST of following Jesus today is much different than in His day. Those of us in the Western world have little notion of the consequences these people faced. There are many places in the world where following Jesus may cost you your life, but in America the *cost* amounts to little more than someone rolling her eyes or leaving you off the party list. If you allow God to develop in you the perspective that we have seen in Jesus during this study, the *cost* will more than likely be linked to how *other believers* treat you. Today, the church has become the enemy of herself. The greatest fights are between believers, not with secularists, evolutionists, or Muslims. If you submit yourself under the leadership of Jesus, and let's say, He impresses upon you to dramatically downsize your lifestyle, you won't get flack from the secular community, but from fellow believers. If you decide to believe that intimacy is what God desires, not more hard work for the kingdom, you will be viewed as uninvolved and lazy by your

The cost of being a disciple is *everything.*

151

friends at church. If you believe the biblical definition that you are a righteous, holy, forgiven saint, rather than a worthless sinner (Day 5), guess who will debate you and tell you that you are off base theologically?

THE COST is not generally what we think it is. Sure, it involves behavioral matters, like when your ethical standards cause you to miss out on an attractive deal or pay taxes that you could probably have ignored. But it's more. It means saying *yes* to God's agenda; it means staying focused on enjoying Him and passing up the chance to impress others with your tireless works. Instead of winning all the time, it might mean showing the world how to lose graciously. It might mean loving and caring for others without anyone ever knowing but God.

———

PART VI: JESUS' JUDEAN MINISTRY

Jesus had been rejected in His own hometown, but generally, the multitudes weren't able to make up their minds about Him. He speaks with great authority, and yet He is not formally educated, just a common man. Jesus will now spend time in the towns throughout Judea. He performs the third messianic miracle; in Jerusalem, He directly confronts the Pharisees, exposing their hypocrisy, and presents Himself as the Good Shepherd. He further claims that He and the Father are one. The Jewish leaders begin to think more strategically concerning how to seize Jesus without arousing the emotions of the multitudes. He had verbally thrashed them on several occasions and they are now seeking ways to trick Him into saying and doing that which will invalidate His authority.

DAY 45

Turmoil in Jerusalem Over Jesus' Teaching at the Feast of Tabernacles

READ: John 7:11–52

The Feast of Tabernacles (also called the Feast of Booths) was both a celebration of the harvest that had just been gathered and a memorial to Israel's wanderings in the wilderness. It began on the fifteenth day of the seventh month and lasted eight days. The houses in Jerusalem were covered with the branches of trees, symbolizing the tabernacles the Israelites had built to shelter them from the elements in the desert (Lev. 23:39–43).

Two important ceremonies during Jesus' time will help us understand what is happening in this passage. The first was a priest-led procession that began at the temple mount and proceeded down to the pool of Siloam. Here they would fill golden pitchers with water, and proceed back up the Kidron Valley to the temple, where the water was poured out at the altar. The ritual was followed by great rejoicing. The pouring out of the water was so important that it gave the festival its name, "House of Outpouring." It symbolized the pouring out of the Holy Spirit. The second ceremony was the lighting of the golden lampstand in the Holy Place of the temple. This symbolized the *pillar of fire* that God had provided to keep the Jews warm by night in the wilderness. Jesus used these two ceremonies to illustrate His teaching.

> *Hearing that Jesus has arrived in the city, the Jews argue among themselves concerning His identity. Some said, _____, while others thought He _____(vv. 11–13).*

Jesus' identity is the central issue of life. If He really is God, then everything changes for me. I can't be neutral or simply yawn and go about my business. My ethics, my lifestyle, my view of life and death—everything will be affected! The Jewish leaders find Him teaching in the temple and bring up His credentials, education, and training (vv. 16–18). Jesus answers them with words that are a constant theme throughout His life: *His words are not His, but the Father's. His deeds are not His, but are done by the Father, through Him.* This is the key to understanding Jesus' life and also to the way our lives were designed to be lived. Jesus asks why they want Him (vv. 19–24). It is clear from their answer that their desire to kill Him is due to their total misunderstanding of the Sabbath's purpose. The Jews had actually come to the point of worshipping the Sabbath rather than God's intent that it be used as a day of rest.

> *The Jews thought that obeying some fifteen hundred oral laws regarding keeping the Sabbath holy would make them more pleasing to God. Question: What is more spiritual, attending a Bible study or preparing your taxes? Why?*

The Jews are deeply conflicted about Jesus and the crowds are divided about what to do with him (vv. 27–49). He flatly tells them that where He is going they cannot come (vv. 33–36).

> *Where is He going?* _____

> *Why can they not come?* _____

"Are you thirsty?" asked the Lion.

"I'm dying of thirst," said Jill.

"Then drink," said the Lion.

"May I—could I—would you mind going away while I do?" said Jill.

The Lion answered this only by a look and a low growl.

"Will you promise not to do anything to me if I do come?" said Jill.

"I make no promise," said the Lion.

"Do you eat girls?" she said.

"I have swallowed up girls and boys, women and men, kings and emperors, cities and realms," said the Lion.

"I daren't come and drink," said Jill.

"Then you will die of thirst," said the Lion.

"Oh dear," said Jill, coming another step nearer. "I suppose I must go look for another stream, then."

"THERE IS NO OTHER STREAM," said the Lion.

—*The Silver Chair*, Chronicles of Narnia by C. S. Lewis

◆ **Jesus Speaks to Them of Living Water (v. 38).**

✡ Jesus uses a visual illustration with which all Jews would be familiar. He illustrates the ceremonial pouring out of the water from the golden pitchers on the altar. As He does so, He claims that He is the Living Water and that all who are thirsty may come and drink.

💡 Picture the scene: The streets are crowded, venders are selling their wares, and animals are being led through the streets. The noise and activity may have been something like a county fair in our country. Jesus stands on a wall, or possibly on a donkey cart that puts Him above the crowd. His voice bellows out across the busy streets, "I AM THE LIVING WATER [as opposed to the water from the pool of Siloam poured out symbolically on the altar]. ALL WHO ARE THIRSTY [FOR LIFE] COME AND DRINK!" When you and I speak of matters of faith, we think of *thirst for the word, for truth, or for God*. However Jesus uses thirst in a general way. He knew most of the people were not moving along the streets conscious of any particular spiritual thirst any more than today. After all, they were Jews, God's special people. They thought that their being children of Abraham secured their salvation. Jesus is saying, *"Whatever it is you are thirsty for, come to Me and I will satisfy that thirst!"* Thirsty for wealth? Jesus can satisfy you so that you will experience contentment with what you have. Thirsty for sex? Jesus can satisfy that by relighting your passion for your spouse or giving you a vision of the beauty of waiting for the one with whom you will spend the rest of your life. How about recognition or appreciation. God may not get you on *The Tonight Show*, but he will quench your thirst by making you a secure man or woman who likes who you are in Christ. Whatever you are thirsty for, Jesus can quench *that* thirst!

The Pharisees were experts in the law and they knew their history, but like all of us, they assumed many things without verifying their source. It would have been easy to find out that Jesus was born in Bethlehem, but they assumed that because He grew up in Nazareth, He was born there. Do you assume that all you read in a best-selling Christian book or hear in a sermon lines up with biblical perspective? No one is right all the time. Dig in for yourself. Critique all that you hear and read in light of the full counsel of God's Word.

◆ **The Jewish Leaders' Confusion Over Jesus' Place of Birth (John 7:41–42).**

💡 We see here in verses 41–42 part of the problem causing their confusion. They assume that because Jesus grew up in Nazareth, He was a Galilean; therefore, He could not be the Messiah. They say that no prophet has ever come from Nazareth. Neither of these assumptions is true. Had they done their homework, they would have known that He was born in Bethlehem of Judea, just as the Scriptures foretold. Second, there indeed *was* a prophet from Galilee. He was from a place called Gath-Hepher (2 Kings 14:25), the Old Testament name for what in Jesus' day was Galilee.

Who was this prophet?

◆ **Nicodemus Reenters the Story and Defends Jesus (John 7:50–53).**

Nicodemus steps forward on Jesus' behalf and challenges his fellow Jews concerning their willingness to break their own laws in order to get rid of Him. He argues that Jesus is not being dealt with fairly. (This is an almost prophetic statement by Nicodemus because we find later that the Jews will break twenty-two of their own laws in order to get Jesus on the cross.)

DAY 46

THE JEWISH LEADERS USE A WOMAN TO SET A TRAP FOR JESUS (JOHN 8:1–11).

The frustrated Jewish leaders leave after Nicodemus challenges their ethics. Jesus and His disciples spend the night on the Mount of Olives (v. 1) and early the next morning He returns to the festival and begins teaching in the temple. Suddenly, there is a great commotion outside. The crowd parts and to everyone's horror, a woman is brought before Jesus probably stark naked, and thrown at His feet. Right away, we can smell a rat! When the Pharisees left in a huff the evening before, they had no intention of giving up. No way! They were simply regrouping to plan another scheme.

◆ **The Leaders Ask Jesus a Question Designed to Trap Him (v. 5).**

Stoning was to be done in order to "purge evil from their midst" (Deut. 17:7; 19:19; 21:21, 22:21). It was like the removal of a tumor so that the rest of the body would avoid infection.

The penalty for adultery was stoning. However, earlier that year, the Romans had taken away the Jews' authority to enact capital punishment. If Jesus says, "Stone her," the Romans will arrest and probably execute Him. On the other hand, if He says, "Do not stone her," He will be committing a sin by breaking Jewish law; and the multitudes will turn against Him, knowing for certain that he is *not* the Messiah. Either answer Jesus gives leaves Him *dead in the water.*

Once again, the Pharisees and scribes try to circumvent the laws that they so firmly defend. Read Deuteronomy 13:6–11; 17:2–7.

> *What key element has conveniently been left out concerning the Pharisee's action toward the woman (Deut. 17:6)?*

Jesus does something that may strike us as rather strange. He stoops down and begins to write in the dirt with His finger. Most commentaries speculate about what He wrote, but we must get inside the mind and culture of a first-century Jew to understand His actions. Read Exodus 31:18.

> *How did God give the Ten Commandments to Moses?*

This would have been *paramount* to a Jew. God gave Israel these special laws for His special people. This was part of their *identity* as a nation and as a people. They were the *wife of God.* What was written in the dirt is *not* the issue. *It was what Jesus wrote with:* His *finger.* **What was He therefore directly saying to every Jew crowded there in the temple?**

Jesus stands up and tells them to throw the first stone if they have never sinned. Does He mean any sin? No! Deuteronomy 17:7 refers specifically to the sin of adultery. Jesus is saying, *"Anyone here who has never committed this sin of adultery, throw the first stone."* Then, as if to remind them before they take action, He stoops down again and writes with the *finger of God.*

> *Based on the Mosaic law, who was to be the first to crush the woman's skull with a stone (Deut.17:7)?* _____

The lengths to which these people stooped in order to use and humiliate this woman for the purpose of entrapping Jesus are sickening. But, once again, God turns the scheme against the schemer!

Jesus uses the term *woman* at least three times in Scripture: twice to his mother (at the wedding at Cana (John 2:4), at the cross (John 19:26), and now to the woman caught in adultery (John 8:10). It was not a harsh or disrespectful term. The closest phrase we have to translate it in English is the term *dear lady.*

By Jesus making an issue of writing in the dirt with His finger, He was in essence saying to the Jewish leaders, "Do you realize that you are actually scheming against Jehovah God Himself?"

◆ **Jesus Turns and Speaks to the Woman.**

He asks her a question and then responds with a statement, both of which summarize His attitude toward sin.

Question:

Statement:

JESUS AGAIN USES THE FEAST OF TABERNACLES TO EXPRESS HIS IDENTITY BY WAY OF PARABLES.

READ: John 8:12–20

As Jesus continues talking in parabolic form, He makes the second of His great "I am" statements concerning His identity. The first appeared in John 6:48. Shortly after He had fed the five thousand, He proclaimed, "I am the bread of life." Now at the Feast of Tabernacles, He says, "I am the light of the world" (8:12). The Jewish leaders call Him a liar (v. 13). Jesus responds by claiming *oneness* with the Father. Though greatly angered, they do not touch Him because the time had not yet come for Him to die.

In addition to the ceremonial outpouring of the water by the priest, there was also the lighting of the Golden Lamp Stand in the Holy Place of the Temple. Jesus used this ceremony as a backdrop to proclaim that He is "the light of the world." *Read Proverbs 4:18. Explain it as it relates to Jesus' statement, "I am the Light ..."*

158

Jesus Exposes the Spiritual Insensitivity of the Pharisees in a Head-on Confrontation (John 8:21–59).

First, Jesus confuses them by saying that where He is going, they cannot go (vv. 21–22). Those who reject the Messiah are not welcome in His Father's kingdom. He then says that He is from above and they are from below and that refusal to believe in Him would result in their dying in their sins (v. 24). Their entire value system was upside down. Temporary things had become more important than the permanent and eternal. Jesus confuses them further by saying that He spoke only those things that He has heard from the Father.

Many years ago there was a popular movie called *The Poseidon Adventure*. It was remade in 2006. A cruise ship was overturned by a huge tidal wave and floated in an upside-down position for the entire movie. A small band of survivors climb through the ship toward the hull, which they were told is the only possible area above water where they might be able to break through and survive. The paradox is that, as they move upward, they are really moving toward the bottom rather than the top because of the ship's inverted position. This is a graphic image of not only the Pharisees' culture, but ours as well. What seems like up is really down, and what seems like down is really up.

List some values in our culture that are turned upside-down.

♦ **Jesus Speaks to the Pharisees about True Freedom (vv. 31–34).**

The Pharisees are indignant hearing about freedom from this itinerant preacher who had not attended any of the required rabbinic schools nor been ordained by them. Once again they completely miss the spiritual implications of the freedom Jesus offers. They flatly tell Him that they have never been slaves to anyone. This is possibly the most ludicrous statement they could make. Consider Jewish history:

- The Jews were slaves in Egypt until Moses led the exodus in 1446 BC.
- The northern kingdom fell to the Assyrians in 722 BC.

- The southern kingdom fell to the Babylonians in 586 BC.
- Persia overthrew the Babylonians in 536 BC (Persian rule).
- Alexander the Great defeated the Persians; and set up the Greek Hellenistic Empire.
- The Romans overthrew the Greeks.
- The Roman general Pompey overthrew Jerusalem in 63 BC (slaves).
- Even as they spoke these words, they were under Roman authority.

◆ **Jesus Takes Dead Aim at the Jewish Leaders' Arrogance (John 8:37–59).**

This so graphically underlines the blindness that sin can cause. In verses 37–59, Jesus holds back nothing as He shreds the core of their identity by saying that He was greater than Abraham, and that He had existed before Abraham was born.

What did the Jews believe about Abraham?

"You belong to the power which you choose to obey, whether you choose sin, whose reward is death, or God, obedience to whom means the reward of righteousness" (Rom 6:16 PH).

Any of us can be blinded by sin in our lives. It is possible for someone to be an insatiable gossip, and because their language is couched in spiritual terms, they are never confronted and made aware of their tendency. A controlling person establishes a pattern of manipulation to always get their way. Everyone has seen it up close and personal, but the offender is often unaware of how destructive they are because no one intervenes. We are a family and need brothers and sisters to love us enough to speak truth into our lives. It involves great risk, but so does saving a drowning person at the beach. The Pharisees, though initially serious and well intentioned, had slowly become a mutual admiration society. Jesus was the only one willing to tell them the truth.

Who in your life will speak the truth in love to you? Write their names below and take a minute to thank God for them.

160

DAY 47

Jesus Heals a Man Who Was Born Blind.

READ: John 9:1–41

Jesus has been at the feast for many days. You can imagine the uproar as word trickles throughout the city of His constant confrontations with the Jewish leaders. His every movement is monitored by the Pharisees who are determined to humiliate Him in front of the Jews who, at least for now, are mesmerized by His teaching and miracles.

◆ **Jesus and the Twelve Encounter a Man Blind from Birth (v. 1).**

◆ **The Disciples Show Their Training by Asking Who Sinned to Cause the Man's Blindness (v. 2).**

What would cause someone to see a disability and assume that there must be a culprit to blame? (Review Day 2.) What was the Jewish mentality concerning things such as this?

◆ **Jesus Tells the Twelve that the Man's Blindness Has Nothing to Do with His Sin or Anyone Else's (v. 3).**

Jesus had healed other blind people. What will be unique about this miracle? (Review Day 15.)

Are you ever amazed at how we have been trained to think that God always reveals Himself through successful people? That is why we get the All-American to come testify about how God helped him score four touchdowns. We get Miss America to tell us how God made her beautiful, or a wealthy businessman to share his success story of how God propelled him to the top.

Go back and briefly review the two encounters with Jesus that we have studied; the woman with the hemorrhage (Day 33; Matt. 9) and the woman at the well

There was great king named Hezekiah (2 Kings 18). He lived during the time when the northern kingdom was taken into captivity in 722 BC. After the Assyrians took the northern kingdom, the king feared they would come south to Jerusalem and do the same. He realized that the main source of water for the city surfaced outside the city walls. He dug a 1,700-foot tunnel. At the end was the pool of Siloam. This amazing accomplishment through solid rock almost 6 football fields long provided water for the city while staying within the security of its walls. Siloam means "sent." Jesus sent the blind man there.

It's the bottom of the ninth, two outs, a man is on second, and your team is down by one run. You're up! Since you are a believer, most of us who write the script will have you hit a dramatic home run so you can give credit to God in the interview after the game. Why? Because we have been taught to believe that God loves winners and success brings Him honor. But what if, instead of being the hero, God would choose to put His glory on display in your life in a different way? Maybe you will strike out and lose the game so that everybody out there who ever lost and whoever failed will have someone to talk to. It's easy to point toward heaven after hitting it out of the park, but why does the same finger not point skyward when we strike out? When the football player hit a knee in the end zone to say a quick prayer after scoring a touchdown, why doesn't he do the same when he fumbles? If we will ever realize that the *strikeout* and the *fumble* can honor and glorify God as much, and even more, than the *home run* and the *touchdown*, this country will turn around!

(Day 14; John 4). Let's say you are in charge of a huge outreach dinner at your church. You need a speaker who will challenge the crowd by telling about the impact that Jesus has made in her and through her. Your choice is between these two women. Think of their personal stories. *Who would you choose and why?*

The truth is, most of us would choose the one with the more spectacular testimony—the one whose conversion led to a domino effect in the lives of others. Therefore, most would choose the Samaritan woman because she got the whole town excited about Jesus. Does that make the testimony of the woman with the hemorrhage any less valid? Instead of the superstar, why don't we get the janitor to come tell us how God sustains him as he mops the floors and cleans toilets? 99 percent of the people you seek to reach, live and relate in this or some similar arena, not the world of superstardom.

Jesus was sent by the Father (v. 3). He is the light that crashes through the darkness (v. 4). In healing the blind man, Jesus will show the spiritual conflict between light and darkness (vv. 4–5). After He heals the man (vv. 6–7), the neighbors and others gathered cannot believe that this is the same beggar whom they have known since he was a boy (vv. 8–10). He tells the neighbors that it was Jesus, but that he does not know who He is. The people take the beggar to the Pharisees and they ask a battery of questions to which he replies, *"All I know is that I used to be blind, but now I can see."*

◆ **The Pharisees Now Interview the Parents of the Man Born Blind (v. 20).**

Notice that the parents identify the man as their son and that he was indeed born blind. However, there is one thing they are afraid to say. We are told in verse 22 that the parents are afraid of the Jews because anyone who confessed Jesus as Messiah would be expelled from the temple. We can be certain that the parents were poor, otherwise they would not have had a son who was a beggar. In those days, the only thing going for a poor person was his involvement in the local synagogue. It was the epicenter of Jewish life. Take that away and he or she had absolutely nothing. But several other unpleasant things would have happened as well:

- No Jew would ever be allowed to speak to them again.

- They would be viewed as a leper (unclean, unacceptable).
- They would never be able to eat with a Jew again for the rest of their lives.
- When they die no one would mourn them or attend their funeral.
- The Pharisees would ensure that stones are cast on their grave in an act of defiance.

♦ **The Beggar's Simple Faith Angers, Embarrasses, and Bewilders the Pharisees (vv. 24–34).**

What do they want the man to say about Jesus (v. 24)?

As they continue the interrogation, what does the beggar say that really angers them (v. 27)?

♦ **The Beggar Shames the Pharisees (vv. 29–30).**

What the beggar is saying in verse 30 is something like this: *"I've never seen you guys, but I know your voices. I have sat and listened to you talk about the coming of the Messiah my whole life. I have heard you teach about the three messianic miracles He will perform so we will know it is He. Now this man, Jesus, comes and performs all three, including this miracle with me, all of which* you said *would one day occur. Now you have the gall to stand there and say to me that you don't know who He is or where He is from. Are you kidding me? And all this time I thought you guys were smart!"*

♦ **They Expel the Man From the Synagogue and Jesus Reveals to Him Who He Is (vv. 34–41).**

Once again, we do not witness a success story, at least from our cultural viewpoint. The beggar stood his ground against the ruling lawyers and elders of the city, but he was the only one in the crowd that day who actually *met* Jesus as far as we know. Because of his belief in Jesus, he was banned from all of the things we just mentioned. Yet, this is one of the great stories of courage

When a person gives his heart to Jesus, rather than instant success, he will more than likely face a landslide of opposition and temptation. Jobs may be lost, financial fortunes may be reversed, and families may even be torn apart. A new moral compass, a new level of honesty and courage, and new priorities may undermine that which a person has held together for years in his own strength. Those outside the circle of faith may never understand.

and the power of God throughout the Scriptures. We need to rethink our ideas of success and stop telling people that when they accept Jesus they'll get a huge raise, be instantly cured, or get a pony.

DAY 48

JESUS CALLS HIMSELF THE GOOD SHEPHERD AND CREATES DIVISION AMONG THE JEWS.

READ: John 10:1–21

◆ **Jesus Contrasts Shepherds with Strangers.**

What is a distinguishing characteristic of a shepherd as opposed to a stranger in relation to sheep (vv. 1–5)?

✡ The sheepfold was built on the side of a house and had one door through which sheep could enter at night to sleep. The surrounding walls kept the sheep from wandering and protected them from wild animals. *In describing those who seek to enter the sheepfold by another door, what is the "door" and who are these thieves Jesus alludes to?*

In what ways were these "thieves" trying to spiritually circumvent the "door"?

After describing the difference between a true shepherd and a fraud, Jesus claims that He is the Good Shepherd. Notice the contrasts between what the Good Shepherd and the Pharisees who are pretenders offer the sheep.

THE GOOD SHEPHERD		THE PRETENDERS	
10:3–5		10:5	
10:9		10:10	
10:10		10:12	
10:14		10:16	

♦ A Debate Ensues Among the Jews Concerning Jesus' "Spiritual Integrity" (vv. 19–21).

The essence of their division was _____.

The term *abundant life* (10:10) has, for the most part, become a spiritual cliché. John 10:10 is one of the first verses we memorize, but it is seldom defined without using other clichés. John 1:4 tells us that life is found in Jesus Christ. If that is so, why are so many of us simply existing day to day with what we could scarcely describe as *life* with any measure of spiritual abundance? We are tired, stressed out, depressed, and possess an enthusiasm that ebbs and flows with the circumstances around us. The same pills the unredeemed take are in our medicine cabinets. We are often told to *imitate Christ* and that abundance will develop, but I have a question: How is it going in your quest to imitate the Savior? Are you having a lot of success?

Paul said that Jesus Christ actually *was* his life (Col. 3:4). Yes, he did say in Ephesians 5:1, "Therefore be imitators of God, as beloved children," but consider this: If you write down every characteristic of Jesus throughout the Gospels, then check these against your daily behavior, will you experience abundance of life or total depression? Look at Ephesians 5:1 again. God has a beloved Son, Jesus. When we received the Son we also became *beloved children*. As *a* beloved child, how did *the* beloved Child live His life on this earth? He lived it, as we have said previously, *solely by the life of His Father.* Even the words He spoke were not His own, but His Father's (John 14:10). His works were done *by His Father, through His Father's life.* Therefore if you are interested in imitating Jesus, don't grit your teeth and go down an impossible list trying to create those character traits in your life. It will never happen! Simply yield your life to the Son in the same manner that the Son yielded His life to the Father. Get over this idea of trying to produce abundance that you are not capable of producing. Abundant life is not dependent on your discipline or how good you try to become. It is you simply allowing Christ to live His life within you. Your job is to enjoy your friendship with Him and allow Him to give you the abundance you could never produce on your own. *This is imitating Jesus: depending on Him just as He depended on the Father.*

SEVENTY ARE SENT OUT TWO BY TWO AND RETURN WITH GOOD NEWS, AND JESUS REJOICES.

READ: Luke 10:1–24

Jesus had previously sent out the twelve apostles two by two (Matt. 9; Luke 6; Mark 9). Now He sends out His original twelve along with fifty-eight more who were now His disciples. It is important to note that these seventy were not sent out by Jesus to "harvest souls" or to *evangelize* as we are often made to believe. Their evangelistic efforts would come much later. Jesus specifically tells these men that the fields are white (ripe) and ready for harvest. The disciples are to *pray* for laborers to be sent into *His* harvest. Whatever is harvested is not because of the messenger, but because of God *in* the messenger. Jesus knows that if these seventy will *pray* for laborers they will also *become* laborers.

Real discipleship does not happen in a classroom. It is more relational than academic. It is about a life on a life. It is about allowing people to fail and even to see you fail in order to help them recognize that failure is actually more important to spiritual growth than success.

- *They are to go as lambs in the midst of* _____ *(v. 3).*
- *They are to carry no* _____, *no* _____, *no* _____, *and greet no one along the way (v. 4).*
- *They are to stay in the house that receives them and* _____ *what they are given (v. 7).*
- *They are to eat* _____ *in each city that receives them (v. 8).*
- *Heal the sick in those cities and say, "The* _____ *has come near to you" (v. 9).*
- *When you are not received,* _____ *in protest (vv. 10–11).*

Some of these instructions are straightforward and others may seem a little puzzling, particularly if someone has not studied the Gospels chronologically as we have. For instance, Jesus had just spoken to the disciples about His being the Good Shepherd who lays down His life for the sheep. If you read His first instruction without knowing that, it would seem ludicrous to *go out as sheep among wolves.* Wolves eat sheep for breakfast! But Jesus has just finished teaching them that the Good Shepherd protects the sheep from their enemies. This being so, the sheep have only to go out and focus on being sheep, leaving the matter of the wolves to the Good Shepherd, who is prepared to do anything and everything to ensure their safety.

Why would Jesus tell them not to carry any money, luggage, or extra sandals and not to greet anyone along the way (Luke 10:4)? It was a way of saying, *"This is a training mission. I don't want you to take along things that you can lean on. No security blankets. Time is short before I must go to Jerusalem. There will be time to socialize later, but this is a mission where you will learn to trust me."*

♦ **Jesus Explains the Consequences to those Cities that Reject the Seventy (vv. 12–16).**

♦ **The Seventy Return from an Obviously Successful Mission (v. 17).**

Demons had been subject to them, and they had been given power over their enemies (vv. 17–19). They were ecstatic! But, Jesus quells their excitement. Why? (See v. 21.)

DAY 49

A LAWYER TESTS JESUS, WHICH RESULTS IN THE PARABLE OF THE GOOD SAMARITAN.

READ: Luke 10:25–38

CONSIDER AND DISCUSS: Have you ever found your enthusiasm and excitement leaning more toward the gifts of God than toward the person of God?

This mission of *the seventy* ensured that there were at least thirty-five homes that had received Jesus' message. It would be these very homes that Jesus would personally visit on His last trip before going to Jerusalem to be crucified.

♦ **An Expert in the Mosaic Law Asks Jesus What He Must Do to Inherit Eternal Life (v. 25).**

What is your assumption about this man as you read his question to Jesus. Is he a genuine seeker or simply trying to back Jesus into a corner? What does John 7:30 tell us?

Jesus is apparently teaching, because the lawyer "stood up" and asked a question about eternal life. Jesus turns the question back on him since the man was an expert in the law. The lawyer answers Jesus by giving the *great commandment*. Jesus agrees and says, "*Do this* and you will live." The key to understanding what is happening in this dialogue rests on *one word* which was used once by the lawyer in verse 25 and once by Jesus in verse 28. However the same word has vastly different meanings. The lawyer says, "What must I *do* to inherit eternal life?" The Greek word *do* is in the *aorist tense,* meaning a final, one-time action like the slamming of a door. The man is therefore asking, *what big one-time splash can I make that will be good enough for me to gain eternal life?* Without commenting, Jesus calmly asks him what the law says. He answers, saying that we are to love God with all of our heart, soul, strength, and mind, and love our neighbor as ourselves. The answer is correct, but Jesus responds by saying, "**Do** this and you will get what you are seeking." Here the word *do* is used by Jesus in a different tense. **Do** is in the *present tense*, meaning continual action. What is Jesus saying to the lawyer? *Live out this great commandment every second of every hour of every day for the rest of your days on earth and you will have eternal life.* Impossible? Absolutely! That was Jesus' point. He couldn't do it; that is why he needed a Savior!

♦ **Seeking to Justify Himself to Jesus, the Lawyer Asks, "Who is My Neighbor?" (v. 29).**

♦ **Jesus Tells Him the Parable of the Good Samaritan (vv. 30–37).**

To a Jew, any mention of a "good Samaritan" would have been an oxymoron to the tenth power. A Jew would have never said the word *good* in the same sentence with *Samaritan*. (See Day 14.) The scene takes place on a 17-mile road stretching from Jerusalem to Jericho. The elevation goes from 2,500 feet above sea level to about 800 feet below. The terrain is rocky desert and easy for robbers to hide and lay in wait for travelers.

We can see the bigotry surface in the lawyer's life as he answers Jesus' questions as to which man along the road was a true neighbor. Notice the lawyer's answer when Jesus asks, *"Who was the neighbor: the one who showed mercy?"* Notice he won't even say the word "Samaritan" (37).

Jesus tells the lawyer to go and do likewise knowing that he is completely incapable of living out the great commandment. Why would Jesus not give the man the plan of salvation right there? Why would He send Him away knowing that he lacked the resources to love God or his neighbor? Consider the entire story before you respond.

In Bethany, Mary and Martha Illustrate Opposite Perspectives Concerning Faith.

READ: Luke 10:38–42

One of the homes prepared by the seventy for Jesus to visit was that of Lazarus and his two sisters, Mary and Martha. Both women are deeply honored to have Jesus in their home, but their enthusiasm expresses itself in very different ways. Martha wants everything to be perfect as she scurries around breathlessly preparing a gourmet meal. Mary's excitement, on the other hand, causes her to want nothing more than to sit at Jesus' feet and cling to every word He says. To be close to Him is enough for her.

Which one of these two perspectives of following Jesus more closely resembles you? Is your tendency to try to work for God or to simply hang out with Him?

What is the purpose of the Christ-centered life: accomplishment or relationship? Service or intimacy? Activity or rest? The debate seems to rage, but the answer is very clear in Scripture. It is said in various ways by various people, but the fundamental idea is the same:

Moses said we are to _____ God (Deut. 6:5).

Sometimes it's a good thing to let a person hit the wall and realize that they are incapable of being what they want to be and doing what they want to do. Maybe after repeated failures and headaches they will realize their need to completely trust Jesus and live by and from His life. This seems to be what Jesus is doing with the lawyer.

Most of us have been taught that our purpose on earth is to serve God, but serving is actually a by-product of the biblical goal of intimacy. If you fall in love with Jesus, you will naturally grow into a desire to serve Him—not necessarily so the other way around. A healthy married couple doesn't have children because they need more help around the house. Children are a result of an intimate relationship. As the children grow, work around the house that was a nonnegotiable duty in their youth and immaturity should become a natural response to the love and respect they have for their parents. God wants companions not helpers.

Isaiah said we are created for _____ *(Isa. 43:7).*

Jeremiah said we are to _____ *God (Jer. 29:13).*

Paul said, "That I might _____ *Him" (Gal. 1:16).*

John said, "That we may have _____ *with God" (1 John 1:3).*

Peter said _____ *Christ as Lord in your hearts (1 Peter 3:15).*

One of the more interesting characters in the Bible is a man that we know almost nothing about. His name is Enoch. He was the father of Methuselah, and the Bible says that he walked with God for 365 years (Gen. 5:21–24). The writer of Hebrews tells us that "he was *pleasing to God*" (Heb. 11:5), and yet we know of nothing noteworthy that he ever did in those 365 years. God apparently just really liked him. He liked walking along and talking with him in the cool of the evening. They were friends, companions. One day, God's desire to spend time with Enoch was so great that He decided to skip death and a funeral, and take Enoch. Can you imagine a greater thought than that God would enjoy your friendship so much that He didn't care if you accomplished anything or not? He simply longed for your company and wanted to be with you every minute?

Martha meant well, but she missed the main attraction. In an instant, Mary had figured out that the essence of life is to enjoy the Savior. Serving God is *not* the purpose for our life. It is a natural by-product of a loving relationship. Can you imagine a man saying to his new bride as they slave away, painting the house, *"Honey, this is too much for the two of us. Why don't we get you pregnant and have some kids!"* What marriage would last if you had children so they could help you do your chores? Children are the result of a natural affection for your spouse. Why does God want more and more children? Not so they can serve Him and help Him with His chores. If we fall in love with Him, the natural outcome will be a desire to have the same heart to care for people as He does.

◆ **Jesus Says That Only One Thing Is Necessary and Mary Found It (v. 42).**

Do you think this experience will impact Martha's life? We'll see …

DAY 50

JESUS TEACHES THE TWELVE TO PRAY, THEN CASTS A DEMON FROM A MAN WHO WAS MUTE.

READ: Luke 11:1–36

The disciples, though raised in Jewish homes and under Jewish religious instruction, knew little about prayer. Through pharisaic instruction, they were taught prayer as a ritual rather than a relationship. The Pharisees read their prayers from a prayer book and gave much attention to the sound of their words rather than the cry of their hearts.

- ♦ **One of the Disciples Asks Jesus to Teach Them How to Pray as John Had Taught His Disciples.**

The question is most likely asked by one of the Twelve who had not formerly been disciples of John. He would have had some understanding of a spontaneous, relational conversation with the Father. Jesus had already taught them the models of what we refer to as the Lord's Prayer during His Sermon on the Mount. This occurred immediately after Jesus had chosen them and they had probably retained little at that point. The intriguing question is, What made this disciple ask that question almost three years into His earthly ministry?

STAND IN THE DISCIPLES' SANDALS: Be these men for a minute. *What have you* seen *and* heard *in these three years of following Jesus?* **List Below.**

Is there a connection between the character, the authority, the love, and the compassion you have seen in Jesus and His need and desire to spend time daily with His Father? The Twelve had finally put it together. All of the attributes of the Son came from the Father. Jesus was *utterly dependent* on the Father. *This was His secret.* Seeing Him roll out of His sleeping bag early in the morning, following Him, and seeing Him on His knees before His Father had finally kicked in with the Twelve. Who Jesus was as a man was directly connected to the intimacy He had with His Father. The natural question then is, *"Will you teach us to pray the way You do? We finally get it!"*

♦ **Jesus Then Teaches and Illustrates Persistence in Prayer (vv. 5–13).**

It's easy to think of prayer as a magic wand that we wave over the problems of the day. Jesus wants these men and us to realize that God may sometimes delay an answer in order to prepare us to receive it. He wants His disciples to learn patience and to be persistent. The greater importance of prayer is that it changes *people* rather than merely changing *circumstances* in life.

JESUS AGAIN PERFORMS A MESSIANIC MIRACLE AND RECEIVES THE SAME REACTION (LUKE 11:14–36).

The crowds were amazed (11:14) and some try to test Him for a sign (11:16). Jesus responds just as He did in Matthew 12 (Day 30), telling them again to *get off the fence*, for "whoever is not for Me is against Me." There are two basic differences in these accounts. The Jewish leaders reject Jesus in Galilee in Matthew 12, while the multitudes reject Him in Luke 11 in Judea.

After casting out a demon from a man who could not speak, Jesus is again accused of doing it by Satan's power. He answers in the same way as in Matthew 12, but with one added phrase. Jesus now asserts verbally in Luke 11:20 what He had done graphically with the woman caught in adultery.

Jesus refutes their allegations once again saying that He casts out demons by the _____ (v. 20).

♦ **Jesus Lowers the Boom, Saying that the Last State of the Jewish Nation Will Be Worse than the First (vv. 24–26).**

What on earth does that mean? Look at it through Jewish eyes. John the Baptist had in essence taken a *spiritual broom* and swept the house of Israel clean. Jesus followed, bringing a fuller expression of truth *putting the house in order*. The Jews rejected Jesus, and now the dust had begun to collect again in the house of Israel. Before Jesus' rejection, the *first state (or circumstance)* of Israel was their being overthrown by Pompey in 63 BC, when they were made subject to Roman authority. Forty years after the crucifixion, the *second state* will come upon them and 1.1 million people will be slaughtered in the siege of Jerusalem by the Roman armies. Therefore, "the *last state* [AD 70] will be worse than the *first* [AD 63]."

◆ **Jesus Concludes by Again Saying There will Be No More Signs Except the Sign of Jonah (vv. 29–32).**

✡ Why had Jonah refused to go to Nineveh when God told him to go? Most people say he was *prejudiced*, but it was more than that. Nineveh was the capital of Assyria. Jonah was a prophet who was born and raised in the northern kingdom. A prophet before Noah had prophesied that the northern kingdom, his homeland, would one day be taken into captivity by none other than Assyria. Jonah could not stand the thought of bringing the truth to the very people he knew would later devastate the land of his birth and take his people captive.

JESUS HAS LUNCH WITH A PHARISEE, THEN WARNS HIM STERNLY CONCERNING THEIR PRACTICES.

READ: Luke 11:37–54

By this point in Jesus' ministry, the scribes and Pharisees are well acquainted with Jesus' position concerning their oral laws. He will always obey every law of God, but He does everything He can to break those laws and traditions concocted by the Pharisees. Why? They were *add-ons* that were heaping great burdens on the people and distorting the truth.

Now He is invited to have lunch with a Pharisee. Jesus is *not* his new best friend. The Pharisee offers the invitation in the hope of using the opportunity to find fault. The Jewish leader is surprised that Jesus had skipped the ceremonial hand-washing ritual before the meal. Jesus may have purposely done this to set up an opportunity to challenge him on the habitual emphasis on external rules instead of the issues of the heart (vv. 39–41).

◆ **Jesus Pronounces Three Woes or Denunciations Upon the Pharisees.**

Woe 1 (v. 42)

What could you ever do to make God or His Word better? What could you add on to the truth to make it more true? Obviously nothing. Even the best of things falls short. Yet, just like the Pharisees, we do this constantly without realizing it.

When we add to Jesus at least four things happen:

• We diminish who He is

• We dilute the truth.

• We distract from the real issues.

• We divide the body of Christ.

Oswald Chambers said, "Jesus plus anything is heresy."

The Pharisees would actually count out meticulously a percentage of the herbs in their garden and their crops as part of their tithe, but could have cared less about the people in their charge.

Woe 2 (v. 43) _____

Woe 3 (v. 44) _____

The Jews would whitewash their tombs so that no one would touch one by accident and therefore become defiled (Num. 19:16).

We can clearly see the hypocrisy of the Pharisees as it related to the ancient prophets, whom they appeared to revere and honor. They built and rebuilt memorials to them, but rejected the Christ that the prophets boldly proclaimed. Their lives reflected little of what the prophets taught. They were just like their ancestors, who rejected and killed these great men.

Jesus hated religion! If you have any doubts about that, you've either been nodding off during the last fifty days or smoking something. This luncheon, disguised as an *olive branch* toward Jesus is anything but. Jesus will turn the tables by looking the Pharisee right in the eyes and condemning everything that he and his colleagues are about. No parables this time … just industrial strength truth!

It will help to think of this luncheon as is a classic encounter between Jesus and religion (the Pharisees.) Look at the following chart.

JESUS	RELIGION
A person is free to live and enjoy God's creation.	Fearful of freedom … uncomfortable without many rules, hates liberty.
Delights God by enjoying His presence.	Seeks to please God by religious activity, biblical knowledge, etc.
Understands resting in God.	Thinks rest is laziness, inactivity.
Draws attention to the Life within Him.	Draws attention to self, prideful, worries about personal image.
Creates spiritual hunger in others.	Can reproduce only themselves.
Confident in the Spirit within.	Insecure, never at peace.

Don't beat yourself up, but stop a moment and reflect on each of the above contrasts between religion and Jesus. Many of us have been exposed to most of what we see in the right column. God cannot change what we refuse to acknowledge. Sincere people may have unknowingly guided us away from a *person*.

Does any of the above ring a bell with you? What do you want God to change? (Don't try to do it yourself … that's religion!)

DAY 51

JESUS TEACHES ON NUMEROUS ISSUES TO THE DISCIPLES AND TO THE MULTITUDES.

READ: Luke 12

After Jesus levels the Pharisees with three specific woes, they become extremely hostile and begin to plot against Him (Luke 11:53–54). Despite the turmoil, Jesus continues to teach the Twelve in plain language, while speaking in parables to the multitudes. The disciples will be dealing with the Pharisees long after He is crucified, and He wants them to know what they are up against. He warns them to "beware of the *leaven* [or *hypocrisy*] of the Pharisees" (v. 1). The disciples' honesty must be above reproach, because what is said in private will be revealed in public (vv. 2–3). They must trust God, not men (vv. 4–5), and confess Jesus, never denying Him (vv. 8–9). When brought before the rulers and authorities they would be given the words to say by the Holy Spirit (vv. 11–12). Jesus will address several issues, including *covetousness,* warning the masses against greed (v. 15), but His method would still be parables (v. 16). He warns them against the sin of *wanting more than they needed* to live (vv. 16–21), and to seek first the kingdom as their top priority in life. In verses 35–40, Jesus encourages believers to remain alert, for He will return at a time when He is *not* expected.

NOTE: Some of the material in this section was covered during our few days in the Sermon on the Mount; therefore, it is only briefly mentioned here.

Jesus again speaks to the multitudes and chides them, saying that they could *predict the weather,* but in spite of His miracles, they had failed to see that He was the Messiah (vv. 55–56) They should make their peace with God before it is too late (vv. 57–59).

JESUS ADDRESSES CAUSE-AND-EFFECT RELIGION (LUKE 13:1–9).

The question is posed to Jesus concerning the idea that anyone who suffered a violent death or, as we saw early in our study, anyone who struggled with an infirmity suffered this because they were being punished for their sins. An evil and bloodthirsty man, Pilate had at some time murdered some Galileans while they were in the temple offering their sacrifices and their blood had mingled with the blood of their sacrifices (v. 1). Jesus refers to a tower at the pool of Siloam that fell on and killed eighteen people (v. 4). There is nothing stated elsewhere in Scripture about these two incidents, so we have no knowledge as to the reason they occurred. Were these things a punishment from God because of some great sin committed by those people? Jesus flatly says no and unless they repent, those who declare such things will "likewise perish."

 This notion that a death, an illness, or a failed business is the result of unconfessed sin in a person's life is a very prevalent thought today in some circles. It has been the source of great confusion and needless pain in numerous lives. In this passage, Jesus flatly states that those who perished had no greater sin than any other. To be certain, sin carries with it natural consequences for the believer in this life. However, if you have a friend who cheats on his wife, and a year later, loses his child to a fatal illness, to imply that this is God's punishment is the worst kind of hocus pocus. If your teenage daughter made a huge error in moral judgment and became pregnant, would you, as her parents try to get back at her by taking the life of her beloved dog? Would you find a way to make her pay? A good parent would certainly allow her to "own" the consequences of the choices she made, but a healthy parent would see this as an opportunity for her to grow and mature rather than an opportunity for retribution.

Jesus, in fact, concludes with a parable in verses 6–9 describing how the nation of Israel, even amid this great rejection, would be granted additional time to repent; but if no repentance results, she would pay the natural consequences (v. 9) in AD 70. (God tarries because of His deep, forgiving love.)

Jesus Again Heals on the Sabbath, Defends His Actions, Then Claims Oneness with the Father.

READ: Luke 13:10–21; John 10:20–29

- ◆ **A Woman, Eighteen Years with an Evil Spirit and Bent Double, Is Healed by Jesus as He Teaches on the Sabbath (Luke 13:10–13).**

In those days, an unredeemed person thought that "demon" meant any supernatural being, whether good or bad. Such a demon could cause a mental disorder (John 10:20), a fit of violent action (Luke 8:26–29), bodily disease (Luke 13:11, 16), and rebellion against God (Rev. 16:14). In this case, the description of the woman's problem suggests that the bones of her spine were rigidly fused together.

- ◆ **The Woman Stood Erect Praising God, but Causing a Negative Reaction from a Synagogue Official (v. 14).**

- ◆ **Jesus Rebukes the Official for His Hypocrisy (vv. 15–16).**

  Notice the synagogue official's statement in verse 14. Paraphrase the absurdity of what he is saying:

When man-made rules take precedence over people and their deepest needs, the rules become the enemy. God gives commands for basically two reasons: to *protect* us and to *provide* for our ongoing welfare. There is *nothing* negative about them. Again, we see religion trying to kill life. Religion says you work six days doing good and then rest on the seventh, being particularly spiritual. Real life means resting "in Jesus Christ" 24-7, honoring Him each day in all you do (1 Cor. 10:31). In other words, every day is a day of rest *in Jesus.*

- ◆ **It Is Now Winter, and Jesus and His disciples attend the Feast of Dedication in Jerusalem (John 10:22–29).**

After the death of Alexander the Great, his top generals divided the kingdoms he had conquered. Two of these generals were the *Ptolemys,* from Egypt and the *Seleucids* from Syria. The Seleucids were in control of Jerusalem in 165 BC when a king named *Antiochus Epiphanes* came into Jerusalem and made a complete mockery of the Jews and their beliefs. He desecrated the temple and killed every circumcised Jew in the city. A man named Judas Macabees came with his army and reclaimed the city in December of that year. Each December to this day, the Jews celebrate this great victory with a Feast of Dedication called *Hanukkah.*

As Jesus and the Twelve walk in the temple by the portico of Solomon, the Jews gather around Him and ask one of the most ridiculous questions in all of Scripture. They say, "Teacher, don't keep us hanging. Tell us if You are really the Messiah."

What had Jesus proclaimed verbally for three years?

What three miracles had He performed that unequivocally confirmed His messiahship?

1.

2.

3.

Who had set those miracles as the validation for the coming Messiah?

♦ **Jesus Tells Them That He and God Are Exactly the Same (v. 30).**

These people are not dumb or hard of hearing. Their problem is that they are not Jesus' sheep, so they cannot respond to His voice (vv. 26–27).

Do you ever find yourself getting angry with nonbelievers for acting like pagans? Do you become unsettled when those without Christ, and therefore with no capacity for true goodness, do shameful things? What are you expecting? Do you tend to ask of the world what they are incapable of giving? *(This is good thought to discuss and examine. Also review the end of Day 42.)*

PART VII: JESUS' PEREAN MINISTRY

Jesus will now spend much time in an area beyond the Jordan called Perea. It is the same area where John baptized the multitudes. Emotions are running high among the Jewish leaders, but Perea is beyond the jurisdiction of the Sanhedrin. As He continues His training of the Twelve, Jesus will focus more and more on the cross.

DAY 52

JESUS WITHDRAWS TO PEREA BEYOND THE JORDAN AND IS ASKED A QUESTION CONCERNING HIS MISSION.

READ: John 10:40–42; Luke 13:22–35

The Jewish leaders have reached the boiling point and Jesus will now spend most of His remaining time in Perea, beyond the Jordan, until He makes His final trip into Jerusalem. Perea is the area where John baptized the people during his ministry of preparing the way for Jesus. This area is significant because it is outside the jurisdiction of the Sanhedrin. The Pharisees cannot touch Him here. This was one of the main reasons why they were unable to prevent John from performing His ministry.

- **Because So Many Had Rejected Him, Someone Asked if There Were Only a Few Actually Finding Salvation (Luke 13:23).**

Though it may have been an innocent observation by one of the multitude following Jesus, it must have been a biting question for Jesus to hear. A modern version of the same sentiment by a news reporter might be, "Hey, Jesus, I notice that You have been run out of town several times over the past few years. It doesn't look like things are working out the way You planned. Doesn't seem like many are going for Your program. Care to comment for our listeners?"

- **Jesus Answers by Speaking of the Narrow Way and Says That They Must Strive to Enter It Before It Is Too Late (Luke 13:24–30).**

Unaffected by the implications of the question, Jesus responds indirectly but warns that many will try to enter the kingdom after it is too late. A key word in this passage is *strive* (v. 24). Jesus is *not* suggesting that they must work harder to find salvation. His message all along has been that salvation is all about God's work on our behalf and not because of any striving we could do to obtain it. Jesus has continuously referred to the "leaven" or the *erroneous teaching* of the Jewish leaders and that these hordes of Jewish humanity will have to *strive* to *unlearn* what they have been taught in order to see the truth.

Are there things that you are coming to realize in this gospel study that you have been taught, but do not line up with biblical truth? Begin a list here:

THE WIDE WAY AND THE NARROW WAY: This was discussed on Day 28 in Matthew 7, but some further comments may be helpful. What if we thought about this passage as if we were first-century Jews? Of the two routes to God that people attempt, which is easy and which is hard? *Draw a line to match up the two ways and the level of difficulty.*

Wide way		difficult
	is	
Narrow way		easy

The wide way leads to _____. The narrow way leads to _____.

Explain why you drew the lines you did:

Jesus says that the wide way leads to death and the narrow leads to life. But why did most of you say that the narrow way is the hard way and the wide way is the easy way? It seems like a logical assumption, doesn't it? It's the way we were taught. Read the passage again. Does it say that? The word *strive* is what throws us off because the word is not attached to the *wide way*. We assume the wide way is easy and we are trained that the best things in life are difficult, *so work hard and squeeze through the narrow door.*

Consider what we have studied in context. Jesus' main argument with the Pharisees is that they are *striving* for righteousness by their own merits. This is why they pray more, give more, memorize more, and make rules on top of rules. Will their efforts to approach God be easy or hard? Actually, neither. It's *impossible!* The wide way is the way the Jewish leaders took and it was a road to nowhere. The narrow way is the easy way in that a person has only to *believe on the Son.* It has nothing to do with his or her own efforts. What makes the narrow way *seem* difficult is that a Jew would have to renounce all of these things he had been taught and go against pharisaic teaching in a world dominated by pharisaic perspective.

- ♦ **The Pharisees Tell Jesus That He Should Flee Because Herod Wants to Kill Him (v. 31).**

    Based on their ongoing relationship with Jesus, what would you say is the Pharisees' motive for warning Jesus about Herod (v. 31)?

- ♦ **Jesus Responds, but They Cannot Understand. He Alludes to His Resurrection (v. 32) and Death in Jerusalem (v. 33).**

This is Jesus' way of saying that it won't be Herod who kills Him, but the Jews in Jerusalem, just like they had killed the prophets (v. 34), referring to the events of AD 70. Jesus tells them that their house will be left desolate. They would not see Him again until Israel repents and says, "Blessed is He who comes in the name of the Lord" (v. 35), in other words, calls Him back in faith (Hos. 5:15; Rom. 11:26).

DAY 53

AFTER ANOTHER SABBATH DEBATE, JESUS DISCUSSES THE COST OF DISCIPLESHIP WITH THE CROWDS (LUKE 14:25–35).

Over 1,500 additional oral laws concerning the Sabbath had been heaped upon the Mosaic law, and thus, on the backs of the Hebrew people.

READ: Luke 14:1–35

Of the seven recorded miracles that Jesus performed on the Sabbath, Luke records five of them. Being a Gentile, he seems intrigued at the absurdity of the Jewish traditions being the cause of the people turning a deaf ear to the cries of the hurting in favor of these endless rules.

Actually, there is nothing in the Mosaic law or the oral traditions that prevented acts of mercy from being performed on the Sabbath. The Pharisees' insistence on this kind of legalism is further evidence of how far their obsession with the law had taken them so far off course.

◆ **Jesus Confounds the Pharisees with Questions About Healing on the Sabbath (Luke 14:1–6).**

Jesus breaks bread with a leading Pharisee in his home and is under close scrutiny (v. 1). In front of Him (obviously a set-up) was a man with dropsy (v. 2), a condition of the heart that affects the entire body. Knowing that He was being tested, Jesus asks the Pharisees if it is lawful to heal on the Sabbath. They do not answer, so Jesus heals the man and sends him on his way.

In verses 7–11, Jesus tells a parable that addresses the sin of *pride* and *self-promotion*. He finishes commenting on this subject by saying that all who exalt themselves will be humbled, but those who humble themselves will be exalted (v. 11). *Explain your perspective on this principle in a sentence or two.*

◆ **Jesus Teaches Unconditional Friendship (vv. 12–14).**

The thought of extending kindness without any expectation of reciprocation would have been a foreign idea to the Pharisees. Because of their preoccupation with image, social events that they initiated would come with subtle strings attached. Only the wealthy and prominent who could return the favor would be invited. Jesus goes to the opposite extreme, telling them to have a dinner and invite the despised of the world, those who had no means to give back. He tells them that they will be rewarded at the resurrection (v. 14).

Jesus concludes with a parable. The key thing about understanding a parable is to determine who the people represent. Sometimes we try to force an application to our own lives when it may have only concerned a specific message to the Jews of that time. In this parable (vv. 16–24):

Who is the man giving the big dinner? _____

Who are the people making excuses about attending? _____

Who are the poor and lame now invited? _____

Who comes in from the highways and hedges? _____

What will be the fate of the excuse makers? _____

Answers
on next page

Think for a moment about social gatherings, large or small, that you have hosted in your home. Have you ever considered your motives concerning those you invited? Was it to be invited to their home in return? Was the motive business related? Status related? No one has ever seen a motive, but pure motives that are unconditional in nature not only build character but reap rewards in heaven. Have you ever thought of giving a dinner and inviting the poor and those who are never invited to such gatherings? Would it change their situation? Probably not, but you would have given them a night to remember, and it just might change your life.

◆ **Jesus Discusses the Cost of Discipleship with the Crowds Following Him (Luke 14:25–35).**

• A Disciple's Love for God Must Exceed Every Other Love (v. 26).

The word hate *here can be confusing, but it is used for a purpose. Read verse 14 again, but insert the phrase "in comparison to loving God" in front of the verse. Now, paraphrase what Jesus is saying:*

Answers
from previous page
___
God the Father

Jews who reject the
Messiah

Jews who believed

Gentiles who believed

They will never enter
the kingdom.

Read Romans 9:13: "Jacob have I loved, Esau have I hated." Did God really hate Esau? Think of it this way: In Exodus 24 God *married* Israel. Jacob's descendants happen to be the Jews; Esau's descendants are the Edomites. Paul is saying that God loved Israel more than the Edomites. Is that fair? You bet! God had to have a son to redeem humankind, so He had to have a wife. God married Jacob's descendants at Mount Sinai. If you have a healthy marriage, is there any woman or man you love more than your spouse? No! Does it mean that you hate all other women or men? Of course not! So when Paul speaks of God's love for Jacob and not for Esau, he is speaking about nations, not individuals. God *married* Israel. He's supposed to love his *bride* more than any other. Therefore are not you and I to love Jesus Christ to such a degree that by comparison, we would "hate" the next greatest love in our lives?

- A Disciple Must Carry His Own Cross (v. 27). (Reread Day 40.)
- A Disciple Must Calculate the Cost Before Following Jesus (vv. 28–32).

Think back to when you first gave your life to Jesus. On a scale of 1 to 10 (10 being the highest), how much were you informed or aware of the cost of following Him? _____ (Discuss this if you are in a group.)

In a so-called *Christian subculture* like ours, the emphasis is placed so firmly on conversions and "winning people to Jesus" that the cost is rarely understood by the person considering this step. There is a big difference in a *decision* for Jesus and a *conversion* to Him. The idea of *winning* someone in the first place is ludicrous. How can one man or woman win another person's heart to God? This is purely the work of the Spirit of God. All I can do is be available, be ready to explain the truth, and pray. The *winning* or *convincing* is entirely up to God. Jesus never pushed for a quick decision. In this passage He stresses that people understand the cost going in.

- A Disciple Must Be Detached from His Possessions or He Will Lose His Cutting Edge (vv. 33–35).

Does this mean that we should give away everything we own?

Why would my possessions potentially cause me to lose my saltiness (vv. 33–35)?

DAY 54

THE PHARISEES GRUMBLE OVER JESUS RECEIVING SINNERS. JESUS ANSWERS WITH THREE PARABLES.

READ: Luke 15:1–32

Tax collectors and prostitutes are clustered around Jesus trying to hear the things He has to say. During meal times, He would stay around and eat with them. The Pharisees could never have understood this had they lived to be a thousand years old. It leaned against everything they believed. They taught that these people were beyond redemption. They believed God had washed His hands of them. How, then, could a man who claimed to be the Messiah carry on with them as if He liked being with them as much as being with the righteous? Without responding directly to their critical remarks, Jesus tells three parables, both to dismantle the Pharisees wrong perspective and to teach the Twelve about the compassion and forgiveness of the Father.

The parable of the prodigal son would have been the hardest of all for the Pharisees to swallow. They believed that God rejoiced when a sinner bit the dust. The Mishnah states, *"There is joy before God when those who provoke Him perish from the world."* Let's see how these parables would offend them.

- Concern for the individual: A typical number for an average flock of sheep was one hundred. The shepherd would count them every night. Upon discovering one missing, the shepherd would leave the remaining ninety-nine to search for a stray. This would be absurd to a Pharisee. If a sheep was dumb enough to wander from the shepherd's care, God would be happy to be rid of him.

The same would be true of the lost coins. Palestinian women would often receive 10 silver coins as a wedding gift. They held sentimental value and would usually be kept in a secret place for a special time of need. A woman would light a lamp and search the dark corners of the house and would not stop until she found the valued coin.

- Cavorting with prostitutes: The prodigal would have disqualified

The word *receive* in Luke 15:2 is used in two ways in Greek. The first is "to welcome into fellowship" (to be willing to sit and talk). The second means "to accept as a friend." The receiving of tax collectors and prostitutes would have made the Pharisees break out in hives. Eating with them in Middle Eastern culture meant not only defilement, but was a sacramental act signifying acceptance on a very deep level.

I highly recommend the book *The Cross & the Prodigal*, by Dr. Ken Bailey. In it, he points out that in a village society, the younger son demanding for his inheritance meant that he was impatient for his father to die. The request is a form of mutiny. He cares nothing for the rest of the family. How would the father pay him his share? Not with a check or cashing in mutual funds. Everything was in land, houses and livestock. To sell off his portion would create unspeakable hardship on the rest of the family. He is also rejecting his family and his heritage and breaking fellowship with his father. This makes the gracious acceptance of the son even more graphic.

185

himself from returning to his father by associating with such people.

- Losing his wealth: The Pharisees believed that wealth was a sign of God's favor regardless of how it was gained. To lose it in riotous living would have been to incur God's wrath.
- The Father's mercy: Pharisaic Judaism taught that salvation was based solely upon works or merit. Jesus was teaching that salvation was based on the Father's mercy alone.
- The ring, the robe, and the fatted calf: To seemingly reward slothfulness would have caused the Pharisees to hyperventilate. People get what they deserve. The older brother should receive the praise. For the Jewish leaders, restoration without reparation paid was unthinkable. This grace was not only *amazing*, but to them, *infuriating!*

NOTE: You can see that this is a picture of the law trying to counterfeit itself as Grace. Jesus wanted this picture to stay in the minds of His disciples.

JESUS CONTINUES SPEAKING IN "CODE" LANGUAGE.

READ: Luke 16:1—17:10

The parable of the prodigal son dismantles the Pharisees' theological perspective concerning the nature of God, salvation, and wealth.

Jesus tells three parables illustrating stewardship that make more sense when considered in light of the big picture as it relates to the nation of Israel. Consider what God had done for Israel. She was His *wife!* He had given the law for her *protection* and *provision*. The Jewish leaders were to *preserve* this sacred trust to help guide the people. They distorted God's laws by adding their own and, in doing so, had put great burdens on the people's backs rather than helping them. Jesus will drive this home in these three parables.

MEMORIZE: "Herein do I exercise myself to have always a conscience void of offense toward God and toward man" (Acts 24:16).

The parable of the unjust steward: As we take an aerial view of the parable, notice the similarities with the Pharisees.

- A manager (_____) is given stewardship over a large estate (_____) does a lousy job and the owner no longer trusts his leadership, so he fires him. The steward tries to do something to help himself before he is relieved of his duties. He goes to each of his master's debtors and cuts them a deal figuring they will be grateful to him and help him later when he is destitute. The master praises the unjust steward for his shrewdness.

The unjust steward is shrewd, but does he have integrity? _____

He is praised because he thought ahead. Does planning indicate a lack of faith? What is the balance?

Do the debtors have integrity? _____ . *Why or why not?*

Is there any difference between this and someone doing a "handyman job" for me and asking to be paid in cash to avoid taxes and I comply?

Think of the things that we highly esteem in our culture. Take power, for instance: Power is not evil. The question is, How was it derived? Was it sought or was it given by God? If it comes naturally, it will be seen by the person as a stewardship. If it is achieved in a person's own strength, God will oppose it and it will not be a source of blessing to the people.

Jesus' point is that God will not entrust spiritual riches to one who does not properly handle material resources. Also, He emphasizes that a man cannot have two masters, God and money (v. 13). He must make a choice.

◆ **The Rich Man and Lazarus (vv. 19–31)**

A poor man named Lazarus and a wealthy man both die near the same time. Their souls go to Hades. (Review in Day 39.) In Hades, Lazarus goes to Abraham's bosom, which is the *redeemed side*, and the rich man goes to the other side, which is *hell*. Immediately this gets the Pharisees' attention. Why? They thought that having wealth garnered the favor of God and was a guaranteed ticket to heaven. The rich man can see Lazarus across the great divide, but cannot cross over because Abraham will not allow it. Confronted with this horrible reality, the rich man thinks of his unredeemed brothers. He asks Abraham to let Lazarus, whom his brothers know is dead, go back and tell them to repent. This is crazy thinking and Abraham knows it. He tells the rich man that his five brothers have the Scriptures (Moses and the prophets) to know the truth if they really want to know. Theatrics will not convince them.

Do you think if Lazarus had gone back from the dead and talked to the five brothers, they would have believed? Many of us know people who will not believe regardless of the evidence they are presented. It is a matter of a person's *will*, not their *inability* to believe. *Commitment* comes before *knowledge*. This was the Jews' problem; they continually asked for a sign, yet Jesus had given sign after sign and they still would not believe. This is why Abraham said no to the rich man's request.

Take a minute to think of several people you desperately want to know Jesus. List their names below and ask God to awaken their spirit to His Spirit.

DAY 55

JESUS RAISES LAZARUS FROM THE DEAD.

READ: John 11:1–44

We are studying the Gospels chronologically (as the events occurred). Although the Lazarus that Jesus spoke of in yesterday's study is not the same Lazarus that Jesus will raise from the dead, it is not coincidental that these two events happen back to back. Just as Abraham knew that for Lazarus to go warn the rich man's brothers would *not* ensure that they would believe, we will see that even though Jesus will raise *this Lazarus* from the grave, the Jews will still not believe. This confirms the fact that old Abe knew what he was saying. This will be the first public miracle Jesus will perform validating His messiahship since Matthew 12:39–40 (Day 30).

The Twelve try to talk Jesus out of going to Bethany, not because of any lack of concern for Lazarus, but because they knew that in order for Jesus to go there, He would be forced to return within the jurisdiction of the Sanhedrin.

Jesus had said that no more signs would be given except for one the sign of _____, soon to happen here in John 11.

Jesus is in Perea when He receives word that His friend Lazarus is deathly ill. Perea is about a two days' journey from the town of Bethany. Lazarus had been dead two days when Jesus arrives. Had He not waited an extra two days, He may have reached His friend before death. After forty-eight hours, He leaves Perea against the advice of the Twelve, and is now within the jurisdiction of the Sanhedrin. He knows that He is vulnerable, but He also knows that He *must* die at the Passover in Jerusalem. When Jesus finally arrives, He is met by an irate

Martha. As you remember, she is the worker bee, a very type-A, take-charge kind of person. In her quest to make things happen, she often misses the real point, which is certainly true in this case. She *hates inefficiency* and feels that, considering Jesus' friendship with her brother, the *least* He could have done was to hurry! She criticizes Him for not coming sooner (vv. 20–21). Jesus is calm and nondefensive, assuring her that her brother will rise again. She thinks of this statement somewhat like the clichés you hear at a funeral: *"He's in a better place,"* and *"You'll see him again one day."* She has no real understanding of who He is or what He is referring to.

Verses 5–6 give us a slant on real love that few understand. It says that Jesus loved Lazarus and his sisters, so when He hears that time is critical, He stays in Perea two more days. *Explain how that expresses and defines real love.*

Why do the disciples fear leaving Perea? _____

Martha and Mary both tell Jesus that if He had been there, Lazarus would not have died, but their approach is different. *Describe the differences.*

Martha:

Mary:

◆ **At the Tomb of Lazarus, Jesus Commands That the Stone Be Removed (vv. 38–39).**

In order for there to be a resurrection there must be a death!

Picture the atmosphere. With Bethany located only two miles from Jerusalem and Lazarus being well known and loved by many, throngs of people are at the house and surround the site of the tomb. Professional mourners are wailing away like coyotes in a western movie, and there is much confusion. Knowing that Jesus would certainly come to honor His friend, the Jewish leaders probably came initially, but had obviously given up and gone back to Jerusalem (v. 46) when Jesus failed to show up within a couple of days.

For Jesus to *prevent* death by curing an illness at the eleventh hour meant that He was a great healer. But for Him to *overcome* death meant that He has power, dominion, and authority over life and death.

An understanding of the Jewish concept of death is critical. When Jesus told the people to remove the stone, a loud gasp of horror went out from those gathered, just as you would if someone ordered a casket opened that had been in the ground for days. For Jews, there was still hope until a certain point after death. Jews believed that the spirit of the person hovered over the body for three days and then departed, leaving them room for hope until after the third day. Jesus purposely arrives on the fourth day so that when He raises His friend, no one can explain away the fact that He is the Messiah.

Mary and Martha understand that Jesus can *prevent* death, because they have witnessed it many times. What they did not understand was that Jesus could *overcome* death. This is the focal point of the story as John relates it. For Jesus to merely be seen as a *great healer* and a *wonderful teacher* limits who He is. He is "the Resurrection and the Life." If they don't see this, they have missed everything, no matter how much they may know!

When Martha protests having the stone removed from the entrance of the tomb, Jesus makes a very profound statement about the nature of truth: "If you believe, you will see the Glory of God." This is another "opposite of God's mind." Man says, "Seeing is believing," but God says, "Believing will give you eyes to see."

◆ **Jesus Commands Lazarus to "Come Forth" (v. 43).**

Lazarus emerges, tightly bound with winding clothes used for burial. Jesus tells them to "unbind him, and let him go." An instructive parallel can be drawn from this. When we meet Jesus, we go from death to life. However, many of us continue to be bound by certain addictions, habits, and phobias, unable to really experience life. Had Jesus not said, "Unbind him," death could well have been a better deal for Lazarus. How was he bound? Specifically, his head, his eyes, his mouth, his hands, and his feet. If you look at these five parts of the body from a spiritual vantage point in your own life, how might you presently be bound and need to be set free?

- Head: The way you think: _____
- Eyes: What you expose yourself to: _____
- Mouth: The way you express yourself: _____
- Hands: The quality of your workmanship: _____
- Feet: Your walk; your lifestyle _____

DAY 56

THE RESURRECTION OF LAZARUS CAUSES SUCH UPHEAVAL THAT THE SADDUCEES AND PHARISEES JOIN FORCES.

READ: John 11:45–54

The Sadducees and Pharisees are usually mentioned together, yet they were bitter enemies. The Sadducees were the wealthy aristocracy, and the Pharisees were generally made up of average people. Great jealousy and many theological differences existed between the two groups. The Sadducees were the priestly group, and the Pharisees were the keepers of the law. The Sadducees did not believe in the resurrection of the body. They relied heavily on logic over faith, did not believe in angels or demons, and did not believe that the entire Bible was God's Word. What brought the two groups together was their anger and fear over the raising of Lazarus. They can wait no longer. They must come up with a definitive solution to get rid of this troublemaker who sways the people and could provoke the Romans and cost them their position and authority.

What is the sentiment of the crowds after the raising of Lazarus (vv. 45–46)?

◆ **The Jewish Leaders Meet and Their Hearts Are Revealed (vv. 47–48).**

We finally see the real agenda. All this time we thought their concern was for the flock under their care. What was their real concern (v. 48)?

◆ **Caiaphas, the High Priest, Makes a Prophetic Statement without Even Realizing It (v. 50).**

Why is Caiaphas's statement in verse 50 prophetic?

Here in John 11:48 we see the true agenda of the Jewish leaders. This fear of losing their "place" drives their actions from their first expedition to the desert to hear John the Baptist through Jesus' death and throughout the book of Acts.

MEMORIZE: "The king's heart is like channels of water in the hand of the Lord; He turns it wherever He wishes" (Prov. 21:1).

191

Why did Caiaphas say this? Proverbs 21:1 helps to explain it. Paraphrase in your own words.

CONSIDER: Does the verse say anything concerning our elected leaders, be they Democrat or Republican? (See Rom 13:1.)

From that day on, the Jewish leaders begin to specifically plot Jesus' death (v. 53). Jesus and His little band depart for Ephraim, no longer walking publicly (v. 54). He will not return to Jerusalem until the week of His crucifixion. Jesus knew the heart of a man like Caiaphas. He knew he would make a decision that would benefit his personal agenda.

JESUS HEALS TEN LEPERS THEN DISCUSSES HIS RETURN.

READ: Luke 17:11–37; 18:1–14

◆ **Jesus Encounters Ten Leprous Men Who Beg Him for Mercy (vv. 12–13).**

After a brief stay in Ephraim, Jesus and the Twelve journey through Samaria and Galilee toward Jerusalem. Ten lepers see Him and cry out from a distance. (Lepers were not allowed to approach an uninfected person.) As you would expect, Jesus heals them, but differently this time. He tells them to show themselves to the priest, which, as you remember, was instructed in the Levitical law (see Day 17). Along the way, they find that their healing has occurred. Only one of them turns back and falls at Jesus' feet, glorifying God. Just as we saw in Luke 5:12–16 (Day 17) when Jesus performed His first messianic miracle, by Levitical law these ten men will have to be examined by the high priest and undergo an eight-day cleansing.

Who is the high priest? _____ What had he just stated (John 11:50)? ....

Much time and planning would be required to carry out the plot to kill Jesus. Now, however, because Jesus had healed the ten lepers, Caiaphas, the high priest, will have to pull aside from his devious plans for eight days and perform the ceremonial cleansing for each man! By declaring that the men have been healed at the end of the eighth day, he will in essence be saying that Jesus actually is the Messiah … even though he is presently plotting His death.

◆ **Jesus Discusses His Second Coming with His Disciples (vv. 22–37).**

This and other areas of Scripture in the Gospels have been debated for centuries. Though we do not have the time or space to discuss these passages in our study, it is a fascinating subject that you would do well to study on your own.

Have you wondered why David was "a man after God's own heart?" "Then David, the King went in and sat before the Lord and said, 'Who am I, O Lord God, and what is my house that thou hast brought me this far'" (1 Chron. 17:16).

◆ **After Teaching on the End Times, Jesus Speaks About Prayer in Two Parables (Luke 18:1–14).**

If you had just heard Jesus address the conditions that will exist surrounding His return, you would probably have been both excited and traumatized. Those who wait for His return will need to be men and women of prayer. He tells two parables that reflect the two-pronged posture of a person whom the Father hears.

- A widow comes back time and again asking for protection from a judge who neither feared God nor respected man. *What finally won him over was her* _____ *(vv. 1–8).* So, if an unrighteous judge is compelled to help the woman, how much more will the righteous Father answer those who cry out to Him in weakness?
- A Pharisee's prayer life is contrasted with a tax collector's. The Pharisee's prayer was essentially an "ode to himself," expressing how fortunate God was to have him on the team. The tax collector's prayer was much different; he knows his unworthiness and his need for mercy. *His was a prayer of* _____.

Once again we see this recurring theme of humility. If pride is, as C. S. Lewis stated, "The Great Sin," then humility must be the "Great Pleasure" of God. We see it all through the Scriptures, and yet arrogance seems to continually characterize much of the modern church. We must continually ask ourselves the tough questions:

- Whose kingdom am I seeking to build—mine or God's?

- If an unprecedented outpouring of God's Spirit happened in my city and neither I nor my church had any role in it, would I be happy or sad?
- In my heart of hearts, can I honestly echo with John the Baptist, "He must increase and I must decrease"?

DAY 57

JESUS LEAVES GALILEE AND ENTERS PEREA. THE PHARISEES QUESTION HIM ABOUT DIVORCE.

READ: Matt. 19:1–12; Mark 10:1–12

To get the full impact and flavor of the Gospels, we must have some basic understanding of our sinful nature—that nature which we possessed before we are redeemed and made a new creation (Rom. 6:6). The Pharisees ask Jesus about divorce at this particular point for a reason. This isn't in order to get a nice sound bite on His perspective. Don't forget, they were plotting to kill Him (John 11:53). Why would they ask a question about divorce in the midst of a murder plot? Let's figure it out.

Why was John the Baptist arrested? (Briefly review Day 36.)

Where is the location of Jesus when they ask this question?

"When a man takes a wife and marries her, and it happens that she finds no favor in his eyes because he has found some indecency in her, and he writes her a certificate of divorce and puts it in her hand and sends her out from his house" (Deut. 24:1).

Who is Tetrarch of Galilee, and who has jurisdiction where Jesus is?

Obviously, they had no interest in what Jesus believed about divorce. It was merely a device to try to get Him to say something that would enrage Herod Antipas and hopefully aid them in their plan to take Jesus' life.

194

The subject of divorce is a difficult and volatile issue in our society. We will attempt to show what appears to be a healthy biblical posture from the full counsel of the Word of God. Historically there was disagreement even among the Pharisees concerning grounds for divorce. Look at Deuteronomy 24:1.

✡ The great debate centered on the meaning of the phrase *"has found some indecency in her."* There were two schools of thought concerning divorce we earlier mentioned briefly. The first was the school of Shammai. This was the conservative school that believed divorce should only be granted in cases of adultery. The second was the school of Hallel. This more liberal position held that a man may divorce a woman for almost any cause. The Mishnah gives reasons as trivial as "burning the food" or "finding any impurity in her." This could be anything from bad breath to smelly feet. If a man saw someone "fairer" than his wife, he could leave her and remarry. The disagreement over how to interpret this phrase *"any indecency in her"* was paramount. It is interesting that throughout the dialogue, the Pharisees focus on *divorce,* while Jesus focuses on *marriage.* The Pharisees see divorce as a *legal* issue, but Jesus sees it as *spiritual.*

- **The Pharisees Ask Jesus if Divorce Is Lawful for Any Cause (Matt. 19:3).**

  The phrase "any cause at all" (v. 3) tells us the Pharisees asking the question are from the school of _____.

- **Jesus Responds by Quoting the Scripture (vv. 4–6).**

  Paraphrase in your own words Jesus' answer.

- **The Pharisees Ask Why Moses Commanded to Give a Woman a Certificate of Divorcement (v. 7).**

  Jesus corrects them by saying that Moses _____ *divorce because of* _____.

 Look at the parallel account in Mark 10:8. Read it carefully. Here Jesus introduces a new wrinkle in the ongoing debate. Notice who the man com-

In the Old Testament, adultery was not grounds for divorce; it was grounds for stoning.

Did the Pharisees get the answer they wanted that would anger Herod? Yes and no. Jesus firmly endorses John's condemnation of Herod's marriage to his brother's wife. However, because Jesus correctly quoted the Scriptures, there was little they could do.

195

mits adultery against: *the woman!* In Jewish thinking, if a married man and a woman slept together, the woman commits adultery against the man as well as her own husband. The adulterous man's culpability was against the adulterous woman's husband. In other words, the man was always the victim, and the woman was always the perpetrator. Now Jesus is saying in Mark 10:11 that a man can commit this sin against a woman. In verse 12, He adds a shocking piece to the debate by saying that the woman had the *same right* to divorce as a man.

Jesus does *not* legitimize divorce in any way. He does, however, challenge the thinking that the woman is always at fault. Most observant Jews today still hold to the tradition that only the man can file for divorce. To comprehend Jesus' position on divorce, we must understand God's original purpose for marriage. According to Moses and Jesus, marriage is based upon *exclusiveness.* When that is broken, the contract can be considered null and void. What was on God's heart when He instituted marriage? Dick Woodward, a dear friend and pastor in Virginia, explains it this way:

"God wanted to populate the earth with adequate *people. His plan was to take two* persons *and make them* partners *that they might become* parents. *Those parents produce* little persons *who will one day become* partners *and* parents *who will produce* little persons *until the earth is populated. The adequacy of the* persons *produced depends upon the adequacy of the* parents. *The adequacy of the* parents *depends upon the adequacy of the* partnership, *and the adequacy of the* partnership *depends upon the adequacy of the* two people *who made it up."*

This is simple, but profound. To fail to understand this is to fail to see that marriage is *not* simply about what is in it for the man and woman. The critical issue is, *what is in it for God?* What does He stand to gain from this union and what would He stand to lose from its dissolution? If God brings it together, God can keep it together. God is *always* on the side of reconciliation.

Woodward adds, *"Marriage is a* permanent *tie because of what we might call 'children's rights.' Children have a right to a stable, permanent context within which they might receive nurture and the education that will prepare them to face life. They will only have this launching pad into life if the marriage that brought them into the world provides that context of nurture by demonstrating commitment, love, and permanence to that child."*

Here we see humility approached through the back door. We become so absorbed in how everything will affect us that we seldom consider what is at stake for God. What about His reputation? Pride and arrogance consider "my rights," never the rights of the spouse, the children, and certainly not God. Humility always asks the question, "How will my actions and decisions impact others?"

- ♦ **Hearing That Marriage Was Intended to Be Permanent, the Disciples Wonder if It Might Be Better to Remain Single (v. 10).**

Jesus gently tells them that celibacy is a gift of God. In other words, if the desire to marry is there, don't put a guilt trip on yourself.

> NOTE: Interestingly, on the heels of this, Jesus rebukes the disciples for trying to keep the children from "bothering" Him (Matt. 19:13–15). His great love for children has much to do with His postition on marriage and divorce.

DAY 58

A RICH YOUNG RULER SEEKS OUT THE TEACHER. JESUS USES THE ENCOUNTER AS A TOOL TO TEACH THE TWELVE.

READ: Matt. 19:16—20:16; Mark 10:17–31; Luke 18:17–30

A man comes to Jesus and asks how he can have eternal life. In Luke 18:17–21, three things are stated about him and two are implied. *The man was:*

_____   _____

_____   _____

This man has a lot going for him. You might ask, *What more could you want?* However, because he came to Jesus we know that this member of the Sanhedrin council had a *hole in his heart!* Keep in mind that he had bought into three great lies that were the foundation of his belief system. He had been taught that *wealth* made him acceptable to God and that his *worth* and *value* were dependent on his *performance* in keeping the law. Mark's account says he ran and knelt before Jesus, showing respect toward Jesus as well as indicating the intensity of his question. Jesus asks the man why he refers to Him as "good," since only God is "good" (10:18). The inference is, If you are willing to call Me "good," are you also willing to call Me "God"? People often see the qualities of Jesus' life but will not deal with the implications of that recognition. Jesus then quotes the last six of the Ten Commandments and the man says he has faith-fully followed these since he was a child (probably meaning since he had his bar mitzvah at age thirteen).

> *Why would Jesus then tell him to sell his possessions, give the money to the poor, and come follow Him? (Remember, He knew the man's teaching.)*

The young man can not abandon his pharisaic teachings, so he goes sadly on his way. Jesus will now use this as a backdrop to teach the disciples about being wealthy and following Him at the same time. Jesus is not opposed to wealth, but in many cases, the way people became rich was through a pattern of greed and selfishness. It is not an indictment, but simply a fact. Wealth and the desire for more is very difficult to harness and bring into submission to Christ.

◆ **Peter Shows His Spiritual Immaturity (Matt. 19:27).**

> *What does he ask of Jesus?*

> *How does a spiritually mature person think?*

◆ **Jesus Redefines Being "First and Last" in the Kingdom (v. 30).**

> *Who were "first" in Jesus' day?* _____ *Who were "last"?* _____

Though Jesus uses money in dealing with the rich young ruler, money has little to do with Jesus' point. The man's problem was his perspective, the way he looked at God. Jesus is saying, "Change your mind about how you see God." Money, performance, or anything else has no value in terms of your worth to God. In this particular case, money was too important to the young man and blocked his ability to see the Father.

JESUS SPEAKS OF THE CROSS AND RESURRECTION AND JAMES AND JOHN MAKE A SELFISH REQUEST.

READ: Matt. 20:17–28; Mark 10:32–45; Luke 18:31–34

As Jewish children, the disciples would have learned about the coming of the Prophet of Deuteronomy, the Messiah. However, pharisaic influences were very great and the idea of a "suffering Savior" was something the Jewish leaders did not buy. But Jesus had told the Twelve on a couple of previous occasions that He would be killed. Notice the following prophecies telling of the Messiah's suffering and death. The Twelve didn't understand anything about Jesus' mission and coming crucifixion (Luke 18:23).

> **THE MESSIAH WOULD SUFFER AND DIE**
> - He would be executed, and die (Isa. 50:4–9; Isa. 52:13–53:12; Ps. 22).
> - He would be legally tried and condemned to death (Isa. 52:13–53:12).
> - He would die (Ps. 16:1–11; Ps. 22).
> - His death would be substitutionary (Isa. 52:13–53:12).
> - His death would result in the destruction of the temple (Dan. 9:24–27).
> - He would be buried in a rich man's tomb (Isa. 52:13–53:12).
> - He would be resurrected (Isa. 52:13–53:12; Ps. 16:1–11; Ps. 22).
> - He would bring justification to those who believed in Him (Ps. 110:1–7).

◆ **James and John's Mother Makes a Selfish Request (Matt. 20:20–21).**

 A very controlling and insecure woman sidles over to Jesus and tries to push her boys to the front of the line. She, like most Jews, expected the Messiah to set up a new political order that would get the Romans off their backs. James and John's mother sees an opportunity to get on the inside track in the *new administration*. Remember, Peter, James, and John had already had the *Who will be the grand poobah?* discussion (Day 41). Jesus tells this mother that she has no idea what she is asking (v. 22). He speaks of the "cup" (see sidebar) they will have to drink, and they basically say, *"no problem."* Their response is not only naïve, but arrogant and irresponsible.

This is a scene that anyone whose son or daughter has played sports has witnessed many times. A dad wants his son to pitch and hit third in the

THE "CUP" THE TWELVE WOULD DRINK

Matthew: killed by a lance in Ethiopia

Nathanael: beaten and crucified in India

Thomas: stoned and speared in India

Philip: scourged and crucified in Greece

James (Son of Alpheus): crucified in Greece

Thaddeus: killed by arrows in Egypt

Simon the Zealot: crucified in Turkey

Judas: hanged himself outside Jerusalem

Peter: crucified upside-down in Rome

James: beheaded in Jerusalem

Andrew: beaten and crucified on an X-shaped cross.

John: an attempt to boil him in oil failed; exiled to island of Patmos, Greece, and died a natural death

We set our children up for failure by always trying to give them an unearned "leg up" on the competition. This bears no resemblance whatsoever to what they will face in the real world.

lineup, a soccer mom insists that her daughter be a starter, or a dad wants to coach his kid to make sure he makes the all-star team. Parents who refuse to let their children *earn* their position and *pay the price* to excel are creating a monster. Look at the result of the mother's request:

Notice the reaction of the other disciples (20:24)?

Parents think they are helping their children, but the fact is, they cause alienation among their children's friends and classmates. Have you witnessed this?

◆ **Jesus Uses This as an Opportunity to Teach about Humility and Taking the Posture of a Servant.**

DAY 59

THE HEALING OF BLIND BARTIMAEUS AND THE ENCOUNTER WITH ZACCHEUS

READ: Matt. 20:29–34; Mark 10:46–52; Luke 18:35–43; 19:1–28

Notice that the two men refer to Jesus as "Lord." They had referred to Him as "Son of David." This gets His attention, but He heals them on the basis of their personal faith when they call Him "Lord."

 Jesus and His companions are now on the Jericho road, which means they have left Perea and are once again within the Sanhedrin's jurisdiction.

✡ One Jewish historical note: You will notice an apparent contradiction if you look carefully in the Matthew (20:29) and Luke (18:35) accounts. Matthew says they were *leaving* Jericho and Luke says they were *approaching* Jericho. This is easily reconciled when we understand that there are two places called Jericho about one-and-a-half miles apart. Jesus was leaving the Old Testament Jericho (where Joshua fought his famous battle) and was walking to New Testament Jericho, built by Herod the Great just prior to Jesus' birth.

◆ **Two Blind Men Cry Out to Jesus for Healing (Matt. 20:30).**

Two blind men are sitting by the side of the road begging for money from those passing by. They hear a commotion and ask what all of the excitement is about (Luke 18:36–37). They are told that Jesus of Nazareth is coming. Without hesitation, they cry out to Him, using His messianic title, "Son of David" (Matt. 20:30). Jesus stops and asks them what they want of Him. "Lord, we want our eyes opened," they say. Moved with compassion, Jesus touches their eyes. They gain their sight and follow Him.

JESUS' ENCOUNTER WITH THE TAX COLLECTOR

READ: Luke 19:1–28

PUT ON ZAC'S SANDALS: You will add much empathy and flavor to this story if you study it autobiographically. As we have seen previously, using what Dr. Richard Halverson used to call a "sanctified imagination" can help us get inside the life and thought of this man and maybe feel some of what he feels before, during, and after he encounters Jesus. We are all basically alike. This is why the Scriptures have the same effect at any time in history and in any culture. If you understand anything of human emotion, desire, and need, you will find that you know much more about Zaccheus than you think. Be this man as we look at this great encounter with Jesus.

You were raised in a typical Jewish home. As the other kids grew physically, you seemed to go nowhere. The older you got, the more insecure you probably were around the others. Many of them teased you and you found that you seemed to always find out after the fact about social events and things the local kids were doing around Jericho. The rejection made you bitter at life, at people, and if you are honest, at God as well. Your parents had dreams for you, but you became more distant as you grew older. You had accumulated some money over the years and heard that the Roman government had a few job openings for young, enterprising Jewish men. The job offered great financial potential, but was considered by the Jews to be in the same category as a prostitute because it required selling yourself out, as well as your fellow Jews. You would have to bid for or put up bribe money to get the job from the Romans. Everyone who looked at you as you came around to collect various taxes hated your guts. If you had ever thought you were left out before, it was minor compared to this.

Luke 19:10 is a fundamental summary of Jesus' purpose for coming into the world: "to seek and save that which was lost."

Now you're completely ostracized! Even your parents are shamed and ridiculed. You are banished from the synagogue and only spoken to out of necessity. By Jewish custom, your parents had chosen a wife for you when you became eighteen, and you know that was the only way you would ever have had a wife. The money came rolling in as you charged a commission for yourself over and above the tax in this wealthy Galilean region. Before many years passed, you were promoted to chief tax collector, in charge of the others (Luke 19:2). But where does a wealthy, despised, little man spend all of that money in a city like Jericho? You have alienated the owners of the restaurants, the bakers, the fishermen, the bartenders, and all of your neighbors. Your wife and kids are shunned because of what you do and who you've become. There is no place to go, no social life, no friends, nothing but your work, and even your employers the Romans think you are a pathetic little pimple on the rear end of humanity. You are useful to them and nothing more.

♦ Jesus Comes to Town.

You have heard about this man they call the *Nazarene*. He is everything you are not. Though you have long ago given up on religion, you are intrigued by this man Jesus. There is an explosion of activity as He enters the city and people are scurrying toward the main street to catch a glimpse of Him. Many are carrying the lame and assisting the blind in hopes of getting near Him. Nothing has ever been bigger than this. By the time you arrive, the streets are jammed on both sides. The people do not merely watch as He passes; they follow! You try to squeeze your way up to the front, but people seem to enjoy blocking your way. You even get a few "accidental" elbows to the ribs. Finally, about fifty yards up the street you climb a sycamore tree to get above the crowd. It's pretty embarrassing because the only people in the tree besides you are children.

♦ Face-to-Face with the Messiah

As Jesus passes under the tree, He suddenly stops and looks up. At first, He is amused, seeing you jostling with the kids for the best spot on the limb. Then a winsome look comes over His face. It's not the typical look you have seen from other people. Jesus speaks to you. He asks you to come down and have dinner with Him. This, too, has never happened before. You show up at your home with this guest and your wife is so stunned she can barely speak. *A guest—in our home—and what a guest!* It was an indescribable evening where hearts were opened, sorrow turned to joy, bitterness gave in to forgiveness, and hope was ignited for the first time. To show that it was real, restitution was promised to those whom you had cheated. It was not a *clean slate*, it was a *new slate*, and best of all, your wife and children discover the Savior as well. That night, for the first time, a scruffy little tax collector smiles in his sleep.

- ◆ **Realizing That the Disciples Are Confused About the Kingdom, Jesus Tells a Parable (vv. 11–27).**

As we have seen before, the disciples thought the messianic kingdom was imminent (v. 11). Jesus tells about a nobleman (Jesus) who left his servants (believers) in charge of his estate while he went on a journey.

Where is Jesus going? _____

What will he leave for which we are to be stewards? _____

What tools are we given with which to care for His church?
_____ *(1 Peter 4:10)*

When the nobleman returned, he found that the servants had invested well and earned a dividend on what they were given. However, one servant was fearful and hid his in a handkerchief, earning no money. He had not understood the heart of the nobleman and missed out on a great reward.

When Jesus is crucified and resurrected, He will leave these men to invest in the lives of people. When He returns He will reward the faithful who have been good stewards of what they were given (1 Cor. 3:10–15; 2 Cor. 5:10).

PART VIII: THE FINAL DAYS OF JESUS' PUBLIC MINISTRY

There was much speculation among the people concerning whether Jesus would come to the Passover celebration in Jerusalem. He was a marked man and the multitudes knew that He was in grave danger. Jesus knows it will be His last Passover and that He must make His triumphal entry into the city riding on a donkey. He will continue to "cross swords" with the Jewish leaders, but with each attempt to trap Him, they fail miserably. These will be the last few days of His public ministry.

DAY 60

JESUS' TRIUMPHAL ENTRY INTO JERUSALEM BEGINS HIS FINAL DAYS OF PUBLIC MINISTRY.

READ: Matt. 21:1–11, 14–17; Mark 11:1–11; Luke 19:29–44; John 12:12–19

Jesus and His disciples arrive in Bethany, which is just outside of Jerusalem. It is six days before the beginning of Passover and exactly one week before Jesus will be crucified (John 12:1). The date is the eighth of *Nisan*, AD 30, the first month in the Jewish calendar. This date corresponds to March 31 on our calendar. This will be the fourth Passover Jesus has attended during His ministry of about three-and-a-half years.

◆ **The Lamb of God Was Found to Be Flawless!**

Read Exodus 12:1–14 and you will see why Jesus enters Jerusalem on the tenth of Nisan. (Note: Before the captivity in Babylon, the first month on the Jewish calendar was called *Abib*, and from then on, *Nisan*.) Moses had instructed the people at Passover to put up a lamb on the tenth day of the first month. It had to be unblemished, without flaws. From the tenth until the fourteenth, this lamb was to be inspected to make certain it was perfect. Then, on Passover, it could be proclaimed suitable for sacrifice. This is exactly what is happening, by God's design with Jesus. He rides in on a donkey on the tenth of

Nisan. He will be examined and questioned in every way during the next few days. There will be a point where the Jewish leaders give up on their examination of Jesus and will therefore unknowingly be proclaiming Him the *unblemished Lamb of God.*

The crowds in Bethany are staggering. The news has spread throughout the region about the raising of Lazarus. Jesus has become a national icon, although they do not yet understand who He is. People come not only to see Jesus, but Lazarus as well (John 12:9).

How do the Jewish leaders feel about Lazarus (John 12:10)?

Why? (See 12:11.)

◆ **Jesus' Triumphal Entry into Jerusalem**

Bethphage means "House of Figs."

Before going into Jerusalem, Jesus gathers with his disciples at the Mount of Olives. He sends two of them into *Bethpage*, which is nearby. They are to secure a young donkey and say only that *the Lord needs it.* This colt has never been ridden, and yet, when Jesus mounts it, it does not buck. This fulfills Zechariah's prophecy (Zech. 9:9). Everything was just as Jesus had said. When they return, they drape their garments over the donkey's back, an act of homage to royalty (2 Kings 9:13), and Jesus begins His historic entry into Jerusalem.

As Jesus approaches the hordes of people lining the streets, they begin pulling palm branches from the trees and laying them in the streets, along with pieces of clothing. This fulfills Leviticus 23:40. The rabbis had always taught that when the Messiah comes, the people are to make this symbolic gesture. A fascinating note about Jesus riding in on the colt of a donkey as prophesied in Zechariah 9:9: After the Jews were allowed to return to their homeland in 536 BC after the Babylonians were defeated, they rebuilt the city, including the temple. As the years wore on, the workers became lethargic and discouraged. God sent two prophets, Haggai and Zechariah, to give them encouragement. It was Zechariah who gave them hope by telling them that the Messiah would ride

The waving of palm branches was a symbol of Jewish nationalism and solidarity. When the Romans figured this out, they later minted Roman coins with the image of a Roman soldier standing over a kneeling slave holding a palm branch to demonstrate their disdain and disrespect. It is also taken from the Scriptures: "Now on the first day you shall take for yourselves the foliage of beautiful trees, palm branches and boughs of leafy trees and willows of the brook, and you shall rejoice before the Lord your God for seven days" (Lev. 23:40). (This is the length of Passover.)

into this very city on a donkey. Every first-century Jew would have understood that a man riding on the fold of an unbroken donkey that did not buck, *must* be the Messiah.

◆ **The Multitudes Shout, "Hosanna, to the Son of David; Blessed Is He Who Comes in the Name of the Lord; Hosanna in the Highest!" (Matt. 21:9).**

Why do the people in Jerusalem suddenly hail Jesus with these words taken from Psalm 118:25–26 (a sign He had said He would give in Matthew 12)?

Keep in mind that the people have begun to view Jesus' entry into Jerusalem as the beginning of the messianic kingdom where He would rule as King. The multitudes appear to be completely sincere, but are they really convinced? This will be the same crowd who will stand outside the Praetorium when Pilate offers to release Jesus, and yell, "Crucify Him!"

If you were a Jew, what would the messianic kingdom have meant to you?

The term *Hosanna* means "Lord save us!"

Why could this not be the time of the messianic kingdom?

With the rage and animosity of the Jewish leaders searing in on Jesus, how else but by the sovereignty of God could he have entered Jerusalem on the tenth of Nisan and not be arrested until the fourteenth?

STEP INTO THE SANDALS OF THE JEWISH LEADERS: You are witnessing all of this commotion, knowing full well that the people are in a complete frenzy ever since the raising of Lazarus. You also know that you have only the authority that the Romans allow you to have. If there is a riot, they will come down on you like a meat cleaver. You will lose your job and your authority, which is what you live for. How do you control or subdue a crowd of thousands that are so certain that the messianic kingdom is here? You have to get rid of Jesus, but it must be done before Passover begins and it must be done quietly. You will have to find a way to incite Pilate, the Roman governor, so that he sees Jesus as a political threat, not simply as a Jewish prophet who has offended your religious sensitivities. He couldn't care less!

Jesus Curses the Barren Fig Tree Between Bethany and Jerusalem, Then Cleanses the Temple Again.

READ: Matt. 21:18–19a, 12–14; Mark 11:12–18; Luke 19:45–48

♦ **Jesus Curses the Fig Tree (Mark 11:12–18).**

Again we will see the value of studying these events chronologically. Immediately following Jesus' triumphal entry, the multitudes hail Him as Messiah and King. The next event Matthew records is the second cleansing of the temple (vv. 12–13). However, the next thing that actually happened is recorded in Mark 11:12–18. Jesus walks by a fig tree in full leaf and to the disciple's dismay, after examining it, He curses the tree and it withers (vv. 19–20). It is Monday, the eleventh of Nisan, six weeks prior to the time when figs would burst forth.

Why do you think Jesus would curse a tree for not having fruit when it was not yet the season?

Prior to figs blooming, small nodules appear on the tree that are edible. This tree, however, had no nodules. The leaves were full and green, indicating a healthy, fruitful tree; but the nodules were not present and Jesus knew the tree would never bear fruit.

Think of what had just happened as Jesus rode into Jerusalem. The multitudes hailed Him as Messiah and King. The Pharisees and everyone else assume their proclamation is real. But Jesus knew that these very people will scream, *"Let His blood be on us and on our children"* in less than four days (Matt. 27:25). A fig tree is a symbol for the nation of Israel. The tree, from its appearance—with green healthy leaves—is proclaiming to be a fruit-bearing tree just like the Jews who hailed Jesus as Messiah. Both, however, were giving a false proclamation.

Like the multitudes who, with great emotion and religious fervor, say all the right things, how easy it is for us to do the same. Our culture is geared toward language. Saying things *right* is paramount whether you are in the hip hop culture, at a dinner party, or in church. Nowadays it's called *political correctness.* Tomorrow it will be called something else. If you say the right things, you qualify! You're in! If you pray the right prayer you will be saved, if you use the right clichés in your testimony you can be one of us, and if you speak the right language you can pass as a godly person. We are dangerously close to living like those we are studying from two thousand years ago.

◆ **Jesus Reenters Jerusalem and Cleanses the Temple (Matt. 21:12–14).**

Had there been much change since the first cleansing of the temple back on Day 13? The Pharisees are beside themselves with anger, but this time it is mostly because what group of people are singing His praises (Matt. 21:15–17)?

DAY 61

AFTER NON-JEWS SEEK HIM, JESUS TEACHES MORE CONCERNING HIS PURPOSE.

READ: John 12:20–50

When Jesus uses the term *Name*, it means "character." Jesus' intent was to always bring glory to the Father by showing people a full expression of His character.

Several Greeks, who were obviously proselytes of Judaism, were coming to the Passover Feast to worship (v. 22). They ask Philip if they might speak with Jesus. Philip got flustered over what to do. Knowing that Jesus had come for the Jews, he goes to Andrew and they approach Jesus together. Jesus' answer appears to ignore the question, but as He speaks of the fruits of His crucifixion, we realize He is saying that this will be the very thing that will open the door to salvation for all people, Jew and Gentile alike. He uses the analogy of a grain of wheat dying in order to reproduce life (v. 24). This principle would most easily be understood by people in an agrarian culture. He continues by using, as we have seen before, the word *hate* as a comparative analogy. Try to squeeze all the *gusto* out of life that you can and it will be lost. Allow Jesus to be your life and you will live (v. 25). Jesus confesses to the Twelve that He is troubled about what He will face, but instantly focuses in on the fact that this is the purpose for which He came (v. 27).

Suddenly, as He speaks of glorifying the Father's name, a voice comes from heaven. There were only two other times when God spoke in His presence. When?

1. _____ *Day 9*

2. _____ *Day 40*

The crowd's reaction is interesting. What two ways do they react (v. 29)?

1. _____

2. _____

Who are these people standing around when God speaks from heaven? They are the same people who hailed Jesus as Messiah at the triumphal entry. Wonder why they can't hear the Father when He speaks? Your thoughts?

The truth is, God's most intimate thoughts are available to every believer. However, those who reject Him cannot hear or understand His words.

◆ **"If I Be Lifted Up from the Earth, I Will Draw ALL Men to Myself" (v. 32).**

Jesus is speaking of the cross, which is His ultimate exaltation. The cross will be the vehicle that will draw people to Him regardless of background, nationality, color, or status. It is also critical for His followers to remember that if we lift up Christ alone, without all the Christian attachments, He will draw people to Himself.

A critical thing to learn in working with people is that *what you win them with, you will win them to*. If you try to draw people with great music, great music will win their allegiance, and it will have to be better each week. If you draw young people by famous athletes and unlimited pizza, that is what you will win them to; and the pressure will mount to get better athletes and pizza the next time. If you lift up Christ, and Him only, He will draw them to Himself and they will be satisfied.

◆ **Walk in the Light and You Will Never Lose Your Way (v. 35).**

◆ **John Summarizes Jesus' Faithful Obedience to the Father (vv. 44–50).**

The Pharisees Press the Issue of Authority.

READ: Matt. 21:19–22; Mark 11:19–26; Matt. 21:23—22:14; Mark 11:27—12:12; Luke 20:1–19

Keep in mind that the constant attempts of the Jewish leaders to trap Jesus with trick questions relates directly to the Passover requirement that the "lamb" would be examined from the 10th through the 14th of the month to determine its suitability for sacrifice.

On the following day, Thursday, the twelfth of Nisan (April 4) Jesus and His disciples pass by the fig tree that He had cursed on the previous day. Seeing the disciples' amazement, Jesus uses this as an opportunity to teach them about prayer (Mark 11:23–26). He wants them to know that effective prayer is directly linked to forgiving those with whom we have a problem. Later that day, Jesus is teaching in the court of the temple and is approached by the scribes and elders concerning the matter of authority (Matt. 21:23). The Jewish leaders want to know by whose authority He speaks and acts. Jesus turns the question back on them by asking if John the Baptist's authority was from heaven or from men (Matt. 21:25).

Why could they not answer?

The question of Jesus' authority was just another way to try to discredit Him before the masses. Jewish theology declared that no teaching was authoritative unless it had been approved and sanctioned by the rabbis. It is obviously a trap because they had already declared in Matthew 12:24 that Jesus' authority came from the Devil. Had they come to Jesus with sincere hearts, He would have answered them, but as it is He says nothing.

The Pharisees were men with great intelligence, but lacked wisdom. Is there a difference between being smart and being wise? If so, what is it?

210

This would have been a great time for the Pharisees to shut up, but because they lack wisdom, they continue to talk, wading deeper into the mire of their own making. Jesus tells them the parable of the two sons (Matt. 21:28–32), which is about them, but they are unaware of it. Notice their answer in verse 31; they are actually condemning themselves.

Have you ever engaged in a war of words with your spouse or with a friend and realized too late theat you should have just quit talking. Instead, you kept going and you dug yourself a deeper hole?

Jesus is not finished with them. He tells them the parable of the wicked landowner. Again they condemn themselves. He states that He is the Chief Cornerstone of the nation of Israel, who has been rejected by the builders, the Jews (v. 42). This, they realize, is speaking of them, but they fear the crowds and decide not to seize Him at this time. Jesus concludes with the parable of the marriage feast. Let's figure this one out. Read Matthew 22:1–14.

The king (_____) gives a wedding feast for his son (_____) (vv. 1–2). Those who were invited (_____) refused the invitation (vv. 2–6). The king is justifiably angry and destroys their city (v. 7). He sends out his slaves to invite any and everybody (the _____), both good and bad, to fill the banquet hall (vv. 8–10). One guest shows up without wearing the wedding garment, which was always supplied by the king, so he is bound hand and foot and cast out. The garment represents _____, freely given by the king. The _____ refused it, desiring their own garment to be acceptable.

Answers on next page

DAY 62

Jesus Silences the Pharisees and Herodians When Questioned About Paying Tribute to Caesar.

READ: Matt. 22:15–22; Mark 12:13–17; Luke 20:20–25

The Herodians and the Pharisees hated each other. The Pharisees adamantly opposed Roman rule, and the Herodians just as adamantly supported the Roman government. In the same way we saw the Sadducees and Pharisees join forces to plot Jesus' death after Lazarus was raised, we see hatred briefly unify these two groups in order to try and trap Jesus.

Having failed miserably in seeking to corner Jesus, two groups come along thinking they can do better. This attempt involved the paying of a poll tax to Caesar (Matt. 13—14). For Jesus to agree that it was a lawful tax would incite the Pharisees because they considered it as worshipping Caesar in place of Jehovah. To say no would be seen by the Herodians as rebellion against Rome.

"The state is divinely sanctioned, and religion is divinely sanctioned, and both are equally the ordinance of God. On this principle did apostolic authority regulate the relations between Church and State, even when the latter is heathen" (*Jesus the Messiah* by Alfred Edersheim, Book V; p. 386).

♦ **Jesus' Answer Forms the Basis of Our Modern Concept of Separation of Church and State.**

Jesus asks them to bring Him a denarius, which was the common Roman coinage. (A soldier's wage was one denarius per day.)

Notice that Jesus uses the phrase "bring me" rather than "give me" or "hand me" *a* coin. No Jew would have been carrying a Roman coin. On one side was a portrait of Emperor Tiberius and on the other side the inscription in Latin, "Tiberius Caesar Augustus, Son of the Divine Augustus." These coins were minted by Tiberius and used to pay taxes to him. It was more than the issue of a graven image, it was the blasphemous inscription.

Jesus gives a brilliant answer, clearly establishing that Caesar is in no way divine and that the things that interest Caesar do not interest God. Again, no response.

Answers from previous page

THE WEDDING FEAST PARABLE

God

Jesus

the Jewish nation

the Gentiles

righteousness

the Jewish leaders

JESUS SILENCES THE SADDUCEES AFTER THEY ASK A QUESTION ABOUT THE RESURRECTION.

READ: Matt. 22:23–33; Mark 12:19–27; Luke 20:27–40

✡ There is some interesting Jewish history behind this question concerning the resurrection. The Sadducees denied both the resurrection of the dead and a future life after death. The Pharisees vehemently disagreed, and a running debate existed between the two groups. The illustration given by the Sadducees to Jesus was their *ace in the hole*, which they had always used to intimidate the Pharisees because they could never answer it.

The Sadducees think they can kill two birds with one stone with the illustration they give to Jesus. They are hoping to shame the Pharisees, whom they hate, and to poke holes in Jesus' theology at the same time, exposing Him to the multitudes.

How does Jesus shred their argument (Luke 20:34–35; Matt. 22:29–32)?

Jesus not only blows the Sadducees' theology out of the water, but for a brief moment, the Pharisees are in Jesus' corner, ecstatic over His answer (Luke 20:39). He has settled an age-old debate that had backed the Pharisees into a corner for generations. Again, the scheme turns against the schemer.

A LAWYER ASKS JESUS, "WHAT IS THE GREATEST COMMANDMENT?"

READ: Matt. 22:34–40; Mark 12:28–34

Remember, all of these questions and attempts to back Jesus into a corner are part of the examination of the Lamb of God as the Passover draws near.

✈ There are 613 laws recorded in the Torah, the first five books of the Old Testament. Add to that thousands of oral laws created by the Pharisees and you can get a glimpse of what most Jews would be wondering. A Pharisee would have had to memorize most, if not all, of the Torah beginning at age six and starting with the book of Leviticus. Keep in mind, however, that his question was not out of any sincere desire to know, but only to test Jesus (Matt. 22:35). He answers the lawyer by quoting Deuteronomy 6:4.

✡ The first word of this quotation by Moses became known as the *Shema*. In Hebrew, it means "hear." The *Shema* became the Jewish confession of faith, which was recited by pious Jews every morning and evening. Even today it begins every service in a Jewish synagogue. Jesus adds to the *Shema* the commandment from Leviticus 19:18 in order to show that loving our neighbor is a natural extension of loving God. In fact, Jesus basically equates the two. He also adds that on these two commands hang all of the law and the prophets (Matt. 22:40). Mark tells us that the lawyer affirms Jesus' answer (Mark 12:32–33) and Jesus tells him that he is not far from the kingdom (v. 34).

Jesus concludes by discussing David with the Pharisees. He states that in His humanity He is David's *descendant,* and in His Deity He is David's Lord. *From that day on, no one dared ask Him any more questions* (Matt. 22:46).

How does that last verse compare to the inspection of the Passover Lamb (Day 58)?

DAY 63

JESUS MAKES HIS FINAL PUBLIC ADDRESS, UNMASKING THE PHARISEES' BRAND OF LEADERSHIP.

READ: Matt. 23:1–39; Mark 12:38–40; Luke 20:45–47

This is Jesus' final public address to the crowds. He takes dead aim at the Pharisees, blasting their theology and attacking their incompetent and dangerous brand of leadership. In Matthew 23:1–12, Jesus warns the people not to imitate the hypocritical Pharisees and in verses 13–39 He pronounces eight specific woes or denunciations against them.

◆ **How *Not* to Lead People Spiritually (Matt. 23:1–12)**

Read these verses carefully and briefly write in your own words the Pharisees' erroneous ideas of leadership according to Jesus:

23:3:

23:4:

23:5:

✡ Phylacteries are small wooden boxes worn on the arm and forehead. They contain four Scripture passages (Ex. 3:1–10; 13:11–16; Deut. 6:4–9; 11:13–21). The precedent for this comes from Deuteronomy 6:6–8.

23:6:

"Chief seats in the synagogues" refers to the bench in front of the "arc" that contained the sacred scrolls. Anyone who sat on this bench could be seen by all of those who worshipped in the synagogue.

23:7:

How does Jesus contrast a real leader with what He had just described (vv. 8–12)?

♦ **Stepping Over the Line: Eight Woes upon the Pharisees (vv. 13–39)**

- Their rejection of Jesus influenced the Jews to reject Jesus as well (v. 13). *Does our sin have consequences for others as well as us? Yes! An entire generation of Jews bit the dust because they put themselves at the _____ of teachers who possessed no spiritual _____:*

> The Pharisees could never understand that what matters to God is the intent of the heart.

Answers
on next page

- They took advantage of widows, strictly forbidden in the Old Testament (v. 14).
- They improperly instructed Gentiles proselytes making them worse than themselves (v. 15).

- They paid homage to that which was sanctified rather than the God who sanctified it (their values were upside-down) (vv. 16–22).
- They were unable to discern the important from the unimportant (vv. 23–24).
- They had corrupt hearts and were obsessed with external righteousness (vv. 25–28). (The 6th and 7th woes are combined here.)
- They rejected Jesus as Messiah because they did not believe the Old Testament prophets (vv. 29–36).

JESUS CONTRASTS BIG GIVERS WITH A GIVING HEART.

READ: Mark 12:41–44; Luke 21:1–4

While sitting by the treasury in the temple, Jesus watches as one wealthy person after another, including the Pharisees, drops impressive sums of money in the treasury boxes. This would not have amused Jesus, because it was this type of outward performance that had spelled spiritual disaster for the Jewish nation. In addition, Jesus knew that much of this money had come from unsuspecting widows who had been duped by these pseudo-pious men. A poor widow walks quietly, and probably sheepishly, up to the treasury, embarrassed by the little she has to give. She drops in two mites (copper coins worth very little).

The treasury was located in the court of the women. Both men and women were allowed to come there, but women could go no further than the temple buildings. There were thirteen trumpet-shaped receptacles into which people would drop money. As we saw in our study of the Sermon on the Mount (Day 25), dropping in many coins made a distinctive noise; it was called "sounding the trumpet." This was a favorite indoor sport of the Pharisees because of their desire to showcase their external virtue.

♦ **Jesus Instructs the Twelve by the Widow's Example.**

Obviously, numbers are never the issue with Jesus. Unfortunately, numbers and amounts are everything to us in the modern church. It is usually the basis for the way we judge the success of an event, the validity of a ministry, or the effectiveness of a project or program. This brief episode is not simply a sweet story of an elderly lady giving out of her lack; it is much more. We are less

In Mark 12:40, Jesus points to the Pharisees' mistreatment of widows, even as they prayed long pious prayers to appear righteous. They would receive greater consequences in that the Old Testament says much about the treatment of widows and orphans. In fact, if you know anyone who has plans to rip somebody off in the future, tell them to make sure it is not a widow or an orphan. God takes special offense to the abuse of these two groups of people.

Answers from previous page

mercy
discernment

than three days from Jesus' crucifixion. Imagine what must have been on His mind. Why would both Matthew and Luke include this simple story at such a critical time in Jesus' life? There were certainly bigger fish to fry in these last seventy-two hours than arguing over a widow's two mites!

Why is this woman's example so critical to Jesus? What does He want the disciples to understand in calling them over to praise this widow?

Have you ever considered how uncomfortable and insecure you are when you are unable to measure results? How does this line up with trusting God? (If you're in a group, discuss this topic.)

PART IX: PREPARATIONS FOR THE CROSS

It is four days until Jesus' crucifixion. He will spend considerable time answering the questions of His disciples concerning the end of the age and His return. He will instruct Peter and John to prepare the Passover meal, Judas will cut a deal with the Jewish leaders to betray Him. As we study, pay close attention to the way the sovereignty of God overcomes the evil intentions of men.

DAY 64

JESUS' DISCOURSE ON THE MOUNT OF OLIVES: EVENTS LEADING TO THE END OF THE AGE

READ: Matt. 24—25; Mark 13:1–37; Luke 21:5–38

Matthew devotes two full chapters to what is commonly called the Olivet Discourse because it was given on the Mount of Olives. The date is Tuesday the twelfth of Nisan (April 4). Jesus will explain in these chapters the signs associated with His return and will speak of other events that will occur in preparation for His coming. NOTE: These chapters have been highly debated for many years and will continue to be in the future. Depending on the theological perspective of your church or denomination, the order of events leading to Jesus' return is at issue. Also, whether all of these events are literal or spiritual is a matter of theological debate as well. It is not the purpose of this study to take a strong position in this area, but to give a full perspective and flavor to all that is transpiring as we look at these last days of Jesus' life. We will therefore take a brief *aerial view* of this portion of the Gospels. You can do more extensive study on your own at a later time.

To be Savior, Jesus *must* die on a cross. Why? Deut. 21:23 says anyone left hanging on a tree is under God's curse. Jesus had to become a curse in order to set us free (Rom. 7:4). On the cross, our curse, inherited from Adam (Eph. 2:3), was transferred to Jesus so His death could set us free. How Jesus died and when He died was not determined by the Jews or the Romans, but by God.

♦ **As the Disciples Leave the Temple with Jesus, They Are Awestruck by Its Magnificence (Matt. 24:1–2).**

When Roman General Pompey attacked Jerusalem in 63 BC, great damage was done. Herod the Great began to refurbish the temple in 20 BC and the project was still in process in AD 30. In fact, it would not be completed until AD 64, just six years prior to its complete destruction. The level of the temple's magnificence has only recently been documented through archeological evidence. One stone alone at the southwest corner was thirty-six feet long. "Whatever was not overlaid with gold was purest white," wrote Josephus. For one of the decorations, Herod gave a golden vine with grape clusters as tall as a man. It was a magnificent edifice!

Jesus quelled the disciples' enthusiasm for the building's opulence and man-made beauty by stating that *not one stone would be left standing* on another (meaning AD 70).

◆ **Jesus Answers Three Critical Questions Asked by the Twelve (Matt. 24:3–51).**

By the time they had reached the Mount of Olives, a full discussion had ensued. The disciples ask Jesus three questions (Matt. 24:3):

1. When will these things be *(relates to the signs pointing to the destruction of the temple)?*
2. What will be the sign of Your coming *(addresses the signs corresponding to Jesus' second coming)?*
3. What will be the sign of "the end of the age" *(confirming that the end of the age has begun)?*

Jesus will answer the third question first, the first question second, and the second question last.

Concerning the question about destruction of the temple in AD 70, Jewish history is fascinating in terms of how messianic Jews escaped the siege of Jerusalem with their lives. *Write out Luke 21:20–21:*

In AD 64, not long after the temple was finally restored, the Jews staged a great revolt against Rome and actually drove the Romans from the city. They were finally free from Roman domination, at least for awhile. In AD 66, a Roman governor from Syria named Cestius Gallus surrounded the city with his great army and waited. Without warning, or for any apparent reason, he mysteriously withdrew his troops after a time and left the area. It was then that the Jewish believers in the city fled Jerusalem into the mountains and did not return. Why did they leave? They had access to Luke's gospel manuscript (21:20), which would have been completed by that time. When the Romans returned and destroyed the city, not one messianic believer perished because they had heeded Jesus' warning recorded by Luke and fled the city (21:20–21).

◆ **Jesus Speaks of the Signs That Will Precede His Return (Matt. 24:43—25:46).**

Jesus discusses the signs that will warn of His return, and many scholars—as well as *nut cases*—have attempted to interpret these signs specifically in terms of modern day places and events. The truth is, we don't know and can only speculate, but the value for us today is that every day should be lived in preparation for and in light of His coming. For those "in Jesus Christ," it will be nothing to fear or be apprehensive about. It will be the most glorious thing imaginable. In Mark 13:33–37 and Matthew 24:43—25:46, Jesus teaches seven parables. Each of these concerns preparation of the faithful for His return.

As the Leaders Plot Against Him, Jesus Tells the Disciples That He Will Die in Two Days.

READ: Matt. 26:1–5; Mark 14:1–2; Luke 22:1–2

It is Tuesday evening, which is the beginning of Jewish Wednesday. Jesus and the Twelve are either still on the Mount of Olives or possibly in Bethany. It is important to know that for a Jew, each new day begins in the evening rather than after midnight as it does for us. This is actually a biblical position taken by the Jews. Read Genesis 1:1–5. Notice especially verse 5: *"There was evening and there was morning, one day."* This understanding will be important as we look at the events of Jesus' death, burial, and resurrection.

In the last part of Matthew 25, Jesus discusses the judgment of those who have not rested their faith in Him. It is obvious that there will be many who have done numerous good works on His behalf and who have a spotless reputation. Some of these will be greatly surprised when Jesus says, "I never

In Matthew 25, Jesus gives a series of parables that we do not have time or space to cover. They all emphasize our being ready and prepared for Jesus return. Notice in Matthew 25:14–30 how Jesus once again discusses faithfulness with the resources with which God has entrusted us.

A "talent" was not money as many suppose; it was a unit of weight. As it was used by Jesus in the parable of the talents, it was most certainly either gold or silver. Many have speculated about the actual value of the talents, but we really can't be sure, since we do not know if the measurement refers to silver or gold. What we do know is that it represented a huge sum of money.

knew you." His mind is now fully on the *cross* and He discusses it again with the Twelve (Matt. 26:1–2). Meanwhile, the scribes and elders gather at the court of the high priest to plot how they might kill Him *secretly* (vv. 3–5). They had ruled this out during the Passover for fear of a riot (v. 6), so they must do their deed before the Sabbath begins.

The Jewish leaders have a dilemma on their hands. They want Jesus dead, but they can't do it themselves. That same year, AD 30, the right or authority to enact capital punishment was taken away from the Jews by the Roman government. Stoning had been the typical way of taking life. Now they realize He must die by Roman execution, which will be crucifixion. But how will they convince Roman authorities that Jesus' "crimes" are worthy of death? They must get to Jesus and arrest Him in a *private setting* away from the crowds. They need someone on the *inside*. A great political drama now begins.

MARY ANOINTS JESUS FOR BURIAL IN THE HOME OF SIMON THE LEPER.

READ: Matt. 26:6–13; Mark 14:3–9; John 12:2–8

Later that same evening, Jesus enters the home of Simon the leper. He was apparently a well-known leper in the area who had previously been healed by Jesus. We first met Mary back in Luke 10 (Day 46), in the home of Lazarus. Now she brings an alabaster vial of expensive oil, worth a year's wages, and begins to anoint the head of Jesus (Matt. 26:7).

What is the reaction of the disciples? _____
(Matt. 26:8–9)

What disciple takes issue with this "waste" of resources? _____
(John 12:4–5)

This could well be the final nudge that pushed him over the edge in his betrayal.

In fairness to the Twelve, we should note that at this point, they are not prepared to accept the fact that Jesus is voluntarily walking toward the cross. After all, to them, His death would solve nothing. They may be thinking

Jesus says that Martha was worried about many things. This is the tragedy of performance faith, working for God. We never know when we've done enough. So we do more and more and experience greater and greater stress. All of our activities are temporary, but intimacy with God is permanent.

that some last-minute escape could be possible. But, there is *someone* in the room who seems fully aware of what He must endure and it prompts her actions.

What is Martha, Mary's sister, doing all this time (John 12:2)?

Had she yet taken to heart anything Jesus taught her in Luke 10?

Why did Mary understand what none of the disciples nor her sister did? Wisdom comes not by serving, but by sitting at the feet of Jesus as Mary did. Serving is a mandate for every believer, but it is never a substitute for intimacy.

Jesus had taught her, but she had not yet hit the wall in terms of coming to the end of herself. Therefore the teaching was still *information* to her and had not become *revelation*.

Consider for a moment the extravagant love displayed by Mary. The cost of the perfume is not an issue to her. It is very much in character for what we know of her. She was hopelessly in love with the Savior and this kind of extravagance seemed normal to her. *What might this love look like in a marriage?*

DAY 65

JUDAS GOES TO THE JEWISH LEADERS FOR THE PURPOSE OF CUTTING A DEAL TO BETRAY JESUS.

READ: Matt. 26:14–16; Mark 14:10–11; Luke 22:3–6

Don't cheat yourself.... Read all of the parallel passages listed to get the most flavor from each of the writers.

◆ **The Price Offered by the Jewish Leaders Is 30 Pieces of Silver (Matt. 26:15).**

What is the value of 30 pieces of silver? It was the value the Jewish leaders placed on the life of God and the value accepted by Judas (read Zech. 11:12–13). Technically it was equivalent to 120 denarii. Normally laborers or soldiers received one denarii for a day's work. Even more shameful is the fact that if a slave was accidentally killed by an ox, the value that the owner of the ox was to pay to the slave owner was 30 pieces of silver (Ex. 31:32). So, *the life of God to these men was worth the value of a dead slave!*

How could a man who had followed Jesus for this long and have seen what he saw stoop so low (Luke 22:3)?

For what three reasons did the Pharisees and Sadducees need Judas?

1. *To _____ Jesus and manipulate circumstances where He could be apprehended in a _____ .*

2. *To bring _____ against Jesus, they need an _____ so that Pontius Pilate will order a cohort of Roman soldiers to arrest Jesus.*

3. *To be an official _____ for the civil trial of Jesus.*

Answers on next page

JESUS SENDS PETER AND JOHN TO PREPARE THE PASSOVER MEAL.

READ: Matt. 26:17–19; Mark 14:12–16; Luke 22:7–13

It is now Thursday afternoon, the fourteenth of Nisan, AD 30. Jesus had evidently spent most of Wednesday alone with His disciples. He tells Peter and John to go and prepare the Passover meal for Him and the other disciples. They want to know where. He gives them specific instructions (Luke 22:8–13). They enter Jerusalem and everything is exactly as Jesus had said it would be.

A lamb was no longer used in the Seder meal after the destruction of the temple in AD 70. Today Jews use a roasted chicken as a substitute.

How do Peter and John prepare the Passover meal? First, these two disciples take an approved lamb to the temple to be killed. According to the Mishnah, a very precise ceremony is performed by the priest, ending with the lamb being skinned, the entrails removed, washed, and placed back inside the animal. A portion of the lamb is then burned on the altar and the remaining part taken home and roasted. In addition to the lamb, there are four other ingredients in the Passover meal. Each of these has a very symbolic significance that we should be aware of in order to understand the significance of this meal.

Answers
from previous page

1. identify Jesus;
private setting

2. civil charges, insider

3. witness

The ingredients of the Passover meal may seem somewhat mundane to a Gentile, but to a Jew it is a remembrance of their heritage. Each part of the meal and each ingredient specifically represents the history of God's faithfulness to Israel. It allows them to tell and retell their story in graphic form during Passover.

- THE PASSOVER LAMB: The shankbone or forearm of the lamb symbolizes the *outstretched arm of the Lord,* who brought the Jews out of bondage in Egypt (Ex. 6:6; Deut. 4:34).
- WINE: There are four cups of wine associated with the Passover Seder. It is naturally fermented wine without the use of yeast for fermentation. Although the Jewish community did not condone intoxication, all four cups must be consumed at specified times throughout the meal.
- UNLEAVENED BREAD: Three small loaves called *matzah* would be brought to the table in a three-compartment bag. The middle loaf would be broken in half. One half is placed back in the bag, and the other is wrapped in a linen cloth and hidden away. This half is called the *fikoman.* The symbolism of its being hidden away until later in the meal represents Jesus being buried for three days and then resurrecting. It is returned after the main meal, broken into pieces the size of an olive, and given to the participants. This was the breaking of Christ's body, which we see in the Scriptures.
- GREEN VEGETABLE: Called *carpas,* a green vegetable—usually celery, lettuce, parsley or radish tops—is dipped in salt water and eaten. Parsley is most often used because of its similarity to hyssop which was used to apply the blood of the lamb to the door posts of the homes in Egypt (Ex. 12:22). When dipped in salt water and shaken off the parsley, it looks like *tears.* Vegetables are used because their greenish color represents the spring of the year, which is a symbol of early development or youthfulness. The meaning here is that Israel was young when God parted the waters of the Red Sea and they made their escape from Egypt.
- BITTER HERBS: The *maror,* usually horseradish, is dipped in *charoset,* a grayish mixture of apples, nuts, honey, cinnamon, and wine. The bitter herb bring tears to the eyes in *remembrance* of the bitter tears the forefathers shed in Egypt due to their slavery and the loss of their sons in the Nile.

Today there are fifteen ceremonies associated with the Seder meal including the *rachtzah,* a ceremonial washing of the hands, the *maggid,* the telling of the Passover story, and various blessings that are said. The meal concludes with the singing of the *Hallel,* which is the singing of Psalm 113—118. These psalms are viewed by the rabbis as containing the central teaching of Judaism.

Jesus Chooses Not to Wash the Disciples' Hands, but Their Feet.

READ: John 13:2–11

Reclining at the table, Jesus prays over the first cup of wine, called the "Cup of Blessing." He tells the Twelve to share it among themselves (Luke 22:17–18). He then says that it will be the last time He tastes the "fruit of the vine" until He drinks it in the messianic kingdom. As we saw yesterday in Luke 22:3, Satan had already captured the heart of Judas. The betrayal was in place (John 13:1). Jesus knows this, but rather than avoid Judas, He gets up during supper, girds Himself in a towel, and takes the posture of a *servant* with a basin of water. After all of His teaching on humility and servanthood, this should have been done upon arrival by one of the disciples. Jesus gives them time to see if any would respond. When no one does, He takes the position Himself.

Consider the potential *insecurity* of knowing you are about to be betrayed and that the betrayal will cost you your life. What is it that made Jesus so secure that He could serve the others in the wake of such a dramatic time? How could He bring Himself to wash Judas's feet? *Look carefully at three things in John 13:3:*

1.

2.

3.

How can these three principles be the key to overcoming insecurity from within ourselves?

According to the Mishnah, reclining at the table points to the fact that Jews were freed from slavery through the Passover in Egypt. In antiquity, slaves had to eat standing or sitting straight up. Those who were free reclined as they ate. They leaned on their left elbow into one another's breast simply because most people are right handed.

225

◆ **Peter Resists Because His Master Takes the Role of a Servant (vv. 6–8).**

Consider Peter's objection in light of what he has seen and heard over the past three years. He had watched Jesus' example of incredible humility day after day. He had heard Jesus teach that the greatest is the one who serves. He has seen Jesus' glory uncovered at the transfiguration, and he has proclaimed, "You are the Christ, the Son of the Living God" at Caesarea Philippi. Does he get it? Not by a long shot. He still does not understand Jesus as the suffering Servant of Psalm 22 and Isaiah 53. (The Pharisees did not believe in a suffering Messiah and Peter, like the others, had learned under their teaching.)

Can you think of biblical principles that you have heard and even spoken of for years that had little or no impact on your own life? Then one day, years down the road, you see a truth starkly for the first time. All of those years spent spouting words and ideas that you may have believed intellectually, but had little bearing on your personal life. This is Peter. His statement about Jesus being the Christ was the foundation of the church, and Jesus had given him the keys to the kingdom, and yet he does not want Jesus to wash his feet.

List one or two biblical truths that you may have espoused for years, but actually learned way down the road.

◆ **Jesus' Response Causes Peter to Overreact (vv. 8–10).**

It is more blessed to give than to receive, but it is sometimes more difficult to receive than to give. Ask Peter!

When Jesus lets Peter know that to disallow Him to serve was to dismiss Him altogether, Peter overreacts and says, in effect, "Well then, give me a bath!" Jesus' response is full of implications for us today. We spent substantial time on Day 5 looking at our true identity in Christ. (Review Day 5.) When we meet Jesus Christ, we are *thoroughly cleansed* (given a bath from sin, if you will). No more baths are necessary, only the washing of our feet when we the "dust and grime" of sin make our behavior unacceptable to God. Jesus is saying to Peter, "You don't need a bath. You are already washed clean; your identity is secure, but your feet will get dirty from time to time and you guys must help each other by washing each other's feet when you sin."

DAY 66

JESUS PREDICTS THAT ONE OF THEM WHO WAS NOT WASHED CLEAN WOULD BETRAY HIM.

READ: Matt. 26:20–25; Mark 14:18–21; Luke 22:21–23; John 13:10–11

After telling the Twelve that one among them would betray Him, each disciple is deeply grieved and asks, *"Surely not I, Lord?"* (Matt. 26:22). Jesus says that it is the one who dips in the bowl with Him at the same time. He follows by saying that He would die as planned, but *"woe to the man by whom the Son of Man is betrayed! It would have been good for that man if he had not been born"* (Matt. 26:24). Judas then asks if he is the one, and Jesus answers in the affirmative (Matt. 26:25). Jesus takes a small piece of bread, dipped it into the *charoset* (apple mixture), and then gives it to Judas, telling him to *do quickly what he must do*. Judas then departs into the night.

> *Where do the other eleven disciples think Judas is going (John 13:28–29)?*

The critical thing to know about the Passover is that it is all about remembrance.

◆ **Jesus Institutes the Lord's Supper.**

After the eating the *main meal,* which included the roasted lamb, Jesus took the *fikoman* (the half loaf of bread that had been hidden away) and broke it, symbolizing the breaking of His body on the cross (Matt. 26:26; Mark 14:22; Luke 22:19). Keep in mind that Judas had already left. (Communion is to be taken by those who have trusted in Christ alone for salvation.) Jesus then takes the cup (this was the third cup, the "cup of redemption") and tells them to drink it all in remembrance. This is symbolic of His blood that will be shed for remission of their sin (Matt. 26:27–29; Mark 14:23–25; Luke 22:20).

We have allowed commercialism to so dominate Christmas and Easter that *remembrance* is largely confined to remembering a gift for Aunt Suzie or what Bobby asked Santa for in the department store. Sadly, today, most Jews have become so secular that they simply go through the motions

A Middle Eastern custom still practiced today is that of taking a piece of meat wrapped in bread and dipping it in a sauce on the table. Eating with someone was a way of saying, "I am your friend and will not harm you." This makes Judas's deed even more contemptible.

during the Seder meal and other remembrances in order not to offend their elders.

♦ **Jesus Teaches the Eleven a Lesson in Greatness (Luke 22:24–30).**

Can you believe that right on the heels of this magnificent demonstration of humility and the serving of the *fikoman* and the wine, the disciples argue over who will be the greatest? How could they be so spiritually insensitive? Probably, the same way we can study contentment in a Bible study and sit there secretly wishing we had a new BMW like our neighbor. The same way every man can hear a powerful sermon on purity and have lustful thoughts about the woman one pew over. These guys were wed to the thinking of their culture. Rank and position was an important value in Jewish thinking, but it was not part of Jesus' value system. The *greatest* is the one who *serves.*

It is remembering the mercies of God in our lives that keep us thankful for what He has done and hopeful for His continued grace on our behalf in the future.

Jesus tells *the eleven* of the glory that will come to both the Father and the Son as a result of His death (John 13:31–33). He also gives His disciples a new commandment. It was new in the sense that they had never experienced a live demonstration of pure love shown to them. They knew they were to love one another, but to allow Jesus to practice that kind of love *in them* the same way the Father had loved *through Him* was a different matter (John 13:34–35).

If you had been one of the eleven, what specific ways would you recount that Jesus had demonstrated His love toward you ever since you had known Him?

What specific ways has He shown specific love to you in recent months?

♦ **Jesus Annuls an Order Given Previously in Luke 22:35–38.**

When Jesus sent the disciples out two by two, He told them to take no purse, bag, or extra sandals. Now He tells them the opposite. Why? Until now, He had provided for their every need. He will still provide, but they have to learn to manage their time, their relationships, and their financial resources. *It was time to grow up!*

DAY 67

JESUS CONTINUES HIS UPPER ROOM DISCOURSE.

READ: John 14

What is known as the *Upper Room Discourse* began in John 13. After their Seder meal, the disciples are relaxed and receptive. As they recline around the table, Jesus teaches them many of the truths that are actually the foundation of the New Testament Epistles. In these next four chapters (14—17), we find some of the richest truths in the entire Bible. We can only highlight the most critical passages in this study, but hopefully you will turn to these passages many times and study them in much greater depth.

In John 14, Jesus will give His own funeral sermon in advance of His death. Why were the disciples' hearts troubled? Was it because He would be leaving? Jesus tells them there is not only a *state of being* after they die, but an actual *place*. He is going ahead of them to prepare this *place* in His Father's house where they will live throughout eternity. In this house there will also be a kind of *inner peace,* where regrets and guilt will be a thing of the past. Best of all, Jesus will be in the same place where they will be. This would have calmed their fears about not liking the *place* where they would be going.

Thomas usually gets a bum rap for being the "doubter," but he, like many of us, is a very pragmatic person. Jesus speaks of their *knowing* where He is going and how they all *knew* the way. None of them has any idea what He was talking about in verse 4, but Thomas is the only one who has the courage to say, *"I don't have a clue where you are going or how to get there."* This prompted Jesus to make one of the greatest statements ever uttered (vv. 5–7).

- He is the only way to the Father (v. 6).
- He is the only source of truth (v. 6).
- He is the only source of life (Col. 3:4).

Arguably, the most consistent objection to faith in Jesus centers around what many claim is "exclusivity." Have you ever looked closely at what other religions espouse? Mohammad said the *Koran* is *the* way (it also must be

If you enjoy memorizing Scripture for your personal growth, one of the most profound and profitable passages you can consider is Colossians 1:15–20, which is a description of Jesus Christ.

"Their stress for the disciples was not only in His leaving, but because of what they had been previously taught concerning the hereafter, 'that those in glory occupied different abodes corresponding to their ranks'" (*The Life and Times of Jesus the Messiah, Edersheim Book V,* pp. 513–14).

studied in Arabic, no other language). Buddha said that *his noble truths* were *the* way; Krishna said his *philosophy* was *the* way. There must be a standard of truth. Jesus said "I am *the* way." When you consider what we have seen in this study, is it narrow to say Jesus Christ *is* exclusive? No one else died for those who hated Him; no one else rose from the dead. No one else can live inside the heart of the believer. Everything He said or did was *exclusive and unique*, yet He welcomes, without qualification, all who will come to Him in simple faith.

◆ **Jesus Tells the Eleven That He Is the Mirror Image of the Father (vv. 7–10).**

Jesus is the _____ *(Col. 1:15).*

The Pharisees basic problem is that they were trying to produce, in their own strength and energy, a life that only God from within is capable of producing.

In verse 10, Jesus reveals the secret to His life and ministry. It is also the basic element in the believer's quest to be a true disciple. This principle is what will keep us from living under law and replicating what we have seen in the lives of the Pharisees.

> "Do you not believe that I am in the Father, and the Father is in Me? The words that I say to you I do not speak on My own initiative, but the Father abiding in Me does His works."

Did you know that *none* of the miracles we have seen over the past two months in this study were performed by Jesus? Have you realized that the authority with which He spoke *did not* come from Him? In this passage, Jesus tells us that it is the Father who *performs every work* and it is the Father who *tells Him what to say.* Jesus opened His mouth, but the Father spoke; Jesus raised His hand, but the storm obeyed the Father; Jesus spat on the ground and made clay, but the Father gave sight. This is exactly what Jesus is saying.

Living for Jesus sounds spiritual, but it is actually bondage in disguise. Living from Christ and the abundance of His resources is true freedom. If we live from Christ and by His life in us, we will automatically live for Him.

Write out John 8:28:

What does this have to do with us? If the secret to Jesus' life was doing *nothing* on His own, how can you and I be disciples by our own determination or by trying to copy Jesus' character traits? Jesus didn't copy the Father. He allowed the Father to live through Him. How can you copy Jesus? The WWJD bracelet (What Would Jesus Do?) is a nice sentiment, but it is *pure law* and has nothing whatever to do with grace. What it says is, *"Show me what Jesus would do in this situation and I will do it."* Who will do it? *"I will do it!"* The emphasis is completely on our personal efforts and discipline. With grace, the emphasis is completely on Jesus. You and I can't live as Jesus did. It's impossible. That's why He came to live *in us* and reproduce His life from the inside. And incidentally, without our help. Why would Jesus need my help to be Himself within me? What Jesus wants from me is to *give up*—the very thing I am told never to do in life. However, Jesus cannot live His life through me unless I yield my desire to live it myself. I must *relinquish* the controls. He does not want to be my *copilot*. He wants control of the wheel with me in the passenger seat. This principle will change your life radically if you ask God to reveal it to you. The secret to Jesus' life was that *He lived by the life of His Father.* This is exactly what He wants from us. (See Day 45.)

◆ **Jesus Promises to Answer Prayer Under One Condition (v. 13).**

What is the condition? _____

"In His name" is not simply what we tack on the end of our prayers. A name defines a person's character. Praying in Jesus' name is praying for the answer that lines up with His will, because His will finds its origin in His flawless character. His will is the *outworking* of His name; to know His will you must understand Him, how He thinks.

DAY 68

Jesus Equates Loving Him with Keeping His Commands (v. 15).

What are His commands?

If you said the *Ten Commandments,* you are in the majority. However, a closer look will reveal that this is *not* what He is referring to here. John also addresses this issue in his first epistle. ***Read carefully and write out 1 John 3:22:***

"Real life is Jesus Christ in you, living His own life through you, without any help or assistance from you."

–Tom Skinner

This affirms what we just read in John's gospel, but it sounds as if it is all up to me. If so, that's *law* and not *grace!* That is what Jesus has spent three-and-a-half years railing against. *But maybe the next verse will tell us something. Write 1 John 3:23:*

What are these commandments John says we are to obey that validate our love for God?

1.

2.

For me to *love* my brother or sister means "to will the best for them." As wonderful a person as you probably are, I am not capable of loving you in that way! Only if I yield to Jesus and allow Him to love you *through me* can I obey this command.

- ◆ **Jesus Gives His Disciples Confident Assurance Regarding Their Future (vv. 16–20).**

    Jesus gives the eleven disciples four assurances they can count on after He leaves:

    (v. 16) _____

    (v. 17) _____

    (v. 18) _____

    (vv. 19–20) _____

- ◆ **Jesus Again Equates Love with Obedience (v. 21).**

- ◆ **Another Judas Asks Jesus Why He Is Disclosing Himself to Them and Not to the World (v. 22).**

Judas Iscariot has already left during the Passover meal. Another Judas, who had obviously joined the eleven after the meal, asks why *everyone* will not be privy to a full revelation of Jesus as their group will be. He is thinking on a

232

physical level. Why would Jesus show to everyone what He would show to those who love and follow Him? Why would He reveal the very thoughts of the Father to those who refuse to believe? This is why He will, again, link loving Him with obedience in the next verse (v. 23). *Revelation* of the deeper truths of God can never come without *intimacy*.

This passage brings forward an important lesson for us. Jesus did not tell everyone everything. He spoke *generally* to the crowds, but more *intimately* to His disciples. Why would you teach your three-year-old about the emerging opportunities in global technology? Truth is truth, but one size does not fit all in terms of the *communication* of that truth. We must be willing to get away from our religious clichés and communicate in the language and manner of those we hope to reach.

What two key things does Jesus say about the words He speaks (v. 24)?

1.

2.

In what two specific ways will the "Helper" aid them when He comes (v. 26)?

1.

2.

◆ **Jesus Will Leave Peace Unlike Anything They Have Known (v. 27).**

What do human beings desire more than anything in life? They want *peace*. You might answer money, fame, power, but at the end of the day it's *peace!* Jesus tells us that the *peace* He leaves is not temporary or dependent upon circumstances like that which the world offers. It won't be a counterfeit, fleeting kind of *peace* that creates a troubled heart. It will be the *peace* of waking up tomorrow morning knowing that *not one fraction of this day depends on you.* This will be a day that you will enjoy your companionship with Jesus and experience Sabbath rest (Heb. 4:9) while He is at work within you. Valium and Prozac can't touch that! It's not that you will circumvent or ignore problems, but you will come to understand that trials create an even *deeper peace* within you as they run their course.

Jesus will soon face the most stressful encounter imaginable and He says to these companions, *I am about to suffer and die as no man has or will ever die. I will demonstrate for you a peace that is real. It is authentic and it really works! This is the kind of peace that I am leaving you.*

They will leave the upper room after this chapter, but before they go, Jesus tells them that the Evil One is coming and therefore the time is short (v. 30). He does not fear Satan because he has no authority over Jesus. He proved this in Matthew 4 and 5. Satan also possesses *no truth* (John 8:44). Consider this thought from Bob Warren: "If Satan possesses no truth, then he cannot possess any wisdom. If he possesses no wisdom, he cannot possess any discernment. If he does not possess any discernment, he is on a *certain* path to self-destruction." Jesus ends by saying that because He has loved the Father, the world would know that the Father was worth loving. *In the simplest terms, Jesus is saying, "I came to prove to you that My Dad is worth your time."*

DAY 69

Jesus' Discourse to the Disciples on the Way to Gethsemane

READ: John 15

The Hallel was the singing of Psalm 113–118. These psalms are a historical recounting of what has transpired in Jewish culture—the law, the Passover, as well as the coming Messiah (Ps. 118). This hymn was in conjunction with the fourth cup, known as the cup of praise.

After Jesus finishes His teaching in the upper room of John 14, He and His disciples sing the Hallel. NOTE: The last verse in John 14 does not come next after Jesus' teaching. We must go to Matthew 26:30. They sing the Hallel to end the Seder meal and then Jesus says, "Get up. Let us go from here" (John 14:31).

The group leaves the upper room and begins their walk to Gethsemane. Jesus will continue to teach them along the way. It may be helpful to break this teaching in John 15 down into three basic areas.

The streets are jammed with pilgrims who have come for the Passover Feast. This was not an optional choice for a Jew. People came not only from Judea and Galilee, but from other surrounding countries. Accommodations were minimal and most families camped out. As Jesus and His disciples left the upper room and began their walk through the Kidron Valley to Gethsemane at the base of the Mount of Olives, they would have seen the flicker of hundreds of campfires dotting the hillside. People were clustered anywhere they could find a place to set up camp. This is one reason Judas was necessary for identifying Jesus. He knew where Jesus would be because He often went to this garden to pray. Under cover of night and with thousands of pilgrims in the area, making correct identification by the soldiers alone would be virtually impossible.

◆ The Relationship of Branches to Vines (15:1–11)

Now Jesus will tell these men who they are and how they will be related to him both here on the earth and throughout all eternity. He uses a very famil-iar analogy for them…that of a vine with many branches. It is a powerful illustration that not only speak of their relationship with Him, but also to one another and to the unredeemed world.

Jesus' focus on their relationship to Him and one another far outweighs their deployment to accomplish a task. This is the central point of this passage. We have missed this terribly in modern evangelicalism. The task of convincing others has become paramount and relationships have become an afterthought. The task is never more important than the relationship because without it we have no model of nurture and affection for this lost world.

Just as He has done in a number of parables, Jesus uses the familiar agricultural symbols to drive home important principles. The *task* must never become more prominent than the *relationship*. There will always be unlimited opportunities in the lives of people, but He wants them to know that their knowledge, their gifts, and their enthusiasm will not sustain them. Jesus is the Vine. He is their connection with life. He *is* their life (Col. 3:4). Fruit can never be produced by talented, well-intentioned branches, no matter how determined they may be. Jesus tells them that when fruit is not being produced, something is wrong. The problem is definitely *not* with the Vine, so it must lie with the *branches*. How is a dormant branch revitalized? The Vinedresser (the Father) must *prune* it.

John 15:2 says that every branch that has no fruit, "He takes away."
What do you think this means?

235

If you said something about the branch being thrown away or judged unsuitable, even sent to hell, you're not alone. This is unfortunately how many of us have been taught: *"Either get with it or get out of the way!"* Again, this mentality promotes the idea that it all depends on *you*. That's law! But what if you knew that: The phrase "takes away" can be translated *lift up, to elevate*, or *draw up*. In the Holy Land, a branch cannot produce fruit while lying on the ground. The gardener or vinedresser would see this, and take a rock and place it under the branch to help enable it to bear fruit. Quite a different picture, isn't it? The first one makes me sweat and try to figure out what *I* can *do* to be more fruitful. The second is what *God does* to *encourage* my growth. Jesus further states that the Father continues to watch the branches as they produce fruit, pruning them regularly to make them even more fruitful.

What is fruit? Is it souls? _____

Read Galatians 5:22–23; Ephesians 5:9; and Philippians 1:11. Whose responsibility is it to bear fruit (John 15:4–5)?

◆ **Jesus Invites the Disciples to Abide in Him (v. 4).**

Consider the idea of *abiding* in light of what we studied in John 14:10 (Day 66). Abiding is not doing something, not even Bible study, prayer, or verse memory. It is learning to live by the life of Jesus Christ. It is yielding our life to His Holy Spirit within us. Fruit in our lives comes not by our activity on His behalf, but by learning to give up and allow the Vinedresser to give life to the Vine as the Vine gives life to the branches (you and me). "I have come to give you life," said Jesus. Life is not a commodity, but a Person. "I have come to give you Me!"

◆ **Jesus Speaks Hard Words That We Must Interpret Properly (v. 6).**

At first glance, verse 6 sounds like we are on the hot seat again: *Either produce fruit or God will burn you up!* However, we always study the Scriptures according to the "full counsel of God." In other words we can't pull a verse like this out of context. It must be compatible with the rest of Scripture. God doesn't speak out of both sides of His mouth. Will believers face a judgment for what they failed to do on earth? No! Romans 8:1 says, *"There is therefore no condemnation for those who are in Christ Jesus."* Jude 24 says that the believer will

236

be presented to the Father *"blameless and with great joy."* What will be judged is the quality of the fruit produced in our lives. Works that were done in our own energy and strength will burn up when tested by fire. That which is produced by the life of Christ in us will be rewarded (1 Cor. 3:12–15; 2 Cor. 5:10). In this verse Jesus is not speaking of fruitless disciples. There is no such thing. If fruit never appears, there is no connection between the vine and the branches. Any authentic disciple will see fruit in his or her life in time.

◆ The Result of Abiding in the Vine (vv. 7–11)

In verses 7–11 we see the results of abiding in the Vine: Prayers will answered because abiding develops maturity, and maturity causes us to pray more meaningfully and in line with God's will (v. 7). Jesus also teaches the eleven that God is glorified when fruit is produced—not by us, but by the Spirit in us. It is impossible to keep Jesus' commandments unless we abide in His love. Intimacy must come *before* obedience or else we will live by *obligation* and *duty*. To obey out of a motive of fear or obligation is *never* pleasing to God. Just *getting it done* is not what God is after. He is capable of *getting it done* without us! He is after our *hearts*. Obedience must spring from *intimacy* with Jesus. When this is intact, joy will be the natural result (v. 11).

Have you ever made this statement: "I have to go do my quiet time"? Ever ask anyone the question, "Did you do your quiet time this morning?" Think about that for a minute. We don't speak that way of any other healthy relationship in our lives. Imagine coming home from work, having dinner, reading a bedtime story to the kids, then walking into the den and saying to your spouse, "Okay, I did my time with the kids, now I'm ready to do my time with you." The only people who "do time" are prisoners. Free people who have intimate relationships long to spend time together. Who wants to be a project that someone else feels good about completing? The more intimate and positive the relationship, the more they will fight for time together—not out of obligation, but out of desire. This is the difference between law and grace.

DAY 70

JESUS ADDRESSES THE RELATIONSHIP OF HIS DISCIPLES WITH ONE ANOTHER (VV. 12–17).

♦ **"Love One Another as I Have Loved You": Exciting Possibility, Impossible Task**

Just as we found in our study of the Sermon on the Mount, if we view this command of Jesus from a legal, *must-do* standpoint, we set ourselves up for guaranteed failure. *First, take a moment to think back on several specific ways that you have seen Jesus love His disciples. We have to know this if we are to love one another the way He has loved us.*

- _____
- _____
- _____

- _____
- _____
- _____

There are many more, but just deal with those you have listed for now. How will you begin to pull this off? How do you make yourself love people unconditionally, putting no designs on their lives? How do you practice justice regardless of the personal cost to you? It becomes like a New Year's resolution that everyone makes but no one keeps. The only way to obey Jesus' command is to do what we have seen over and over—yield to His life within us. Give up resolutions. Intimacy with Jesus will cause His love to radiate through you to others. How else can we love as He loves?

Jesus will soon demonstrate the ultimate expression of love by laying down His life for His friends (v. 13). The confirmation of the disciples' friendship with Jesus is their *obedience to His commands*. As we discussed in verse 12, self-discipline is not enough. It must come from Jesus' life in us.

♦ **The Relationship Between Jesus and the Disciples Has Changed From Slave to Friend (v. 15).**

Why does Paul call himself a bond slave or servant (Rom. 1:1; 2 Cor. 4:5)? What is the difference between a slave and a bond slave? A slave

serves His master because he has _____. *A bond servant is*
_____ *to go, but* _____ *to come back and serve*
_____*.*

Answers
on next page

Before they met Jesus, the disciples were typical Jews trying to do more good things than bad, going through religious rituals, hoping they would one day please God. They meet Jesus and find in Him a friend, a real companion. Now they serve out of *love* rather than *duty*.

♦ **The Disciples Are Chosen to Bear Fruit That Will Remain (v. 16).**

Although there are other passages that may support the doctrine of election, this is not one of them. As you remember from Mark 3:14, Jesus chose the Twelve to be *with Him.* This is about being *chosen* for a specific mission, it is not referring here to *salvation.* To the degree that the disciples' intimacy with Jesus is the priority, their fruit will remain because it will be generated by Jesus. As a result, the Father will hear their prayers because the Spirit within will show them how to pray.

Normally, a potential disciple would choose a particular rabbi that he wanted to teach and train him. This was not so with Jesus. He *chose* His disciples that they might bear fruit.

THE DISCIPLES' RELATIONSHIP WITH THE WORLD (VV. 18–27)

As Jesus turns His teaching to their relationship with the unbelieving world, He fires right out of the gate with a reality that they must understand. They should expect *no better treatment* than He has received (v. 18). Uh-oh! After Jesus is crucified, the world will turn their resentment and hatred toward His disciples, but Jesus also tells them that those who keep His words will keep the disciples' words as well (v. 20). Jesus' words still ring out across the centuries: *"I experienced the ultimate hatred on the cross. If they hated Me and you intend walk with Me forever, what makes you think they would let you stroll through life unscathed?"*

"For consider Him who has endured such hostility by sinners against Himself, so that you will not grow weary and lose heart" (Heb. 12:3).

Think back to when you first began your walk with Jesus. Did anyone ever explain to you the cost of following Him? Have you experienced any real resentment from friends or colleagues because of your faith? Explain.

Answers
from previous page

no choice

free

chooses

voluntarily

Respond to this statement: "Most persecution today comes not because of our commitment to the truth, but because we make ourselves so obnoxious in defending it."

A dear friend named George Sheffer used to say, "The only reason a person doesn't love Jesus is because they never met Him!"

Jesus goes on to say that the world's animosity toward Him is only because they don't know the Father and therefore have no life within them (v. 21). They have had the opportunity to hear the truth, but refused, giving them no excuse (v. 22). He concludes by saying that He will send the Holy Spirit, who is the *Spirit of Truth*. This means they will never be led to do anything by the Spirit that is in violation of the truth.

DAY 71

JESUS SPEAKS OF THE HOLY SPIRIT'S ROLE WHEN HE COMES.

READ: John 16

Jesus had just addressed the subject of persecution and suffering with His disciples as they walked toward Gethsemane (15:18–20). Now, He wants to encourage them as they go through it. Keep in mind that the eleven disciples do not fully believe at this juncture. They won't until after Jesus is raised, but they have in their minds the information that will come alive as revelation in Acts 2. They will come to understand that Jesus was the "seed" in Genesis 3:15, that He was born of a virgin (Ps. 22), that He was the suffering Savior (Isa. 53).

Just as was the case with the blind beggar in John 9, the disciples will also be barred from the synagogues for the rest of their lives on earth because of their allegiance and identification with Jesus.

 As they continue their walk through the Kidron Valley, Jesus tells the eleven that the truth He speaks to them will give them a strong, confident walk (v. 1). They will prevail in spite of being barred from the synagogues and that their enemies will believe that their evil actions against them are doing God a favor (v. 2). Jesus says that He is now telling them things that they were not prepared for earlier (v. 4).

One of the most difficult things to learn as we seek to mentor and disciple others is knowing when to shut up! People can only absorb truth in small doses. Too much at the wrong time can cause damage. This is why the Scriptures instruct us about learning truth little by little as we are ready.

What do the following verses tell us in regard to this?

Hebrews 5:12

1 Peter 2:2

♦ **Jesus Tells Them That His Departure Will Be to Their Advantage. (v. 7).**

BE THE DISCIPLES and hear these words from Jesus. Imagine being told that you will actually benefit more by Jesus' absence than by His physical presence. *"Yeah, right,"* you mumble. *"We're like kids with water guns taking on the whole Roman Empire as well as thousands of hostile Jews. Our leader is going to be executed and we'll be left alone to deal with an angry world."* But, before they can even finish the thought, Jesus explains why this will be so.

Until now Jesus can only be *with* them, limited by time and space. When the Holy Spirit comes, He will then be *in* them, a much better deal.

When the Spirit comes, He will do three things: He will convict the world of _____, _____, *and* _____ *(v. 8).*

Concerning Sin (v. 9): Who among us would ever have seen ourselves as sinners before we met Jesus if the Holy Spirit had not shown us our rebelliousness? Most

MEMORIZE: "Even in laughter the heart may be in pain, and the end of joy may be grief" (Prov. 14:13).

We see the reality of this at the cross. The enemies pumped their fists in the air as Jesus drew His last breath, and they said, "We won!" But their joy turned to grief as God looked down from heaven and declared, "You lost!" The end of joy was grief, but for those who believed, the opposite was also true: The end of grief became joy.

of us compared ourselves with others and came out looking pretty good. It is the Spirit that helps us see the blackness of our hearts against the backdrop of God's purity and holiness.

Concerning Righteousness (v. 10): What human mind would ever be able to understand that our righteous standing before God has to do with what Christ did on our behalf and on nothing we achieved by ourselves?

Concerning Judgment (v. 11): The Spirit will convict the world of the fact that though Satan is alive and active, he operates under the judgment of God. Jesus' death was more than a victory over Satan, it was the beginning of his ultimate demise and the breaking of his stronghold on believers who trust in Jesus.

> *Upon Jesus' death, the disciples will weep and the world will rejoice, but the disciples' sorrow and pain will turn to _____ (v. 20).*

The disciples will weep because they cannot process their Master's death. The unredeemed Jews, however, will *rejoice* because they think they have rid themselves of a fraud. King Solomon said, "The end of joy may be grief" (Prov. 14:13). This will certainly be the case for that generation of Jews. One million, one hundred thousand unredeemed Jews will be slaughtered in Jerusalem forty years later, but not one redeemed Jew would lose his life, because of Jesus' warning in Luke 21:20–24. (Review Day 62.)

As they near the Garden of Gethsemane, Jesus concludes His teaching with words He has said at least twice before; He speaks of the significance of praying *in His name* (according to His character) (vv. 23–24). He tells them that it will be the Father's joy to listen to their prayers because they believe in His Son (vv. 26–27). The disciples then assure Jesus that they now understand and believe that He is from God (vv. 29–30). It was a nice thought, but they still have no idea what they are saying. He tells them that they will scatter like scared rabbits when He is arrested (v. 32). However, He says He will not be alone for His Father will be with Him. He concludes by saying that they will experience peace in the midst of tribulation because He has already *overcome* the world (v. 33).

DAY 72

JESUS' PRAYER NEAR THE GARDEN OF GETHSEMANE

READ: John 17

Jesus and the eleven finally arrive at an area near Gethsemane, which is located at the foot of the Mount of Olives. It was later Thursday night, the beginning of Jewish Friday, or possibly after midnight, when they reach the Mount of Olives. While Jesus prays, Judas and the Jewish leaders, along with a cohort of Roman soldiers, are on their way through the Kidron Valley to arrest Him.

Throughout our study of the Gospels, we have repeatedly seen that Jesus was totally dependent upon the Father for everything He said and did. That posture is never more evident than in this chapter, where we witness Him opening His heart to His Father in complete and unbridled reliance. Everything He has just taught the disciples in chapters 13–16, He will now bring before the Father. He prays for three things:

John 17:1–8	Jesus prays for His glory.
John 17:9–19	Jesus prays for His disciples.
John 17:20–26	Jesus prays for all believers.

◆ **The Time Had Come for the Father to Glorify the Son (vv. 1–8).**

There is no selfish intent whatsoever on Jesus' part in praying for the Father to glorify Him. Why? His full intent is to glorify the Father. Each member of the Trinity does everything for the benefit of the other. No jealousy or competition has ever existed within the Trinity. Jesus will be glorified as the Father completes the purpose for which Jesus was sent.

Jesus had been given authority to give _____ *(v. 2).*

Jesus asks for His glory to be restored (v. 5). During His life on earth, His glory was veiled or hidden from the eyes of the people. Only three men saw it while Jesus was on earth. Do you remember who they were?

_____ , _____ *and* _____ *on*
the _____ .

This veil will be removed at the resurrection. Jesus had displayed His Father's name (character) in every respect (v. 6). Everything Jesus possesses comes from the Father and He has made that known to His disciples (vv. 7–8).

◆ **Jesus Now Prays for the Men God Had Given Him (vv. 9–19).**

Jesus focuses this portion of His prayer on His disciples. He says He has been glorified in them. Are you kidding? They have basically been a *shipwreck* for over three years. They have misunderstood, been arrogant and greedy, and will soon scatter with the wind. Why would He say such a thing? This is how Jesus *thinks*. He dwells *not* on their past failures or on their current fear and ineptness, but on their *potential* and what they would *be* and *do* in the future by the power of His Spirit.

This is not some psychological technique; it is an affirmation of the potential of a person's life in whom the Spirit of God dwells.

Are you able to look at your children or someone whom you are mentoring and see past their laziness and pride? Can you will yourself to believe in what they can become? This is not about human potential. In fact, this kind of forward thinking is not some idea invented by Tony Robbins or Dr. Phil. Jesus thought this way, not because of the disciples, but because He knew the power of the One who would live within them. To the extent they would yield themselves, they were a sure bet! It's the same with your kids, or with you and me! When was the last time you spoke with your children, your spouse, or a friend from a posture of believing what Jesus *will* do in and through them rather than based on their current or past behavior? *Please write down the names of those who need to hear and feel this perspective coming from you. Write beside their name what each needs to hear.*

Knowing the difficulties the disciples would face, Jesus asks that they might be kept in _____ *(v. 11). This means kept in the Father's* _____ .

Jesus asks the Father a number of other things on behalf of His disciples, but four things stand out that should be very instructive to us:

1. That they might be one just as He and the Father are one (v. 11).
Why is the unity of the family of God so important to Jesus?

2. That His joy might be made full within them (v. 13).
Grace is driven by joy; law is driven by obligation. Is it your joy to serve or your duty? Is it your privilege to give or is it an obligation? Write out Hebrews 12:2.

3. That they not escape affliction, but stand firm and not falter (v. 15).
Affliction will mature them and build their character. Have you been able to pray this for your children and really believe it? Why not start now? Write a specific prayer for them on a separate piece of paper that they are not kept out of the battle, but out of harm's way.

4. That they will be sanctified *in* the truth (v. 17).
It is not the truth that will sanctify them (set them apart). Jesus' prayer was that the Father would sanctify them in the truth. He will use the truth as a tool, but memorizing a thousand verses will not make them or us godly people. This is solely God's prerogative.

Look up Psalm 119:9–11. It is a familiar passage that is often taught incorrectly. Write it here:

Is this passage saying that if I treasure God's Word in my heart it will keep me set apart and godly? If you believe that, then you believe the Word is like a *magic wand*. It is *not* the Scriptures that sanctify us. It is God alone, using His Word as a tool to sculpt our lives, to reflect His. The Pharisees thought that studying the Scriptures would make them holy, but Jesus reprimanded them, saying that only He could give them this life (John 5:39–40).

♦ **Jesus Concludes by Praying for All Believers (vv. 20–26).**

He prays that the harmony that exists between the Father and the Son might also be theirs (vv. 21–22).

Religion can produce *unison*, but not *unity*. The most critical element in reaching a lost world is not better programs, methods, or silver-tongued speakers, but a family of believers who love one another. If the Spirit of God lives in me and in you, we ought to be able to bridge our petty differences and walk together. We don't have to agree, but we are commanded to love with unlimited liability.

DAY 73

JESUS' AGONY AT GETHSEMANE

READ: Matt. 26:36–46; Mark 14:32–42; Luke 22:39–46; John 18:1

After Jesus' prayer in John 17, He and His disciples travel over the ravine (brook) of the Kidron and enter the Garden of Gethsemane (Matt. 26:36; Mark 14:32). This brook is located in the Valley of Jehoshaphat, at the base of the Mount of Olives. In the lower slopes of the Mount of Olives sits the Garden of Gethsemane. The term is derived from the Hebrew expression *gat shemen*, which means "olive press." The area was filled with olive trees and presses that extracted the oil from the olives. In a very real sense, Jesus will be *pressed* spiritually like the olives. He will undergo a level of spiritual angst like no one has ever known. Meanwhile, Judas has apparently pulled off the coup of the millennium. As an insider in Jesus' entourage, he has supplied information to the Jewish leaders that will cause Pontius Pilate to view Jesus as more than a religious radical. Reluctantly, while Jesus is in Gethsemane, Pilate agrees to release a Roman cohort to arrest Him and bring Him in for questioning.

♦ **Jesus Experiences a Level of Agony No Man Can Comprehend.**

Jesus takes only Peter, James, and John with Him into the garden area where they had come many times before to pray. This is quite different from His prayer in John 17. This is spiritual warfare of a level none of us can comprehend. He tells the three disciples to keep watch while He goes off nearby to pray (Matt. 26:36–37). Jesus is "grieved and distressed" (v. 37). These words mean "amazed or stunned" at the level of intense spiritual conflict He was experiencing. Verse 38 says He was "grieved to the point of death." His sorrow was dangerously close to shutting down His bodily functions. Luke tells us He was in "agony" (22:44).

A fascinating movie came out several years ago about *death* coming in the form of a human being to claim a wealthy businessman named Bill Parrish. This personification of death, called *Joe Black* (also the movie title) becomes intrigued with Bill Parrish and his family. Subsequently, for the first time in his existence, he (death) falls deeply in love with none other than Parrish's daughter Susan. Fearful for his daughter's future, Joe Parrish confronts Joe Black, saying that as the personification of *death* he has no idea what real love is. They argue and Joe thinks he understands his own feelings, but Parrish says, *"Take that (understanding), multiply by infinity, and take it to the depth of forever and you will still have barely a glimpse of what I'm taking about."* This is an apt description of Jesus' agony. Regardless of the agony we may have faced at any point in our lives, we cannot comprehend what was going on inside the body, emotions, and spirit of Jesus at this moment.

♦ **The Father Sends an Angel to Comfort His Son (Luke 22:43).**

Jesus' grief is so intense that the Father sends an angel to comfort and minister to Him. What did the angel do? What could the angel teach Jesus that He didn't already know? C. S. Lewis once said, "It is greater to remind than to instruct." Some scholars think the angel may have reminded Jesus of what the psalmist and the prophets had said concerning the result of His rejection. (See Isa. 49:1–13.) This may be true, but maybe the angel said very little. Words are often useless. Maybe the angel came to just *be with Him* as He had been with the disciples.

Jesus prays that the "cup" might pass from Him if it is the Father's will. He will pray this prayer three separate times (vv. 39, 42, 44). He will also return to the disciples three times and each time they will be overcome by sleep (vv. 40–41,

Why have none of the disciples asked where Judas is? Remember, when He left the upper room during the Passover meal, they thought he had been sent by Jesus to get supplies or to give something to the poor (John 13:28–29).

43, 45). You would think that at least one of the three would have rallied to the cause at such an important moment, but they still didn't *get it*.

 What was the "cup" Jesus did not want to face? What are the choices?

1. Was Jesus concerned about dying a premature death (John 10:18)?
2. Was it the natural fear of the pain and agony of crucifixion?
3. Was it the reality that for the first time He would become totally detached, separated from His Father?

The "cup" was that Jesus would become a _____ (Gal. 3:13).

He would also become _____ on our behalf (2 Cor. 5:21).

Finally, the agony was so great that the capillaries of Jesus skin burst and blood actually seeped through His pores. This is a phenomenon called *hemohidrosis*. As a physician, Luke wants us to know this (22:44). Finally Jesus will make two statements before His arrest. He tells the disciples that the hour has come for His betrayal, and that the one who will betray Him is now waiting nearby.

Before we continue with Jesus' arrest and trial, we should understand the paradox of the lengths the Jewish leaders will go to get Jesus arrested, tried, and executed. They *had* to get Jesus on the cross and in the ground before Passover began at sundown on Friday. They are at the mercy of the Romans to pull it off for them. They are sworn protectors of their sacred laws. Their goal was to *never* break one. Yet, they will violate twenty-two of their own sacred laws so that they can put to death this *Man,* whom they charge with violating their sacred laws.

TWENTY-TWO VIOLATIONS OF JEWISH LAWS BY THE JEWISH LEADERS IN THE ARREST AND TRIAL OF JESUS CHRIST

JEWISH LAW	VIOLATION
1. There were to be no steps of criminal proceedings after sun-set MISHNAH CAPITAL CHARGES MUST BE TRIED BY DAY AND CONCLUDED BY DAY.	John 18:3
2. There was to be no arrest by religious authorities that was affected by a bribe (Ex. 23:8) See Zech. 11:13 for 30 pieces of silver.	John 18:3
3. Judges or Sanhedrin members were not allowed to participate in the arrest.	Luke 22:52; John 18:3
4. There were to be no trials before morning sacrifice.	John 18:12–13
5. There were to be no secret trials, only public.	John 18:12
6. There were to be two to three witnesses, and their testimony had to agree in every detail.	Deut. 19:15; Mark 14:55–59; Matt. 26:59–61, 65
7. The procedure was to be first the defense and then the accusation: MISHNAH P. 386—CAPITAL CHARGES MUST BEGIN WITH REASONS FOR ACQUITTAL AND MAY NOT BEGIN WITH REASONS FOR CONVICTION.	Matt 26:57–59; John 18:19
8. There was to be no allowance for the accused to testify against himself.	Matt. 26:62
9. All may argue in favor of acquittal, but all may not argue in favor of Conviction: ACQUITTAL, BUT NOT IN FAVOR OF CONVICTION.	Matt. 26:59
10. The accusation of blasphemy was only valid if the name of God itself was pronounced: MISHNAH P. 382—HE THAT HATH BROUGHT AN EVIL NAME (MUST BE JUDGED) BY THREE AND TWENTY, FOR THERE MAY ARISE THEREFROM A CAPITAL CASE. MISHNAH P. 392—'THE BLASPHEMER" IS NOT CULPABLE UNLESS HE PRONOUNCES THE NAME ITSELF.	Matt. 26:65
11. A person condemned to death was not to be scourged or beaten beforehand: BABYLONIAN TALMUD—FLOGGING IS CONSIDERED A SUBSTITUTE FOR DEATH. A PERSON WHO WAS TO DIE WAS NOT TO BE BEATEN OR SCOURGED BEFOREHAND.	Mark 14:65
12. The verdict could not be pronounced at night, only in the daytime: (Friday, MISHNAH P. 387—IN CAPITAL CASES.... THE VERDICT ALSO before dawn) MUST BE REACHED DURING THE DAYTIME.	Matt. 26:57
13. The high priest was forbidden to tear his garments (Lev. 21:10)	Matt. 26:65
14. In cases of capital punishment, the trial and guilty verdict could not occur at the same time, but must be separated by at least 24 hours: MISHNAH P. 387—IN CAPITAL CASES A VERDICT OF ACQUITTAL MAY BE REACHED ON THE SAME DAY, BUT A VERDICT OF CONVICTION NOT UNTIL THE FOLLOWING DAY. MISHNAH P. 389—IF THEY FOUND HIM INNOCENT, THEY SET HIM FREE; OTHERWISE THEY LEAVE HIS SENTENCE OVER UNTIL THE MORROW.	Matt. 26:65–66
15. Charges could not originate with the judges; they could only investigate charges brought to them.	Matt. 26:65
16. A unanimous decision for guilt shows innocence since it is impossible for twenty-three to seventy men to agree without plotting.	Matt. 26:66; Mark 14:65

17. Judges were to be humane and kind.	Mark 14:65
18. A person could not be condemned on the basis of his own words alone.	Mark 14:64
19. Voting for the death penalty had to be done by individual count beginning with the youngest so that the young would not be influenced by the elders. MISHNAH P. 378—IN CAPITAL CASES THEY BEGIN FROM [THEM THAT SIT AT] THE SIDE. Matt. 26:66	Matt. 26:66
20. The only place a Sanhedrin trial could take place was in the Hall of Judgment of the temple compound: BABYLONIAN TALMUD—MAS AVODAH ZARAH 8B. CAPITAL CASES WERE ONLY DEALT WITH BY ANY COURT OF 23 WHILE THE SANHEDRIN SAT IN THE HEWN STONE CHAMBER OF THE TEMPLE.	Matt. 20:57–58
21. The sentence and the guilty verdict could not be announced on the same day; in fact, it had to be separated by three days.	Matt. 26:65–66
22. No trials were allowed on the eve of the Sabbath or on the eve of a feast day: MISHNAH P. 387—TRIALS ARE NOT HELD ON THE SABBATH OR ON THE EVE OF A FESTIVAL DAY.	Passover eve

(Uppercase letters indicate laws that are contained in the Mishnah and Talmud.)

As we study the arrest, trial, crucifixion, and resurrection of Jesus, it is critical that you read each of the parallel accounts to gain the full impact and perspective of all that is happening.

NOTE: These Jewish laws were obtained from the Mishnah, the Babylonian Talmud, Arnold Fruchtenbaum of Ariel Ministries, and Bob Warren of Life on the Hill Ministry.

BE THE JEWISH LEADERS: You do not believe that Jesus is the Messiah, and have therefore rejected Him. You agree with your colleagues that He is a gifted, but misguided and probably crazed, radical. If allowed to continue, He could incite the crowds and bring down the wrath of the Roman government. Even worse, if Jesus were to be made king, you would lose the authority and position you have so diligently sought. Your identity is wrapped up in what you do. Without your position and the weight it carries, you would be lost. There would be no reason to live. Jesus must be eliminated! You must find a way to extract Him from the crowds to avoid the possibility of a riot. You know that Pilate, the Roman procurator, couldn't care less about Jewish religious matters. He would only be concerned if he thought Jesus' popularity could threaten Rome, and therefore his own authority and position. You must devise a way to convince Pilate that Jesus' motives are not only spiritual, but political. The only way to kill Jesus is through Roman authority, since the right to enact capital punishment had recently been taken away from the Jews. You have now cut a deal with a member of Jesus' inner circle. The next step is to do whatever it takes to convince Pilate that Jesus is dangerous to Rome.

DAY 74

JESUS' BETRAYAL AND ARREST IN GETHSEMANE

READ: Matt. 26:47–56; Mark 14:43–52; John 18:2–12

◆ **Judas Reenters the Plot; He Knows Where to Find Jesus (John 18:1–2).**

It worked! Whatever the level of persuasion Judas and the Jewish leaders used to convince Pilate that Jesus was a potential political threat to Caesar, the Roman procurator went for it. Judas brings formal charges against Jesus. Pilate releases a cohort of soldiers (a cohort is four hundred to six hundred men) to make the arrest. Judas knows where Jesus is and must identify Him. Jesus boldly goes out to meet the soldiers and asks them whom they seek, and they respond, "Jesus the Nazarene." When Jesus confirms that He is the one they seek, something strange happens. They fall to the ground as if hit by lightning.

What happened? We can only speculate, but what we do know is that the Roman soldiers had come expecting to arrest a poor Jewish peasant and were confronted with the majestic presence of God. Notice Jesus answer, "I am *He.*" The word *He* in your Bible is probably in italics. This means it is not in the original manuscripts. Jesus actually said, "I am." Any Jew would recognize immediately that this was complete and total identification with God. The soldiers would *not* know this, but they probably tapped out because they were overwhelmed with the awesome presence of God.

After recovering, they ask Jesus again, and He responds the same. He asks that *the eleven* be permitted to leave unharmed. Judas then steps forward and kisses Jesus making a complete fool of himself. Why? Jesus had already identified Himself. Why would Judas need to duplicate that?

In Jewish culture, a kiss on the cheek of a rabbi indicated the desire of that person to submit and be taught by him. It is also worth mentioning that the word *kiss* is the same Greek word used in Acts 20:37 when the apostle Paul left Ephesus and the people hugged and kissed him. The word means "repeatedly, over and over with great affection." This underlines the depth of Judas's hypocrisy.

Immediately there is violation of three Jewish laws:

Law #1: No criminal proceedings could occur after sunset.

Law #2: There could be no arrest by religious authorities effected by a bribe. There could be no nighttime arrest.

Law #3: Judges and Sanhedrin members could not be present.

The healing of the ear of the high priest's servant is the only time in the Gospels where Jesus heals a fresh wound.

◆ Peter Retaliates with a Sword, Cutting off the Ear of the High Priest's Servant (18:10).

 Peter pulls a sword and slices off the servant's ear, and Jesus immediately orders him to put the sword away. He asks Peter rhetorically, "Would you have Me to try to avoid the very purpose for which My Father sent Me?" Then, without a word, He heals the servant's ear as the others watch in stunned silence.

What do you make of this behavior on the part of Peter? Irrational or normal response? Explain.

Nothing Jesus ever taught condoned or promoted violence. The following verses reflect Jesus' thinking on the issue of retaliation.

- Matt. 26:52: _____
- Matt. 6:53: _____
- Matt. 6:54: _____
- Isa. 53:7: _____

Jesus is arrested and the disciples scatter in all directions, but before they take Him, Jesus lets the Jews and Romans know they are not in control.

In many ways we are very much like the religious leaders who come in like John Wayne and the cavalry to arrest Jesus. We act as if we are in control of our lives and our destiny. God must look at us as Jesus did these men and say, *"You've got to be kidding. You have nothing that I have not allowed you to have; you've accomplished nothing for which I have not opened doors; and you have no authority that I have not given you."*

Imagine the absurdity of these men thinking that their numbers and their swords had any ability whatsoever to subdue Jesus if He decided He had wanted to be somewhere else!

PART X: THE TRIAL, DEATH, AND BURIAL OF JESUS

We will clearly see the political implications surrounding Jesus' trial and death. Everyone has a self-protective agenda except Jesus. Pilate fears the Roman authorities who watch him closely. The Jewish leaders fear Jesus, the multitudes, Pilate, and the Romans. If Jesus lives and becomes king in a new political order, they will lose their authority. If He dies and the crowds become uncontrollable, Rome will step in and come down on Pilate, who will in turn curtail the authority of the Sanhedrin. The Jews can do little more than harass Jesus at this point. They must convince Pilate that Jesus' offenses are great enough that he will see Jesus as a political threat. That they have called Jesus a blasphemer is irrelevant to Pilate. They must make Pilate fearful of losing his job. Imprisonment will not satisfy them or remove the threat to their authority. The following events are manipulative attempts to do whatever it takes, including violating their own sacred laws, to get Jesus executed.

DAY 75

JESUS IS BROUGHT BEFORE ANNAS IN THE HOME OF CAIAPHAS, HIS FATHER-IN-LAW.

READ: John 18:12–14, 19–24

Annas had been appointed high priest by Quirinius, the governor of Syria in AD 7. He held the office until he was deposed by Valerius Gratus, the Roman procurator in AD 15. Several sons followed him and served as high priest after he was deposed. Now it is AD 30 and the high priest is a man named Caiaphas, the son-in-law of Annas, who had now held that position for five years. (He would hold the office until AD 36.) By Jewish law, a high priest is appointed until he dies, much like our Supreme Court justices. However, Rome, the ruling authority, had appointed Caiaphas in AD 25, and this is why the Scriptures refer to both men as high priest. From Rome's perspective, Caiaphas is high priest, but to the Jews it is Annas.

Law Violations:

#4: There were to be no trials before morning sacrifice.

#5: There were to be no secret trials, only public.

#7: Capital cases must begin with reasons for acquittal and not reasons for conviction.

#8: There is no allowance for the accused to testify against himself.

253

Jesus is taken directly to Annas. The Jewish leaders hope to charge Him with a religious crime. They had already predetermined that He should die (John 18:14). The Pharisees and Sadducees had even joined together to plot His death after Lazarus was raised (John 11:49–52). Annas asks Jesus about His disciples and about His teaching. Jesus calmly tells him that He has done everything in plain view for all to see (v. 20), and that there were many people who could verify what He taught (v. 21). One of the officials strikes Him, then reprimands Him for what he considered disrespect to the high priest. Jesus says, in effect, *"If what I am telling you is not true, prove it!"* (v. 23). Annas is unable to produce a religious charge, so he sends Jesus to his son-in-law, Caiaphas.

JESUS GOES BEFORE CAIAPHAS AND THE SANHEDRIN.

Law Violations:

#20: Trials were to be held in the Hall of Judgment of the temple compound only.

#22: No trials were allowed on the eve of the Sabbath or a feast day.

#6: The testimony of two or three witnesses must agree in every detail.

#8: There is no allowance for the accused to testify against himself.

#13: The high priest is forbidden to tear his garments.

READ: Matt. 26:57, 59–68; Mark 14:53, 55–65; Luke 22:54

Sometime before dawn on Friday, the 15th of Nisan, Jesus is taken before Caiaphas in his palace. This will be His official religious trial (Matt. 57—58). Many tactics were used in an attempt to accuse Him, but all failed, including false witnesses who were brought in, all to no avail.

Jesus is misquoted as saying He _____ destroy the physical temple (Mark 14:55–59). Another witness quoted Him as saying, "I _____ to destroy the temple" (Matt. 26:51). This contradiction was so blatant and obvious that it should have been thrown out.

◆ **Caiaphas Demands a Verbal Response to the Charges (Matt. 26:62).**

Legally Jesus is not required to answer, so He keeps silent. Caiaphas then puts Him under an oath in order to force a response (Matt. 26:63).

How did Caiaphas put Jesus under an oath?

Because He is under oath, Jesus answers, *"You have said it yourself"* (vv. 64–65). He then quotes Daniel 7:13, which refers to His second coming, and Caiaphas tears his robes, charging Jesus with blasphemy and saying that He is deserving of death (vv. 65–66). All in attendance concur that Jesus deserves to die.

◆ **The Jewish Leaders Begin to Spit on Jesus and to Slap Him (v. 67).**

 Most commentaries never take into consideration that the Sanhedrin continuously *broke* their own laws. They wrongly assume that because the Jews were such diligent guardians of the law they would never violate those laws. They therefore move back the beginning of Jesus' religious trial three days and begin counting from there. It won't work. For the chronology to work, we must realize that these guys violated their own laws by not waiting the required three days between announcing the verdict and the sentencing. The truth is that the Pharisees' tenacity to guard the law was great, but greater still was *their tenacity to preserve their position and authority.* All of these events occurred on the same day!

Under Jewish law:

To strike a person with a fist carried with it a fine of 4 denarii.
To strike a person with an open hand carried a fine of 200 denarii.
To spit in the face of another carried a fine of 400 denarii.

Considering that a soldier's pay was one denarii per day, the financial penalty for what they did to Jesus would have lightened their wallets considerably had they not been allowed to operate "above the law."

PETER DENIES THE LORD THREE TIMES. JESUS IS MOCKED AND BEATEN.

READ: Matt. 26:69–75; Mark 14:66–72; Luke 22:54b–65; John 18:15–18, 25–27

After Jesus is arrested, the disciples run for the hills, including Peter, who had boldly said he would remain faithful even if everyone else bailed out. However, to Peter's credit it appears that he was the first of the eleven to come to his senses, regain his composure, and follow Jesus and the entourage at a distance (Matt. 26:58; Mark 14:54; Luke 22:54).

Law Violations:

#10: The charge of blasphemy was only valid if the name of God was pronounced.

#18: A person cannot be condemned on the basis of his word alone.

#12: The verdict cannot be announced at night, only in the daytime.

#14: The trial and guilty verdict must be separated by twenty-four hours.

#9: All may argue in favor of acquittal, but all may not argue in favor of conviction.

#16: A unanimous decision for guilt shows innocence since it is not possible for 23–71 men to agree without plotting.

#19: Voting for the death penalty must be done by individual count, starting with the youngest so they will not be influenced by the elders.

We switch scenes and find Peter in Caiaphas's courtyard, which could not be accessed by the general public, especially in the middle of the night. How was Peter able to get inside the courtyard? Look back at the arrest in John 18:10. Then read 18:15–16.

What was the name of the high priest's servant? _____.

Who is the only one of the gospel writers who knows his name? _____.

Who was able to get Peter into the courtyard of Caiaphas? _____.

John's family knew Caiaphas the high priest and therefore was able to bring Peter inside his gated courtyard (John 18:15). This is why John knew the name of the high priest's servant (v. 10). John goes inside first, then later returns to speak to the doorkeeper so Peter might enter (v. 16).

Peter will deny Jesus three times before the cock crows twice, just as Jesus had said in the upper room (Matt. 26:34). Notice that with each denial he utters, Peter's response is more adamant and violent. Also, notice that each writer describes the servant girl who questions Peter differently.

- First denial—Peter's response was a simple denial (Mark 14:66–68):
" _____ ."

(The cock crows the first time)

- Second denial—Peter denies at the gateway with an oath (Matt. 26:71–72):
" _____ ."

- Third denial—Peter denies with cursing and swearing (Mark 14:70–71):
" _____ ."

(The cock crows the second time)

As Peter is swearing and cursing, the cock crows. Simultaneously, Caiaphas has just completed his questioning, has torn his robe, and the leaders have blindfolded, spit on Jesus, and hit him in the face. The blindfold is taken off and the door is opened just off the courtyard within a short distance from Peter's tirade. If you saw Mel Gibson's *Passion* film, this scene is chilling and very accurate. As the door opens, Jesus and Peter make direct eye contact as the cock crows in the background and Peter remembers Jesus' words that he would deny Him (Luke 22:62). Peter leaves the palace and goes out and weeps bitterly (Luke 22:62).

Law Violations:

#15: Charges could not originate with the judges; they could only investigate charges brought to them.

#21: The sentence and guilty verdict must be separated by three days.

#11: A condemned person was not to be beaten or scourged beforehand.

BE PETER: Describe your emotions and thoughts when the cock crows and you make eye contact with Jesus in the midst of your third denial:

You and I may have never denied our relationship with Jesus in so dramatic and blatant a fashion, but it is possible to deny Him nonverbally. *List several nonverbal ways you have denied Him. Then put a small check by those in which you have had the greatest growth.*

DAY 76

THE SANHEDRIN TRIAL: JESUS IS OFFICIALLY CONDEMNED.

READ: Matt. 27:1; Mark 15:1; Luke 22:66–71

Everything the Jewish leaders have done was illegal. They have trashed the Jewish legal code and made a mockery of everything they were sworn to protect and uphold. As they begin to realize this, they try to repair some of the damage. They take Jesus before the Sanhedrin to somehow try to make legal some of the charges they have made illegally. This will be an impossible task, as we will see.

◆ The Council of Elders Demand That Jesus Tell Them if He Is the Christ (Luke 22:66–67).

Jesus' answer to the Jewish elders' question should be very instructive to us in terms of our desire to communicate the truth to our families, friends, and colleagues. Jesus replies that *if He tells them, they will not believe Him. If He asks them a question, they will not answer.* What is He saying? He understands well that belief is a matter if the *will*. These leaders saw Him perform the three messianic miracles that *they* had set as the criterion for determining the validity of the Messiah. Still, they *would not* believe. They had schemed against Him at every turn, only to be humiliated. They finally gave up! Why would He answer the questions of those who are unwavering in their intent to reject His answers even before they are given? The validity of any answer is determined by the openness, honesty, and intensity of the question. This is why Jesus said, "Blessed are the poor in spirit" (those who recognize their spiritual poverty). They are people with questions who seek honest answers. But the Jewish leaders have no questions, therefore answers are irrelevant.

Both parents and teachers should find great consolation in this. Even Jesus could not reveal things to *closed* minds. As we discussed previously, *information* is all we can communicate. This study is only *information*. In and of itself, it can change no one. God must make it *revelation*, but it will depend on the *hearer*. Revelation resulting in belief is a matter of the *will*. Jesus said, "If I tell you, you *will not* believe." It wasn't that they *couldn't* believe; it was that they *refused* to believe. They had no real questions about themselves and their lives. You can't say profoundly enough or be articulate enough to engender belief in a human heart. All the pressure comes off of us. We don't need to feel that we have to *pull it off*. We can, pray, prepare well, communicate effectively, but the results are purely up to God, not us!

◆ Jesus Says His Resurrection and Ascension Will Confirm His Identity (v. 69).

Once more they ask Jesus point blank if He is *the Christ* and He says, *"Yes, I am."* Hearing it from His own mouth, they all agree that there is no need for any further testimony. They will now take Jesus for His civil trial. Why would Caiaphas not press for the death penalty with the Sanhedrin? The Babylonian Talmud and the Mishnah both state that forty years before the destruction of the temple in AD 70, the Romans took away the right of the Jews to enact capital punishment. Do the math. The year is AD 30, and the Jews must find a way to get Pilate to crucify Jesus. He has created a logistical nightmare for the Jewish leaders!

> Can you see God's sovereignty running through these events? Had the Romans not taken away the death penalty from the Jews, they would have stoned Jesus (the Jewish form of capital punishment). Had they done that, He could not have been Savior. He *must* hang on a cross as a curse (Deut. 21:23).

JUDAS COMMITS SUICIDE.

READ: Matt. 27:3–10

In the ancient Jewish world, to commit suicide was a certain guarantee of going to the darkest part of Hades.

Judas would not have been allowed to attend the Sanhedrin trial of Jesus, but certainly must have lurked in the shadows outside the court when the verdict was rendered. It is doubtful that he thought things would go this far, and he must have had a lump in his throat the size of a grapefruit. Upon hearing that Jesus had been condemned, he feels *remorse* and returns the bribe money to the Jewish elders (v. 3). He tells them that he realizes now that he had betrayed an innocent man, but their response is, *"That's your problem, deal with it!"* (v. 4). Judas throws the thirty pieces of silver into the temple sanctuary and abruptly leaves.

What kind of remorse do you think Judas was experiencing? Was he truly repentant? Why or why not?

Can we really know Judas's final condition before God as he took his own life? The answer is found in the word *remorse* (v. 3). The Greek word for repentance is *metanoia*. This is the first recorded statement in Jesus' public ministry, "Repent, for the Kingdom of heaven has arrived." The word used here concerning Judas is *metamelomai*, which means that he felt *regret* for what he had done, but is a far cry from true repentance. Jesus also refers to him as the "son of perdition" in John 17:12, saying that Judas was the only one who would *perish*.

♦ **Judas Hangs Himself at Sunrise (v. 5).**

There appears to be a contradiction concerning the manner of Judas's death.

- Matt. 27:5: _____
- Acts 1:18: _____

✡ "According to Jewish law, if there was a dead body in Jerusalem, the city was considered defiled. As a result, the morning Passover sacrifice could not be offered or celebrated. However, jewish law goes on to say that if the body is taken and cast into the valley of Himmon, a place of burning, the city is reckoned as cleansed and the Passover can be partaken of. Later they can return and bury the body." Arnold Fruchtenfaum, Life of Christ series.

💡 Now we can put it together. Both of these statements are correct. Judas *does* hang himself, but apparently inside the city limits. A dead body inside the city limits prevented the Jews from celebrating the Chagigah sacrifice at 9:00 a.m. Friday. Upon their discovery of Judas's body dangling from a tree, they cut him down and throw his body into a ravine in the Hinnom valley, outside the city limits. They will come back and bury him after the Sabbath. The bursting open would have had to do with the impact when thrown over a ledge into the valley filled with rocks and rubble.

The value system of the Jewish leaders is amazing. They have just violated 22 of their own sacred laws without so much as a blink, but now they worry about the illegality of putting bribe money back in the temple treasury.

♦ **The Chief Priest's Dilemma: What to Do with the Blood Money (v. 6)?**

✈ After Judas departs to hang himself, the chief priest and elders must make a decision about the 30 pieces of silver Judas threw down in the sanctuary. They cannot put it back in the temple treasury because it is tainted. What to do?

They obviously could not give it back to the owner, because he was dead. They opted to use it for the public good by purchasing a piece of land that would be used as a public cemetery called a "Potter's Field."

There is another apparent contradiction: Who actually bought the field?

- Matt. 27:7: _____
- Acts 1:18: _____

Once again, understanding Jewish law and custom is helpful. When the donor of the money refused its return or in this case was deceased, the purchase was made and recorded in the name of the donor (Judas Iscariot). This reconciles the statement in Acts. The legal deed listed Judas as the donor of the field, but it was actually purchased by the Jews after Judas died.

ABOUT THIS PIECE OF LAND: In verse 9, Matthew quotes Jeremiah. The only problem is that it was Zechariah who actually made the statement (Zech. 11:12–13). Matthew is not mistaken. He is quoting Jeremiah, who is quoting Zechariah. Why? He wants the reader to know that the 30 pieces of silver actually purchased a *cursed piece of land* and the story of that curse in recorded in the book of Jeremiah.

Read Jeremiah 7:27–34 and 19:1–15, preferably in *The Living Bible* if you have one, before reading the following commentary.

This very land, six hundred years prior, had been the site where Jewish parents had burned their sons and daughters to death as a sacrifice to Baal (Jer. 19:5–6). This field, called Topheth (Place of Burning) was cursed by God for the unthinkable wickedness done there. Matthew is saying that there would come a day when the curse of Jeremiah would be fulfilled. He is speaking of AD 70 when 1.1 million Jews were killed. Topheth then became known as the "Valley of Slaughter," where so many were killed during that Roman siege that there was no place left to bury all of the corpses. Judas, therefore, became the first to be buried in a field that had been cursed six hundred years prior. The fulfillment of that curse forty years later would literally be a "field of blood." These prideful, arrogant Jewish leaders unknowingly *purchased a curse*!

As the trial of Jesus progresses, we will see the political maneuvering on the part of the Jewish leaders, as well as Herod and Pilate. The Jews will stop at nothing to do away with Jesus, but they must convince Pilate that He is dangerous to Rome's authority and continued security. Therefore they must change their charges against Him from blasphemy, which will not faze Pilate, to sedition against Rome. Pilate is being closely watched and cannot afford to misstep. As he interviews Jesus, he begins to realize that the Jews' obsession with Him could potentially end his career if not handled delicately.

DAY 77

JESUS BEFORE PILATE FOR HIS INITIAL CIVIL TRIAL

READ: Matt. 27:2, 11–14; Mark 15:1–5; Luke 23:1–5; John 18:28–38

 After attempting to give some appearance of legality, the chief priest sends Jesus to Pilate for a civil trial. He is taken to *the Praetorium,* the private residence of the Roman governor in Herod's palace. It is some time after daybreak on Friday morning, the fifteenth of Nisan. This will be the first of two times that Jesus will face Pilate. The proceedings were public in accordance with Roman law. This explains why the multitudes were present both times.

A WORD ABOUT PILATE: Pontius Pilate was procurator, or governor, of Judea from AD 26–36. He was an extremely cruel and sadistic man whose hatred for the Jews was only exceeded by their hatred for him. He antagonized them whenever possible, and had little regard for their faith or for their God. He was appointed by a man named Sejanus, who deeply resented the Jews and wanted a procurator over Judea who hated them as much as he. Josephus records that those appointed to this position had no certainty how long they would stay in power, so they fleeced the people quickly and for as much of their wealth as possible. Two particular incidents ignited their hatred: The first was that Pilate used the monies that he confiscated from the temple treasury to build an aqueduct into the city. The second was Pilate's assemblage of pagan statuary around the city as well as standards bearing his image. The Jews were outraged and demanded that the "graven images" be removed from the city. Pilate complied, but not because he was fearful of them. It was because the "eyes of Rome" were watching closely, and his ability to keep peace with the Jews held his job in the balance.

The Jewish leaders lead Jesus to the Praetorium. The Jews will not enter this Gentile place for fear of being defiled and unable to participate in the *Chagigah* sacrifice later that morning (John 18:28). The Jews assume that Pilate would be happy to deal harshly with someone claiming to be king of these people whom he hated so much. However, they are badly mistaken. Their initial charge was that Jesus was a *disturber of the peace*, but Pilate demands a formal charge that must be presented by a prosecuting witness. Big problem! The body of their *star witness* is lying somewhere out in the Hinnom valley. Pilate is far too smart to pass judgment on Jesus without a witness and a formal charge. Besides, he would certainly have enjoyed watching the Jewish leaders squirm. Ignoring their informal charges, he tells them to judge Jesus themselves (vv. 30–31). They respond by saying that they have no authority to put someone to death.

◆ **When Pilate Refuses to Act, the Jews Come Up with Their Own Charges (Luke 23:2).**

1. He is _____ our nation.

2. He opposes _____ .

3. He claims _____ .

Understanding the political "soft shoe" here is important. Pilate's appointment as procurator by Sejanus, a very influential leader in Rome, would actually come back to haunt him. Sejanus was charged with suspicion of treason in AD 31 and executed. He was accused of plotting with others to overthrow Caesar. From then on, all those who had been close to him were under close surveillance. The last thing Pilate needed was for a man proclaiming to be *king* to be set free. Also, notice that the accusations of the Jews concerning Jesus have now been changed from *religious* charges to *political* charges (*sedition* against Rome) at His civil trial. In the religious trial, the charges had been *blasphemy*. This is done to needle Pilate, knowing that he is being closely watched and cannot afford to misstep and risk losing his position.

◆ **Pilate Takes Jesus Aside and Asks Him Privately if He Is King of the Jews (John 18:33).**

Pilate probably has two purposes in speaking privately to Jesus. First and foremost, he would want to satisfy himself that Jesus was no political threat to Caesar, and therefore to his job. Secondly, he may have felt that the Jews had overreacted concerning the severity of Jesus' "crime." When Pilate asks if He is King of the Jews, Jesus responds with His own question (vv. 33–34). He wants to know if Pilate is asking based on what he has been told by the Jews (that He is the Messiah) or from his personal perspective. (Are you a rebel?) Pilate's sarcastic response (v. 35) basically says, "I couldn't care less about these religious charges or whether You caught a pass from Moses in the Rose Bowl, I just want to know if You have political aspirations!"

◆ **Jesus Assures Pilate That His Kingdom Is Not of This World (v. 36).**

Jesus tells Pilate that He is not the kind of king he is thinking of, but that He is "King of the truth." Pilate clearly does not want Jesus executed. From the description he had received from Judas and the Jewish leaders before the arrest, he was expecting a wild-eyed, Charles Manson–type revolutionary who was ready to burn the city to the ground. What he finds is a calm, focused man who asks for no concessions and makes no threats.

The residence of Pilate was normally in the coastal city of Caesarea, but he would come to Jerusalem with his troops during festival times, realizing that these occasions were the most favorable for riots and uprisings.

- **Pilate Goes Out to the Jews and Tells Them He Finds No Fault in Jesus (John 18:38; Luke 23:4).**

The Jewish leaders accuse Him again, but He will not defend Himself (Luke 27:12). Pilate is *amazed* at this (Matt. 27:13–14). As the Jewish leaders levy this barrage of attacks on Jesus, they utter a phrase that is music to Pilate's ears.

Luke 23:5: "He has stirred up people through Judea, _____."

Pilate's jurisdiction is _____. Who is in charge of Galilee?

The moment the Jews say that Jesus had stirred up trouble beginning in Galilee, Pilate realizes a way to get himself off the hook. He sees a way to dump this whole unpleasant issue on his old archenemy, Herod Antipas, Tetrarch of Galilee.

Herod was appointed by and works for the Romans to keep the Jews in line. He is a very insecure man and desperately wants the respect of Pilate. Since Pilate sends Jesus to him, he now feels that he is back on Pilate's Christmas card list. But that is far from the truth.

DAY 78

JESUS GOES BEFORE HEROD ANTIPAS.

READ: Luke 23:6–12

It should be no surprise that Pilate immediately sends Jesus to Herod, given the magic words he had just learned. Herod is very glad to see Jesus. He knows of His reputation and also has some idea of the connection between Jesus and John the Baptist, with whom he had also been intrigued. (His wife hated John and had initiated John's beheading.) He sees Jesus as a kind of religious magician who could do miraculous things. He wants Him to put on a kind of dog-and-pony show for his amusement. Not only will Jesus not perform for Herod's amusement, He will not even answer any questions or accusations (Luke 23:9–10). After mocking and taunting Him, and dressing Him in a purple robe, they send Jesus back to Pilate (v. 11). No formal charges were brought by Herod, but he feels that because Pilate had sent Jesus to him, he now has the respect of the governor and that the relationship is restored.

THE RELATIONSHIP BETWEEN PILATE AND HEROD: Josephus records that Pilate had brought his army from Cesarea to Jeru-salem to make their winter quarters there, in order to abolish the Jewish laws. One night under cover of darkness, Pilate had Caesar's effigies (statues and carvings), brought into the city. The next morning the Jews were horrified to see these graven images covering the holy city. Jews came in multitudes to Pilate demanding that he remove them, but he refused. On the sixth day of rebellion, Pilate had his troops waiting with swords drawn. The Jews flung themselves on the ground, baring their necks, and saying they would die rather than have their laws transgressed. Pilate backed down and had the images removed, but the relationship was strained from then on between he and Herod (Josephus, Ant, XVIII, iii, 2; BJ, II, ix, 4).

JESUS IS BROUGHT BEFORE PILATE A SECOND TIME.

READ: Matt. 27:15–26; Mark 15:6–15; Luke 23:13–25; John 18:39—19:16

♦ **Pilate Calls the Jewish Leaders Together and Tells Them He Does Not Concur with Their Charges, Nor Does Herod.**

BE PILATE: You must judge Jesus based on the evidence available. *Read Luke 23:13–16 and make this brief statement to the Jews in your own words.*

♦ **Pilate Offers to Release a Prisoner to the Crowd (John 18:39).**

What is happening here? Pilate thinks that by sending Jesus to Herod he is covering his bases in case Caesar ever wants to investigate the matter. He can say he sent Jesus to Herod, Tetrarch of Galilee, and that Herod found him not guilty and sent Him back. If a riot ensues, he can blame it on Herod. He wrongly assumes that the Jewish leaders will be satisfied if he scourges Jesus and releases Him. Suddenly he thinks of another option that has *winner* written all over it. It was a Jewish custom to release a prisoner to the crowd at festival time. (Note: This is not a Roman custom and certainly not one Pilate would have agreed to under normal circumstances.) He assumes that the crowd will surely ask for Jesus, and he will be off the hook.

WHAT HAPPENED TO HEROD?

Poor counsel from his wife, Herodius, played a key role in his demise. She had coaxed her daughter to ask for John the Baptist's head on a platter. Then years later, she insisted that he go to Rome to pursue the title of king. He was soon exiled from Rome to what is modern-day France and died a pauper. The sad part is that Herodius's daughter became exactly like her mother! Scary, isn't it?

Not much has changed in 2,000 years. Just like today, people always look for ways to blame someone else. Pilate was trying to cover all the bases so he could not be blamed if something went wrong.

◆ **Pilate Sarcastically Offers Jesus as "King of the Jews" (Mark 15:9).**

Why would Pilate not say, the "alleged" King of the Jews or the man who claims to be the King of the Jews? Because this is an opportunity for him to twist the knife. He is well aware of the insult his sarcasm would be to the Jews.

Pilate is also aware of something about the Jewish leaders. What is it?

The chief priests had delivered Him up because of _____ *(Mark 15:10).*

Elaborate on this:

Sedition against Rome was the charge made against Barabbas. The same charge is made against Jesus, but by the Jews, not the Romans. At Jesus' religious trial, they charged blasphemy, but it changes to sedition when they realize that only that charge will get Pilate's attention.

◆ **We Meet Barabbas: A Prisoner Charged with Sedition Against Rome (Mark 15:6–7).**

◆ **Pilate's Wife Enters the Drama (Matt. 27:19–20).**

Mrs. Pilate's dream changes nothing. Why do you think Matthew included it?

◆ **The Chief Priest and the Pharisees Persuade the Multitudes to Ask for Barabbas (Luke 23:18–19).**

Pilate had found no guilt in Jesus, but was willing to scourge Him, thinking that it would placate the Jewish leaders. Don't get the idea that Pilate is not that bad of a guy. He is a coward who is interested in maintaining his authority and position. He thinks he can blame this whole thing on the Jews, and knowing of Jesus' popularity with the masses, feels confident they will ask for Jesus when he offers to set a prisoner free. The Jewish leaders have obviously moved among the crowd whispering threats and intimidations. To Pilate's astonishment, they ask for Barabbas to be set free rather than Jesus. Pilate has no choice but to comply, and he sends Jesus out to be scourged by a Roman *lictor*. The soldiers mock and abuse Jesus. They drape a purple robe (the color of royalty) over His lacerated back and shoulders and press a crown of thorns on His head (John 19:2–3).

A Roman soldier called a *lictor* would have inflicted excruciating pain upon Jesus' body. Using a whip called a *flagella* with pieces of bone, metal, and rock woven into strands of leather, the blows were directed to the face and upper torso. This fulfills Isaiah's prophecy (52:14): "So His appearance was marred more than any man and His form more than the sons of men." The victim usually passed out and often died. Because it was a Roman punishment, the scourging was not limited to thirty-nine lashes.

Eusebius recorded the following relating to scourging in his day: "For those standing around were struck with amazement, at seeing them lacerated with scourges to their very blood and arteries, so that now the flesh concealed in the very inmost parts of the body and the bowels themselves were exposed to view" (*Ecclesiastical History*, IV, 15).

DAY 79

PILATE AFFIRMS JESUS' INNOCENCE A THIRD TIME (JOHN 19:4–13).

What do you think Pilate meant when he said, "Behold, the Man"?

Pilate brings Jesus out, bloodied and beaten, and wearing a purple robe and a crown made of thorns. Pilate again affirms His innocence, but the chief priests and officers repeatedly cry out, "Crucify Him." Pilate's frustrated response *returns the power to the Jews to crucify Jesus.*

In John 19:6, Pilate says, "_____"

The Jewish leaders' response troubles Pilate. Their true agenda suddenly floats to the surface. They had told Pilate that sedition against Rome was Jesus' crime, because they knew that would be the hot button for him to take action. Now they have painted themselves into a corner. They slip and tell Pilate that they want to put Jesus to death because "He claims to be the Son of God" (v.

WHAT HAPPENED TO PONTIUS PILATE?

Many legends are associated with the events of Pilate's life after Jesus' death, some even stating that he became a believer. Eusebius, a fourth-century historian, records that he committed suicide: "It is proper also, to observe how it is asserted that this same Pilate, who was governor at our Savior's crucifixion in the reign of Caius, whose times we are recording, fell into such calamities that he was forced to become his own murderer and the avenger of his own wickedness. Divine justice, it seems, did not long protract his punishment. This is stated by the Greek historians who have recorded the Olympiads in order, together with the transactions of the times" (*Ecclesiastical History*, II, 7, 43).

7). Pilate hears this and is afraid (v. 8) because he realizes he has been lied to and sucked into the middle of a religious battle that he has desperately tried to avoid. He takes Jesus inside the Praetorium and asks Him once more where He is from. Jesus doesn't answer. Pilate reminds Him that he has authority over whether Jesus lives or dies. Jesus' response is classic and echoes everything we read about authority in the Scriptures: *Paraphrase verse 11.*

Jesus tells Pilate that the greater sin belonged to the one who delivered Him up to Pilate. *To whom is Jesus referring?*

a) Judas   *b) Caiaphas*   Answer on next page

♦ **Pilate Tries to Release Jesus Again, but the Jews Intervene (v. 12).**

How did the Jewish leaders intervene?   Answer on next page

MEMORIZE: "The king's heart is like channels of water in the hand of the Lord; He turns it wherever He wishes" (Prov. 21:1).

Consider the dynamics here: Pilate's stress level must be off the charts by now, with his wife's warning ringing in his ears, Jesus' innocence confirmed by Herod, and his own belief in Jesus' innocence from the outset. How can he explain to Caesar that he released a man claiming to be a king and who may prove to be a political adversary? He knows he is being watched closely because of his close ties with Sejanus. The Jews are aware of this when they tell him that he is no friend of Caesar if he releases Jesus. This is their way of telling Pilate that his job hangs by a thread and they know it! This forces Pilate to act.

♦ **Pilate Takes Jesus Out and Mockingly Presents Him, Beaten and Bloodied, Saying, "Behold, your King" (v. 13).**

In other words, "Here He is. See how pitiful, here's your main man. Aren't you proud?" We are told that it was the sixth hour. This is Roman time, which would mean 6:00 a.m. Jesus must be on the cross by 9:00 a.m. As Pilate presents Jesus to the crowd as "their King," they cry out with one voice, "Away with Him, crucify Him!" (v. 15).

The crowd is in such a frenzied state that they go berserk. Their response is music to Pilate's ears when he asks, "Shall I crucify your King?" (v. 15).

What are the six magical words that get Pilate off the hook?

"_____." (v. 15)

Answer
from previous page

b.) *Caiaphas*; Judas
was only a means.

In their unbalanced state, the multitude commits _____
by recognizing Caesar as sovereign ruler.

Answer
on next page

Now Pilate can see that the crowds will not be dissuaded, so he publicly absolves himself from any responsibility (Matt. 27:24). This display is not as much for the crowd as for the Roman officials who he knows are watching. He says, "I am innocent of this Man's blood; see to that yourselves." The response of the crowds is possibly the most heinous statement ever made: "His blood shall be on us and on our children."

What happens when your ministry or your vocation becomes your life? Anyone who sets up shop nearby becomes a competitor, a major threat!

Think of what these people are saying: "If Jesus' death turns out to be the wrong action, we will take responsibility and will even assign the consequences to our children." That's worse than wagering your children's lives on a shaky hand of cards.

REMEMBER: These are the same people who had hailed Jesus with palm branches five days earlier, saying, "Hosanna to the Son of David."

How did the multitudes come to the conclusion that Jesus was guilty?

Answer
from previous page

They told the people
what to believe.

These people have no idea what they are saying, because in forty years, many of them and most of their children will experience their self-fulfilling prophecy in that men, women, and children would be slaughtered in the streets of Jerusalem at the hand of the Romans (AD 70).

◆ **Barabbas Is Released and Jesus Is Taken Away (Luke 23:24–25).**

DAY 80

JESUS IS LED TO HIS CRUCIFIXION ON GOLGOTHA.

READ: Matt. 27:27–34; Mark 16:15–23; Luke 23:26–33; John 19:16–17

What kind of people would bet so heavily on the unproven guilt of a man that they would be willing to allow their own children to bear the responsibility if proven wrong?

After Pilate releases Barabbas, the soldiers take Jesus and strip Him, dress Him in a purple robe, and place a crown of thorns on His head. A reed symbolizing a scepter is placed in His hand. He is taunted, spat upon, and beaten on the head with the reed they had given Him (Matt. 27:30). Finally, the soldiers remove the purple robe and replace it with Jesus' own seamless robe, then lead Him from the Praetorium into the street (Mark 15:20). He is forced to carry His own cross on the long walk to Golgotha (John 19:17). As the weight of the cross, along with the extreme loss of blood, causes Jesus to stumble, a man named Simon from Cyrene in North Africa is enlisted to help Him (Mark 15:21). Many women follow the procession mourning and lamenting Jesus' treatment. Jesus sees them and tells them not to weep for Him, but for themselves and their children. Again He warns of the coming destruction of Jerusalem in forty years. When they reach the spot on Golgotha where Jesus and the other two men will be crucified, Jesus is offered drugged wine but He refuses it (Matt. 27:34). The offering of drugged wine fulfills Psalm 69:21.

Why do you think Jesus refused the drugged wine?

Answer
from previous page

blasphemy

God uses pain for a special purpose in the lives of those He loves. Our natural tendency is to resent and resist it, doing whatever it takes to bail ourselves out. We see pain as a negative, destructive force in our lives. The truth is, pain is our main channel to growth and maturity. Jesus refused to circumvent it because He knew it was necessary for Him to endure. If we try to circumvent pain, we forfeit the growth that would have resulted from it. Don't resist pain and affliction. Make it a friend, and it will smooth the rough edges in your life and hone you into the person God desires. God loves you so much that if you sidestep pain, He will lovingly require that you repeat the class.

JESUS' FIRST THREE HOURS ON THE CROSS

READ: Matt. 27:35–44; Mark 15:24–32; Luke 23:33–43; John 19:18–27

It is 9:00 a.m. Friday, the fifteenth of Nisan (April 7) AD 30. This is the exact time that Jesus *had* to be crucified. That God engineered this logistical feat is a miracle in itself. Historians and theologians have debated the so-called impossibility of all of these events happening in the time frame and culminating at 9:00 a.m. on Friday for centuries.

Logistically, it was virtually impossible for everything to happen prior to 9:00 a.m., but God chose to accomplish this by using a man named Pilate, who did not know Him and despised His people. Why 9:00 a.m.? That was the time of the Chagigah sacrifice in the temple. An unblemished lamb was placed on the altar at the exact time Jesus is put on the cross as our sacrificial Lamb. "Christ our Passover … has been sacrificed" (1 Cor. 5:7).

Large spikes are driven through the hands and feet of Jesus. Indescribable pain shoots through His body as they lift up the cross and drop it in the hole that will secure it upright. A small protruding piece of wood called the *sedile* was affixed to the upright beam under the buttock to allow the weight of the body to rest so as not to tear the nails through the flesh in the hands. Arms were usually tied at the wrists and nails were driven in various locations of the hands. A piece of wood was placed over each appendage and the nail was hammered through to insure that the limbs would not dislodge. Crucifixion involved not only excruciating pain, but great indignity (Heb. 12:2). Jesus is crucified in a Jewish cemetery, probably without clothes, graphically demonstrating Rome's disdain for the Jewish people. It was a slow death, sometimes taking a day or two to claim its victims. For Jesus, it took only six hours, from 9:00 a.m. until 3:00 p.m.

◆ **From 9:00 a.m. Until Noon Jesus Experiences the Wrath of God.**

From 9:00 a.m. until noon, all of the hate and anger that man's base nature is capable of exuding comes pouring out. Two thieves, probably insurrectionists, are crucified on either side of Jesus. His first thought is to pray and ask the Father to forgive those who have participated in this in ignorance. (This would certainly exclude men such as Annas, Caiaphas, Judas, and Pilate. Their actions were willful and premeditated.) *It appears that God made some allowance for some of the Jewish leaders and Roman soldiers that took part out of duty and in ignorance. See the following verses:*

The word *excruciating* comes from the Latin word *excruciates,* meaning "out of the cross," pointing to the tortuous pain involved in crucifixion.

Acts 3:17: _____

1 Cor. 2:8: _____

◆ **Soldiers Divide Jesus' Outer Garments and Gamble for His Tunic (John 19:23).**

Each of the three men crucified was assigned four soldiers to carry out the capital act. Jesus' garments were divided into four parts, each of the soldiers receiving a part (John 19:23). The Lord's robe was seamless, so rather than divide it, they cast lots, fulfilling Psalm 22:18.

◆ **Pilate Erects an Inscription on Jesus' Cross with the Words "Jesus the Nazarene, King of the Jews" (John 19:19–20).**

The Jewish leaders, deeply resentful of Pilate's "in your face" inscription, tell him that the plaque indicates a title rather than a cause of guilt. Delighted at his ability to annoy them, Pilate brushes it off. "What I have written, I have written." (In other words, What's done is done ... get over it!)

The Talmud records that Jesus was charged with sorcery. This makes sense in light of what we learned in Matthew 12. They accused Him of performing His works by the power of the Devil (Matt. 12:24).

◆ **Four Groups of People Mock Jesus:**

- _____ (Matt. 27:39–40)
- _____ (Matt. 27:41–43)
- _____ (Luke 23:36–37)
- _____ (Matt. 27:44)

◆ **One Criminal Rebukes the Other and Asks Jesus to be Remembered When He Comes into His Kingdom (Luke 23:39–43).**

Here we see a great contrast between the two criminals crucified on either side of Jesus. One taunts Jesus and mocks His deity, while the other rebukes the man, obviously understanding that Jesus is Messiah and that He is being unjustly executed. "Remember me" is all he know to say, signifying that he believes. It is enough for Jesus, and His response assures the thief that before nightfall, they will be together in paradise.

In the little book *Children's Letters to God*, one of the letters, written in crayon said simply, "Dear God, Count me in. Love, Herbie."

If the heart is right, that is enough to take a person from death to life!

Where did we ever come up with the idea that there are special words or prayers that must be said to validate and assure a person's salvation? Such tools as the "sinner's prayer" or "Four Spiritual Laws" are based on biblical principles, but are not in the Bible and therefore should be viewed only as *tools*, not as *prerequisites*. The condition and attitude of the heart is what assures redemption, not any special words that are prayed. This thief on the cross only asks to be *remembered* by Jesus and Jesus *assures* him that he will be with Him in heaven forever.

- ◆ **Jesus Speaks Words of Kindness and Compassion to His Mother (John 19:26–27).**

As the firstborn in a Jewish family, Jesus understood His responsibility to His mother. He places her in the care of John, probably because His half-brothers were not yet believers in His messiahship. Jesus makes a wise choice, because John was the only disciple present when Jesus faced Pilate, and the only disciple we know who was present at the cross. John's love and devotion was obviously something Jesus could count on. He is basically telling His mother to consider John as her son and that he would take responsibility for her welfare just as Jesus had always done. Likewise, He tells John to consider His mother as his own.

DAY 81

JESUS' LAST THREE HOURS ON THE CROSS

READ: Matt. 27:45–50; Mark 15:33–37; Luke 23:44–46; John 19:28–30

- ◆ **At the Sixth Hour Darkness Falls Over the Whole Land (Luke 23:44).**

At noon, the lights went out! A strange and unique darkness fell over the land. The original Greek can be interpreted, "over the whole inhabited earth." This was private time between Father and Son.

For the next three hours, until His death a 3:00 p.m., Jesus experiences the *wrath of God*. He undergoes an agony that no man or woman has experienced or can relate to. It was an agony of the soul where Jesus experienced the "cup" that He had prayed in the garden might be averted. The "cup" would be the Father having to turn His back on His own Son. Jesus becomes sin and the Father has to sever the relationship with His own Son.

What happened on the cross? Write down 2 Corinthians 5:21:

- **Jesus Cries, "My God My God, Why Have You Forsaken Me?"** (Matt. 27:46).

Why would Jesus use the term *forsaken*? The Father saw the Son as sin. His absolute holiness demanded that He separate or disassociate Himself from His Son. Have you ever considered the fact that Jesus *died spiritually*? He didn't just take on sin like a backpack. He *became sin personified!* So the relationship changed from a *Father* to a *Judge*. Notice that Jesus uses "My God" not "My Father" as He had always done previously. No person in all of Scripture had the privilege of calling God "Father." It was Jewish tradition that the firstborn son in a Jewish family would be considered equal to his father. This is why the Jewish leaders were so incensed at Jesus calling God by such a *familiar and intimate* term. It literally meant equality. Today, you and I can address Him as *Father* any time we want to (Matt. 6:9).

- **Knowing That Everything Had Been Accomplished, Jesus Cries, "I Am Thirsty"** (John 19:28).

   Jesus had taught that He was the Fountain of Life and that He would satisfy the thirst of all who come to Him and drink. Now He is thirsty. How is this more than mere physical thirst?

- **A Soldier Offers Jesus a Sponge of Sour Wine on a Reed Fulfilling Psalm 69:21.**

- **Jesus Utters His Last Words: "It Is Finished." He then says, "Father, into Your Hands I Commit My Spirit"** (Luke 23:46).

Notice that Jesus resumes the use of the familial term *Father* rather than *God*, which He used during the dark hours of separation. The relationship is now *restored* and the "Great Accomplishment" is complete! Jesus is spiritually resurrected and now enters back into full fellowship with His Father. As Jesus takes His final breath and His head drops forward, where does His soul go? He had told the thief on the cross, "Today you will be with Me in Paradise." Is paradise heaven? Go back and quickly review the brief description of Hades or Sheol (Day 39). Jesus soul will remain in Abraham's bosom until His resurrection early Sunday morning.

DAY 82

THE EVENTS ACCOMPANYING THE DEATH OF JESUS

Several unprecedented events occurred after Jesus' death. Some of these events are not recorded in Scripture but can be found in the Talmud as well as other Jewish writings. Why would we give any credence to them? They were written by *unredeemed* Jews who did not believe Jesus was the Messiah. They are worth our consideration because they further validate the biblical record. They reinforce and affirm what Jesus' followers already believed. Hopefully, these few events will encourage you.

♦ **The Veil of the Temple Split from Top to Bottom (Matt. 27:15).**

Would you be surprised to learn that the "veil" was made of an extremely thick fabric, making its tearing down the middle even more amazing? Prior to the splitting of the veil after Jesus' death, only the high priest could enter the Holy of Holies and then, only once a year. The veil, which represents Christ's body, was split now, allowing all of the priests to enter. Because of what Jesus did on the cross, every believer now has *complete access* to God (2 Cor. 3:18; Heb. 4:16; 10:19–20, Rev. 1:6).

Since only the high priest could enter the Holy of Holies, how do we know that the veil was split? (See Acts 6:7.)

♦ **The Doors of the Temple Mysteriously Opened by Themselves.**

A phenomenon documented by unredeemed Jews in the Talmud, Josephus also describes this strange happening:

Moreover, the eastern gate of the inner [court of the] temple, which was of brass, and vastly heavy, and had been with difficulty shut by twenty men, and rested upon a basis armed with iron, and had bolts fastened very deep into the firm floor, which was there made of one entire stone, was seen to be opened of its own accord about the sixth

> About the curtain we have learned: Gamaliel said in the name of R. Simeon the Deputy [high priest]: The curtain was a handbreadth thick and was woven on seventy-two strands, and each strand consisted of twenty-four threads; its length was forty cubits and its breadth twenty cubits, and was made up out of eighty-two myriads [of threads]. They used to make two every year; and three hundred priests were required to immerse it (Chullin 90b).

> "During the last forty years before the destruction of the temple … the doors of the Hekal would open by themselves, until R. Johanan b. Zakkai rebuked them, saying: Hekal, Hekal, why wilt thou be the alarmer thyself? I know about thee that thou wilt be destroyed, for Zechariah ben Ido has already prophesied concerning thee: Open thy doors, O Lebanon, that the fire may devour thy cedars" (Yoma 39b).

hour of the night. Now those that kept watch in the temple came hereupon running to the captain of the temple, and told him of it; who then came up thither, and not without great difficulty was able to shut the gate again. This also appeared to the vulgar to be a very happy prodigy, as if God did thereby open them the gate of happiness. But the men of learning understood it, that the security of their holy house was dissolved of its own accord, and that the gate was opened for the advantage of their enemies. So these publicly declared that the signal foreshowed the desolation that was coming upon them. (Wars VI:5;3)

◆ The Legend of Azazel

One day each year, every Jew could know that all of his sins were forgiven. It was called the Day of Atonement. Read Leviticus 16:1–34. On this special day, the priest would take two goats; one of which would be sacrificed and its blood taken by the high priest into the Holy of Holies. The blood would atone for his own sins (31:1–19). A second goat, called *the scapegoat,* was turned loose in the wilderness. He bore the sins of the people (vv. 20–22). The legend of Azazel involves this *scapegoat.* A red ribbon or piece of woven thread was tied around the neck of a goat. The goat was then released into the wilderness. When it was found, the red cord around its neck would have mysteriously turned white. This was a sign that the people's sins had been forgiven (atoned for).

NOTE: After the death of Jesus, according to unredeemed Jews, the ribbon or thread never again turned white.

The "Ner Elohim" (I Sam. iii. 3), was left burning all day and was refilled in the evening. It served to light all the lamps. The Ner Elohim contained no more oil than the other lamps, a halflog measure (1 log contains the liquid of six eggs), sufficient to last during the longest winter night (Men. 89a); yet by a miracle that lamp regularly burned till the following evening (ib. 86b). This miracle, however, ceased after the death of Simeon the Righteous, who was high priest forty years before the destruction of the temple (Yoma 39b).

If you assume it was R. Johanan b. Zaccai [who made the rule], was there in the days of R. Johanan Zaccai a thread of scarlet [which turned white]? Has it not been taught: R. Johanan Zaccai lived altogether a hundred and twenty years. For forty years he was in business, forty years he studied, and forty years he taught, and it has further been taught: For forty years before the destruction of the temple the thread of scarlet never turned white but it remained red. (Rosh HaShana 31b)

◆ The Middle Lamp of the Menorah Was Extinguished and Could Never Be Lit Again.

The menorah, or golden lampstand (golden candlestick) was located on the south side of the Holy Place within the temple. It had seven branches and each branch held a lamp. The middle lamp is called the *Ner Elohim,* the Lamp of God, the western lamp, or the *Shamash* (the Servant Lamp). According to the

Talmud, the three lamps on either side faced the Servant Lamp (middle lamp). The golden lampstand provided light for the Holy Place. In it were the golden lampstand, the table of showbread, and the golden altar of incense (Ex. 40:22–27). According to the *Jewish Encyclopedia*, the miracle of the middle lamp (the *Ner Elohim*) (1 Sam. 3:3) was also mysteriously extinguished forty years before the destruction of the temple. From the death of Jesus until the destruction of Jerusalem (AD 30–70), the golden lampstand *refused to burn.*

DAY 83

AN EARTHQUAKE ACCOMPANIES JESUS' DEATH AND MANY ARE PARALYZED WITH FEAR (MATT. 27:51–56).

As Jesus drew His last breath, with the sky already dark in midafternoon, a rumble erupts from the earth and the ground begins to violently shake. Witnesses to the crucifixion panic and scatter in all directions. Gigantic boulders split, tombs open, and the dead are raised to life. Many people saw them in the streets of Jerusalem (vv. 52–53).

Diogenes, a scientist in Egypt wrote that he saw "a solar darkness of such like that either the deity Himself suffered at that moment or sympathized with one that did." Another writer, Phlegon, of a place called Tralles, wrote that in the fourth year of the 202nd Olympiad, which comes out to roughly 30 AD, there was a great and remarkable eclipse of the sun above any that had happened before. At the sixth hour the day was turned into the darkness of night, so that the stars were seen in heaven. There was a great earthquake at Bithynia which overthrew many houses in modern-day Turkey. He called it an eclipse, but it could not have been an eclipse as we know it, because during an eclipse of the sun, stars do not come out. But this was a unique kind of darkness and there is a record of this darkness from various parts of the Greek world.

BE THE JEWS: You are in the city, and across the street you see two people who look familiar. You walk toward them and your mouth drops open; you think you're dreaming. It's Aunt Frieda and Uncle Cy, who died years ago. Behind them is little Jacob, the kid you took Torah lessons with who died of consumption when you were children. How do you process these things? How do you go back to your normal life after these unprecedented things keep happening and all seem to be related to the death of the Nazarene?

Beating the breast is a traditional sign of mourning, anguish, or contrition.

How do you think nonbelievers can see things like this and remain unmoved and unconvinced? Comment and discuss:

◆ **Some of the Soldiers are Convinced (Matt. 27:54).**

A centurion and other guards nearby shake with fear and proclaim, "Truly, this was the Son of God." Notice that it is not just one centurion who says this, as it is often depicted in movies. Verse 54 says that they *all* made this statement. Others nearby began beating their breasts in fear (Luke 23:48).

Who of Jesus' friends were there when all of this happened?

- Luke 8:3: _____
- Mark 15:40: _____
- Matt. 27:55–56: _____
- John 19:25: _____
- Matt. 27:56: _____

Who is missing? _____   Answer on next page

JESUS' BURIAL IN JOSEPH OF ARIMATHEA'S TOMB

READ: Matt. 27:57–60; Mark 15:42–46; Luke 23:50–54; John 19:31–34

◆ **The Jews Request That Pilate Break the Men's Legs to Expedite Their Deaths (John 19:31).**

Under Jewish law, a dead body must be buried on the day of death so the land could remain undefiled (Deut. 21:23). It was late afternoon on

Friday, only hours before the Sabbath, which would begin at sundown. The Jews approach Pilate to ask that the legs of the crucified be broken (John 19:31) to speed up the death process. (Breaking the legs prevented the one being crucified from pushing upward. He was then unable to breathe freely. Most victims of this agonizing death suffocated.)

The Roman soldiers break the legs of the two thieves, but as they approach Jesus, they find that He is already dead (John 19:32–33). To be certain, they thrust a spear into His side, and blood and water gush forth from the wound (19:34).

How does the soldiers' action fulfill prophecy (Ex. 12:46; Num. 9:12; Ps. 34:20)?

A MAN NAMED JOSEPH OF ARIMATHEA GOES TO PILATE AND REQUESTS JESUS' BODY FOR BURIAL (MARK 15:45).

Answer from previous page
Jesus' mother is not there. Apparently, John took her home after Jesus gave her into his care.

For Pilate to release the body of a man condemned of high treason and to release him to someone other than a family member was very unusual. Joseph probably took no pride in what he did. In fact he may have considered himself a coward. He had secretly believed in Jesus as Messiah, but had been afraid to come out publicly. Claiming Jesus' body and making certain He had a proper burial may have been prompted by the guilt he felt for his lack of courage. He did, however, finally risk his reputation and career when he made this request.

Joseph had feared the reaction of the Jewish leaders. What do we, as believers, fear in our sphere of influence. What makes us stay, in many instances, "secret believers"?

What else do we know about Joseph from Scripture?

Mark 15:43: _____

Matt. 27:51; John 19:38: _____

Luke 23:50–51: _____

Pilate is surprised to hear that Jesus had died so quickly and asks the centurion to confirm it (Matt. 15:44). He releases Jesus' body to Joseph (John 19:38), who had brought linen wrappings with him with which he would prepare the body for burial.

> *Who joins Joseph to anoint the body with myrrh and aloes (John 19:39)?*

> *What do the two men have in common?*

Answer
on next page

♦ **The two men wrap Jesus' body according to Jewish custom (John 19:40).**

They place Jesus' body in a newly hewn tomb owned by Joseph (Matt. 27:60). It was located in a nearby garden (John 19:41). After securing the entrance with a large boulder they leave the tomb area (Matt. 27:60). But in the distance, two pairs of eyes watch intently as the men roll the stone into place and depart.

PART XI: JESUS' RESURRECTION, APPEARANCES, AND ASCENSION

From the perspective of the Jewish leaders, Jesus' death was a great victory. They will retain their power and authority with the people, and they can finally close the book on their more than three-year investigation. From God's perspective, their jealousy, arrogance, and anger were tools used to accomplish His purpose. They, however, are too smart to begin celebrating too quickly. They remember what Jesus said concerning His resurrection. Though they did not believe Him, they fear that His disciples will attempt to steal His body. Rumors will begin to fly, the multitudes' emotions will be rekindled, and order will be impossible to restore. The resurrection occurs, a cover-up is planned, and lies are told, but God's mission is accomplished.

> **Answer from previous page**
>
> Both Nicodemus and Joseph of Arimathea were members of the Sanhedrin and were secret believers.

DAY 84

THE WOMEN PREPARE TO ANOINT JESUS' BODY, AND THE TOMB IS SEALED.

READ: Matt. 27:61–66; Mark 15:47; Luke 23:55–56

As Joseph of Arimathea and Nicodemus prepare Jesus' body and lay it in a garden tomb, who watches from a distance (Luke 23:55)?

_____ *and* _____

After seeing where the body of Jesus is entombed, the two women leave in order to prepare spices and perfumes before the Sabbath begins. They would not have been able to purchase anything needed until after the Sabbath ended. They spend the Sabbath resting in accordance with the commandments of the Torah (Ex. 12:16; 20:8–11).

NOTE: For the next few days in our study, we will shift from scene to scene as events occur simultaneously. Chronology is critical here in order to understand the dynamics of what is happening. Be sure to read all of the parallel accounts before beginning each day's study.

Joseph and Nicodemus had already anointed Jesus' body for burial. Having seen this from a distance, why do Mary Magdalene and Mary the mother of Jesus plan to return after the Sabbath to anoint His body again? Any man participating in this study who understands anything about women will know the answer if you have ever been asked to clean the house. What happens after you attempt to clean it? You guessed it, your wife recleans it. Best guess here is that these two women didn't feel the men did the job properly and went back to do it correctly.

The scene switches to the city. The Jewish leaders have gotten what they wanted, but become nervous when someone reminds them of Jesus' words that He would rise again in three days (Matt. 27:64). They assume that to make good on His promise, His disciples would try to steal the body and claim resurrection, a modern Jewish notion. This could be a nightmare for them in terms of the multitudes, many of whom still believe He is the Messiah. Pilate agrees to put a Roman seal over the tomb and post guards at the entrance in order to thwart any possible deception (Matt. 27:62–66).

Jesus said He would be in the heart of the earth for three days and three nights. Have you noticed that Friday afternoon until Sunday before sunrise is about two days and two nights? Great conjecture has surrounded this issue. However, it can be reconciled if we understand Jewish custom. If you force our Gentile seventy-two-hour requirements on the entombment it will not work. The Jews counted any part of a day as a whole day and a whole night. (See Gen. 42:17–18; 1 Sam. 30:12–13; 1 Kings 20:29; Est. 4:16; 5:1.) Therefore …

- The brief part of Friday before sundown - 1 day; Friday night = 1 night (1 day and 1 night).
- Saturday (Sabbath was day 2 and Saturday night was night 2 (2 days/2 nights).
- Sunday morning was day 3 and also qualified as a night (3 days and 3 nights).

◆ **The Women Begin Traveling Toward the Tomb (Matt. 28:1; Mark 16:1).**

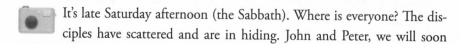

It's late Saturday afternoon (the Sabbath). Where is everyone? The disciples have scattered and are in hiding. John and Peter, we will soon see, are not with the other nine. Mary Magdalene, Mary the mother of James, and Salome have rested on the Sabbath and are preparing to journey toward the tomb. Guards have been stationed outside the entrance.

✡ Arnold Fruchtenbaum of Ariel Ministries points out that the phrase Matthew uses in 28:1, "Now after the Sabbath," can be translated "late on the Sabbath." On Saturday afternoon before sundown, late on the Sabbath, and shortly before the beginning of Jewish Sunday, Mary Magdalene and Mary the mother of James, along with Salome, began traveling toward the tomb (Matt. 28:1; Mark 16:1). While they are walking, darkness falls and the day passes into the first day of the week, Jewish Sunday. (Remember, a new day begins at sundown.) Luke tells us that other women also accompanied them (Luke 24:10).

BACK AT THE TOMB: *What three things are taking place (Matt. 28:2–4)?*

💡 Critical to our understanding of these events is that the women do *not* arrive at the tomb at the same time. Mary Magdalene apparently runs ahead of the other women, arriving at the tomb while it is still dark (John 20:1). In the semidarkness, she sees that the stone has been rolled away from the entrance, but does not see the two angels, probably because of the darkness. Step into Mary's sandals: You can imagine how startled and traumatized you would be to see the stone removed and no one around. (The guards had fled in terror and were on their way to tell the Jewish leaders.) You would naturally assume, as Mary did, that the body had been stolen. Confused and fearful, you do not wait for the other women. You run immediately to tell Peter and John, who are not with the other disciples (John 20:2).

As the other women approach, they are concerned about who will roll the stone away for them. Seeing that the stone has been rolled away, they approach the tomb, go inside, but find no body—but they did find something.

Read Luke 24:3–8 and briefly paraphrase:

♦ **With Great Excitement, the Women Run to Tell the Disciples (Luke 24:9).**

THE STONE

This was a large boulder that would be rolled into a rock-hewn groove in front of the tomb. Its main purpose was to keep animals out and to protect against grave robbers.

DAY 85

MARY MAGDALENE TELLS PETER AND JOHN, WHILE THE OTHER WOMEN TELL THE OTHER DISCIPLES.

ROMAN SEAL

A cord was affixed across the stone and attached to both sides of the tomb so that it could easily be determined if the seal had been disturbed, the penalty being death for both the perpetrator and the guards.

READ: Luke 24:9–12; John 20:2–10

Mary Magdalene tells Peter and John that the body of Jesus had been stolen. (This is her assumption.) The two men immediately begin running toward the tomb. Meanwhile, the other women look in the tomb and are told by the angels that Jesus had risen and is alive. They run quickly to the place where the nine disciples were hiding.

What was the difference between the response of Peter and John and the response of the other nine disciples to Mary Magdalene and the other women?

Peter and John's response (John 20:2–3): _____

The nine apostles' response (Luke 24:11; Mark 16:10–11):

_____

Why do the nine disciples write off what they are told by the women? One reason is surely because they are women. While this is puzzling to us today, it is a great validation for the resurrection when you consider the implications. In the first century, a woman's testimony was not considered valid in court. In fact, pious Jews would thank God every day that they were neither Gentiles or women. God's views are quite different. Consider that He chose women to bring this news to the disciples. He chose Mary Magdalene to be the one to whom Jesus first appeared. If you were to concoct a hoax, wouldn't you validate your story by saying Jesus appeared to the high priest, Herod, or to the Sanhedrin, rather than naming women who had little credibility?

At Caesarea Philippi Peter had proclaimed, Jesus as "the Christ." However he still won't be convinced until after the resurrection. Here he sees the grave clothes and "marveled." Is he convinced? We hear convincing stories about UFOs and may marvel at the evidence, but aren't quite ready to buy in. This may have been Peter's perspective about what he saw.

Meanwhile, Peter and John are running toward the tomb. John outruns Peter and arrives first. He stoops down and looks in the tomb, but doesn't enter (John 20:4–5). He sees the grave clothes *rolled up* on the burial slab, orderly, not in disarray as would have been the result of grave robbery. The face cloth or "napkin" was lying separately (John 20:6–7). Suddenly Peter arrives, but instead of stopping as John had, he goes straight into the tomb and marvels at what he sees. John follows him in, and immediately *sees and believes*. What did he believe? He knew Jesus had resurrected.

Why would John make a point to mention how the grave clothes were arranged on the burial slab? Jesus had resurrected through the wrappings! Apparently the spices and aloes had hardened and retained the shape of Jesus' body, much like a plaster body cast. This is critical to know, because at this point John and Peter only thought Jesus would resurrect spiritually, not physically, and they were not prepared for what they saw. John believes, but what about Peter? Luke 24:12 says, *"He went away to his home, marveling at what had happened,"* but apparently was not yet convinced.

JESUS' FIRST APPEARANCE IS TO MARY MAGDALENE.

READ: Mark 16:9–11; John 20:11–18

Soon after John and Peter enter the tomb, they leave and return home. Mary Magdalene, however, is on her way back to the tomb, hoping to gain some insight from Peter and John about what has occurred. When she arrives, they have already departed. (Remember, they had run there.) Mary is overcome with emotion after she arrives at the tomb (John 20:11). The past few days had been beyond her capacity to comprehend or endure. She had seen the agony of Calvary, the brutality of the Roman soldiers, and the jealousy and hatred of Jewish leaders she had been taught to revere. She and the other women had wanted just one last opportunity to demonstrate their love and compassion by anointing Jesus' body. The thought of His grave being robbed was more than she could handle. She stands outside the tomb "weeping." (This term actually means *wailing*, a loud expression of grief.) Her full sense of loss is beginning to kick in.

Why did Jesus appear to Mary Magdalene first? Possibly because she was the most emotionally needy among all of the women.

◆ Mary Finally Enters the Tomb (John 20:11).

Mary enters the tomb and sees two angels in white sitting at the head and feet of the slab where Jesus had lain. They ask her why she is weeping,

Jesus' appearance to Mary in the tomb is the first of 10 that He will make between His resurrection and ascension.

285

and she tells them it is because someone has taken His body away. Sensing some-one behind her, she turns around and is face-to-face with the Savior, although she does not recognize Him (John 20:14). She thinks He is the gardener and that He has moved Jesus' body.

Read John 20:16–17. Why do you think that only after Jesus says her name does she realize who He is?

Jesus tells Mary to go to the disciples and tell them that He is *risen* and will *ascend* (John 20:17). Mary goes quickly to the disciples and says that she has "seen the Lord," and tells them what Jesus said to her.

Jesus' appearance to Mary in the tomb is the first of 10 that He will make between His resurrection and ascension.

♦ **Mary's Encounter Is the First of Ten Separate Appearances Jesus Will Make Before His Ascension.**

DAY 86

Jesus' Second Appearance Is to the Other Women.

READ: Matt. 28:9–15

Apparently, a substantial amount of time passes between verse 8, when the women ran to tell the disciples, and verse 9, when Jesus appeared to them. Their response was exactly what ours would be. They fall down and wor-ship Him (v. 9). Jesus tells them not to be afraid, but to tell the disciples to meet Him in Galilee. This is the *third time* Jesus has told them to go to Galilee.

Note, that when the Scripture refers to the "the eleven" (as in Luke 24:9), it is used as a generic term and does not mean that all 11 are present at that time. In this case, Peter and John are not among the others. In fact, after Jesus' arrest, the disciples scattered in different directions and were no longer together as a group.

We switch scenes once more. While all of the scurrying back and forth to the tomb is taking place, where are the guards who had been scared out of their wits by the angels? One thing is certain; they would never go back and report to Pilate that they had allowed the seal to be broken and that the body of Jesus was missing. It would mean immediate execution. They are in a heap of trouble and they know it. They are almost like men without a country. Because they had been assigned to the Jewish authorities, they head straight to the high priest, thinking only of getting themselves off the hook. A cover-up is in the making!

♦ **The Roman Guard Seeks Refuge with the Chief Priests (Matt. 28:11).**

Verses 11–15 relate the story concocted by the Jewish leaders for the guards to tell. Anyone who would believe this story also believes Elvis is still alive!

What are the guards to say? (12–15) _____

What will the Jewish leaders do for them (v. 14)?

How could the guards know the disciples stole the body if they fell asleep? Secondly, what kind of influence could the Jewish leaders possibly have with Pilate? He hates their guts. These men have *zero* influence and are shaken to the core; they have seen something they thought did not exist. They feared for their life and were willing to accept the most illogical plan imaginable. Fear causes people to do irrational things. The sad truth is that these guards did nothing wrong except make an error in judgment by going to the chief priests. They were caught in the middle of the self-absorption of Pilate and the jealousy and envy of the Jews. Had Pilate personally guarded the tomb, the same result would have occurred. Were these guards caught and executed, or was their story believed? We don't know their fate, but we do know that the Jews to this day believe that the disciples *stole* the body. People believe what they *want* to believe and reject what they *fear.* Again we see that a person's willingness to accept the truth hinges on the degree to which it will adversely affect his chosen lifestyle.

JESUS' THIRD APPEARANCE ALONG THE ROAD TO EMMAUS

READ: Mark 6:13; Luke 24:13–33a

On Sunday afternoon, the first day of the Jewish week, two of the disciples who had followed Jesus were walking along the seven-mile road from Jerusalem to the little village of Emmaus. Jesus joins them on their journey, but they don't recognize Him. He asks them what they are discussing, and their mood changes to sadness. One of them named Cleopas tells this "stranger" that

He must be the only person in the region who doesn't know what has happened. Jesus plays dumb and they tell Him the whole story (Luke 24:19–24).

Why does Jesus chide them (vv. 25–26)?

Imagine what it would be like have Jesus Himself teach you about Jesus. This is the reason for studying the Bible. It is not to know more doctrine or facts; it is primarily to get to know the One who wrote it.

♦ **Jesus Explains from Scripture the Things Concerning Himself (27).**

When they arrive in Emmaus, they are so taken by this "stranger," they beg Him to stay with them. They dine together, and while they eat and talk their eyes are opened. As they recognize Him, He vanishes from their sight (31).

What happened to them as He taught the Scriptures?

Take a minute to recount the circumstances surrounding the time when your eyes were first opened and you recognized Jesus. (Don't skip this!)

DAY 87

THE FOURTH AND FIFTH APPEARANCES OF JESUS

READ: Mark 16:13; Luke 24:33–35

Remember, the eleven are moving higher on the "Most Wanted" list. Though the Jewish leaders think they have basically solved their problem by taking out Jesus, they know His band of "radicals" can still stir up the people. Jesus had appeared 4 times prior to this, but most of these disciples had not believed in His bodily resurrection at this point, and all had ignored His instructions to meet Him in Galilee.

The day is still Sunday, the Jewish reckoning for the first day of the week. It was probably close to sundown. Whatever plans Cleopas and his friend had in walking to Emmaus earlier that day were quickly aborted after they broke bread and suddenly realized they were having dinner with the crucified Christ. They immediately leave and return to Jerusalem, beside themselves with joy.

The two men know where Jesus' apostles are hiding and go straight to them with the news of what had happened. They burst into the place where the disciples are gathered, only to find that they are there already discussing the risen Christ and the fact that He had appeared to Peter.

Although the disciples refused to believe the women at first, they now are convinced of Jesus' resurrection, but they think it is a spiritual resurrection not a physical one. They apparently think that the encounters with Jesus by the women and the other two disciples were some sort of *ghostly apparition,* and that Jesus could appear and disappear at will. This will become more apparent as we read on. The second point to note is that the gospel accounts do not show Jesus appearing to Peter, but we know from Paul's letter (1 Cor. 15:5), that He *appeared* to Peter some time after he and John saw the *grave clothes* in the tomb.

We can only speculate, but why do you think Jesus appeared to Peter before the other apostles, especially John, who had "seen and believed" at the tomb? Consider Peter's state of mind—his guilt after denying Jesus, the eye contact with Jesus in the courtyard, and his fear of what lay ahead. *What might have been Jesus' reason?*

A. Peter had been given the keys to the kingdom.
B. Jesus likes Peter more than the others.
C. It was a way to get Peter to step up to responsibility.
D. Jesus knew Peter needed encouragement at that point.

Comment on the reason for the option you chose (or another possible reason).

JESUS APPEARS A FIFTH TIME TO THE ELEVEN MINUS THOMAS.

READ: Mark 16:14; Luke 24:36–43; John 20:19–25

As the disciples recline at the table behind closed doors, Jesus suddenly appears in the room. Before they can even gasp, He greets them, saying, "Peace be with you" (John 20:19). They are deathly frightened, thinking they are seeing a ghost (Luke 24:37).

"Peace be with you" was a very common Jewish greeting. However, it means more in the context in which Jesus uses it. Consider the circumstances. They had been in hiding, having heard and yet refused to believe that Jesus had risen. They have no idea what to do or where to go. And their future looked grim. *Go back and read John 14:27 and 16:33. In the upper room and on the way to the Mount of Olives, Jesus talks to them about His peace that He would leave them. How do His words relate to you? How could that reality influence your current circumstances?*

Jesus rebukes them for not believing the others (Mark 16:14). He shows them His hands, His feet, and His side, seeking to assure them that they were not seeing an aberration, but the resurrection of His body (Luke 24:41–43). He shows them His touchable flesh so that it would leave no doubt. John simply says that they rejoiced (John 20:20b).

What had Jesus said to them about this back in John 16:20?

Why would Jesus be upset with them for not believing? It may have been for their failure to *trust* their companions in the faith. Remember this is a fellowship of brothers and sisters who will need each other desperately during the development of the church. They will also have to change their traditional attitude toward *women* and their cultural lack of credibility. There are few things that will solidify and fuse a friendship among a cadre of believers more than absolute *confidence* in the *trustworthiness* of one another. Don't you love to hear a statement like this: *"I know it sounds ridiculous, but Jan and Bob assured me it was true, and if they say it's true, you can bet the farm on it!"*

DAY 88

NOW THAT TEN OF THE ELEVEN BELIEVE, JESUS GIVES THEM THE FIRST OF THREE FINAL COMMISSIONS.

READ: John 20:21–25

- ♦ **Everything the Disciples Had Heard Finally Begins to Come Together.**

In His *first* of *three* commissions to the ten disciples (Thomas is not present), Jesus tells them that He is sending them just as the Father sent Him. They had heard this message before, but now the reality of it comes crashing in on them.

How had the Father sent the Son?

Now, they will be sent in the same way. The words must have caused beads of sweat to break out on their foreheads. Yet before another fearful thought can enter their minds, Jesus breathes on them and says, "Receive the Holy Spirit." Some fifty days later at Pentecost in Acts 2, the Holy Spirit would be poured out on all believers, but apparently this is a very special occasion and a special anointing. They wouldn't be on their own, commissioned like Jedi knights to accomplish this awesome task of taking the truth all over the world after all. Jesus wasn't going to kiss them good-bye and say, *"Do the best you can and write Me when you need help."* He was going to do what He had said over and over again. But until now, they had been incapable of understanding. He would be *in* them, living His own life *through* them. This is why they could be sent as the Father sent the Son. It wasn't up to them!

Where do you and I go with this as modern-day disciples? Every believer will say that he or she wants to be like Jesus and to live as He lived. However, in the next breath, most of us approach life in a manner 180 degrees opposite of the way He lived and commissioned His disciples. Much of the teaching we receive is that *God has acted on our behalf, solely by His grace, but now it is our turn. It is our responsibility to take it from here, with God's help of course, to win the lost and change the world.* It sounds great and it sounds right, but it is the perfect recipe for failure and disillusionment. If there is anything we cannot debate through this study of the Gospels, it is Jesus' *total reliance* on the Father and His desire for His disciples to *depend completely on Him* in the same manner. There is a lost and desperate world out there that needs the Savior. Whose responsibility is it to deliver? There is a huge contingent of good and sincere believers who would say it is *up to us*. Jesus says the opposite! What is more

There is an old Peanuts cartoon I saw years ago that fits well here. Lucy and Charlie Brown are looking out across the horizon and Lucy says, "Well, I guess it's me and you against the world, Charlie Brown. And personally, I think we're going to get creamed!"

paralyzing than to be told day after day that all of your friends and coworkers are headed for hell and it is your responsibility to *win* them to Jesus. Think of the *panic* you feel and the *guilt* that comes when you blow an opportunity to share your faith with them. It is very much like a single woman hearing constantly that she's well over thirty now and that she had better find a husband fast because her biological clock is ticking. What chance would that woman have of patiently and confidently waiting on God rather than desperately going out to try to change her own situation? Stress and desperation would color her whole demeanor in every relationship. The same is true if you and I feel that changing people and society is our responsibility. *It is God's responsibility!*

What, then? Am I to live an uninvolved, passive existence? Absolutely not! People in love with Jesus are proactive, involved people who *listen* for His voice and *yield* to His life within them. What He desires, they desire. The difference is, we don't have to *pull it off.* He wants men and women yielded to Him who respond only to His voice. If you read no further in Rick Warren's *The Purpose Driven Life* than the opening line, it would be worth the price of the book: "It's not about you." This could be framed over Jesus' message and ministry. *It's not about our efforts on His behalf.* In the book of Acts, it is *not* about His disciples and what they can accomplish *for* Him. It is what He accomplishes through lives that are *fully available* to Him!

◆ **The Apostles Tell Thomas That They Have Seen the Lord, but He Refuses to Believe (vv. 24–25).**

Flip back to Day 66. Read John 14:1–6 again. Jesus says He is going away to prepare a place for them. He tells them that where He is they will be also. Then He says that they know where He is going and how to get there. No one says a word. Do they know what He is talking about? Why won't someone speak up and say they don't get it? Thomas is the only one with the guts to say, "We don't have a clue where You are going or how to get there." If old Thomas hadn't said that, we never would have heard these penetrating words, "I am the way, and the truth, and the life; no one comes to the Father but through Me" (John 14:6).

Thomas is a tough-minded pragmatist. He wants bodily proof that Jesus is alive and well. Not only had the women's testimony not fazed him, but even those dramatic statements of Peter and his other companions had left him unmoved. We have labeled him as the "doubter." However, John tells us that he was very *courageous* and *committed* (John 11:16). Matthew says that even after Jesus showed Himself to *the ten* behind locked doors, *some* were still doubtful. Therefore, Thomas was voicing what some of the others believed but may have been afraid to say.

JESUS' SIXTH APPEARANCE IS TO THE DISCIPLES ON SUNDAY NIGHT. THOMAS IS FINALLY CONVINCED.

READ: John 20:26–31; 1 Cor. 15:5

From John 20:26 we learn that a week had passed since Jesus had appeared to the ten apostles. Prior to this, they had failed to go to Galilee because they had *not* believed the reports that Jesus had risen. But now the reason is that they are waiting on Thomas, the lone holdout. To the credit of the nine, they would not move ahead without their brother on board. They would wait.

Question: What is the value of one person? Thomas is not yet on board with the other ten apostles. When someone is struggling, do you move ahead with your mission, ministry, and plans or do you wait? One position is that you can't stall the whole movement of God to wait on a guy who has his nose out of joint. Too many people may pay the price. The other way of thinking is that one person is more important than any ministry; and if you run past this one person, what will keep you from doing it again and again? Jesus always put a person before a program, regardless of its importance. ***Respond and discuss.***

- **Jesus Again Appears to the Disciples, and This Time, Thomas Is Present (John 20:26).**

Eight days have passed. Once again, Jesus appears to the disciples behind locked doors, and once again, knowing their stress and anxiety He says, "Peace be with you" (v. 19). He is fully aware of Thomas's skepticism concerning His resurrection and refusal to believe without physical proof. He stands face-to-face with this tough-minded realist.

What do you imagine the emotions of Jesus were toward Thomas as He looked into his eyes? Was it anger, disgust, frustration, or was it compassion, understanding, and affection?

Holding out His nail-scarred hands and gesturing toward the puncture wounds in His feet and side, Jesus gives Thomas the opportunity he had wanted: "Put your finger here and solve your need for proof that I am who I have said I am from the first day you met me." What is Thomas's response? "My Lord and my God." We don't know if he fell to his knees, hung his head, or what his voice inflection was. What we do know is that John doesn't tell us that Thomas ever actually *touched* Jesus' wounds to be convinced. His statement is the essence of everything Jesus came to proclaim: "Jesus is not only God who created life, He is Lord who will sustain it on a personal basis." This strikes at the heart of John's gospel, which is summarized in John 20:31. *Write the verse and memorize it.*

DAY 89

JESUS' SEVENTH APPEARANCE IS TO SEVEN OF THE APOSTLES BESIDE THE SEA OF GALILEE.

READ: John 21:1–25

Most scholars believe that chapter 21 is an epilogue to John's gospel, written to quell a rumor that he would not die before the Lord's return. Therefore the chapter was added by John to make it clear that no such statement was ever made about Jesus returning prior to John's death. Jesus had told the disciples on *three* occasions to meet Him in Galilee. Because of their fear and confusion, they stayed where they were. Now, they finally journey to Galilee, uncertain of what they should do next. Soon after their arrival, they do what they know best; they return to their former occupations. Down by the Sea of Galilee we find Peter, Nathanael, James, John, Thomas—whose doubt had delayed their departure—and two other disciples whose names are not mentioned. Even having seen Jesus, they still cannot process the implications of His resurrection in terms of how to begin, where to go, and what to do. The foreboding presence of the Roman Empire looms like a giant shadow hovering in front of them, and the sickening guilt and shaken confidence lie behind.

Could it have been more than that? Could some of these guys, especially Peter, have been so disappointed in their cowardly actions after the arrest, trial, and crucifixion that they were considering going back to their former vocations? They knew fishing, they felt in control on the water, but whether they could be effective missionaries in a hostile world was another matter.

What do you think?

BE THE DISCIPLES: Jesus has breathed His Spirit on you just a few days ago behind locked doors. It was euphoric and surreal, but now you are alone again. The reality of no physical presence to guide and direct you almost paralyzes you with fear. You have the Holy Spirit now, but you can't yet grasp what that means. Inner guidance doesn't seem the same as having Jesus with you to observe Him and to answer your questions and teach you. Where do you go when you don't know what to do? You go to comfortable surroundings; you go back to familiar turf. If you're these guys, you go fishing.

♦ Led by Peter, the Seven Disciples Decide to Go Fishing (John 21:3).

Nighttime is often a productive time to fish because fish feed near the surface. As the dawn begins to break, the weary fishermen hoist their nets once again, only to find that they have liberated a few rusty beer cans, a license plate, and an old tire from the bottom of the lake (vv. 1–3). Suddenly a voice pierces the mist rising from the lake, and through the fog the faint image of a man is calling out to them from the shore. Though only a hundred yards from land (v. 8), they are unable to identify the image in the dim light. A question no fisherman wants to hear after being skunked echoes across the water: "Have you caught anything?" Their answer was a firm, and probably testy: "No!" The voice tells them to throw their net on the other side of the boat and it will make their day. (You can just imagine how thrilled these professional fishermen were to be given fishing advice from some guy standing on the shore.)

Why do you think they obeyed the voice from the shore?

What was the probable reason John knew it was the Lord on shore? Go back and read Luke 5:1–11 (Day 17).

NOTE: There has been much speculation by scholars concerning the meaning of the number of fish, but nothing is conclusive. We do know that fishermen would always count their fish and divide them up for personal use and to sell. John obviously wants us to know the contrast of what the disciples achieved on their own as opposed to what Jesus does simply with a spoken word.

♦ Peter Puts on His Clothes, Dives into the Water, and Swims Ashore.

We can only imagine what Peter did when he reached the shore, dripping wet and alone with the Savior whom he had denied.

Do you think Peter …

• was at a loss for words and said nothing?

295

- apologized and asked forgiveness before the others reached shore?

- tried to keep the atmosphere light and avoided dealing with his denial?

- smiled and walked over to warm himself by the fire Jesus had made?

The other disciples arrive on shore with a catch of 153 fish. Even before the fish have been caught, Jesus has started a charcoal fire and was cooking fish for their breakfast. Once again, we can only speculate as to what these guys were thinking. They were once again face-to-face with Jesus and His awesome power, yet what they see here is His gentle, servant heart. As they watch in awe as He fixes their breakfast, the doubts and fears that had lingered since His arrest seem to be slowly abating. As they eat with Him, probably lost in silent wonder, they are reminded of how they had been commissioned by Jesus. They were called to leave the Sea of Galilee and become fishers of men (Luke 5:10) and to begin the new church (Matt. 16:19).

◆ **Jesus Challenges Peter with a Guilt-Removing Question (vv. 14–17).**

There are three uses in the Greek language for the word *love*. Two are used in this passage. *Agapao* which is a love that is unconditional, a love of the will, to will the best for another. The second is *phileo*, an emotional love based on feelings. *Agapao* is clearly the superior of the two.

1st question: "Simon, son of John, do you love [*agapao*] Me more than these?"

It appears that Jesus is asking if Peter's love for Him is not only unconditional, but also to a deeper level than the other apostles'. Why would He ask that?

What had Peter previously boasted (Matt. 26:33; Mark 14:29; John 13:37)?

1st answer: "Yes, Lord, You know that I love [*phileo*] you." (Notice that he answers with a more inferior love than Jesus asked him).

Notice that with each answer Peter gives to the three questions Jesus asks, Jesus' response to Peter's answer brings with it greater intensity and relational involvement.

"Do you love me? Then tend my lambs." Help new believers get started in the faith.

"Do you love me? Then shepherd my sheep." This goes a step deeper: Lead and encourage believers in their walk.

"Do you love me? Then tend my sheep." In other words, help develop them into real maturity.

1st response:	"Tend My lambs." (Help establish new believers in the faith.)
2nd question:	"Simon, son of John, do you love [*agapao*] Me?"
2nd answer:	"Yes, Lord, You know I love (*phileo*) You."
2nd response:	"Shepherd My sheep." (Encourage believers in their walk.)
3rd question:	"Simon, son of John, do you love [*phileo*] Me?" (Jesus uses the love that Peter had used, as if questioning even that level of emotional love.)
3rd answer:	"Lord, You know all things, You know that I love [*phileo*] You." (Peter is hurt, but answers the same as previously, with inferior, feelings-driven love.)
3rd response:	"Tend My sheep." (Mentor, disciple believers into maturity.)

The questions and responses might be paraphrased this way: Jesus asks Peter if he has the kind of love for Him that he had previously boasted. Peter responds by saying, *Lord, You know I really like You a lot.* The second question and answer is the same. Although Jesus' third question appears identical, this time He uses the lesser form of love with which Peter has answered. Peter is hurt because Jesus is basically saying, *Peter, do you even* like *Me a lot?* Though wounded, notice the humility as Peter answers. He is finally broken. Jesus does not ask these questions to chastise Peter, but to encourage and strengthen him. Why does He ask him the same question three times? Peter had denied Jesus three times. With each answer, it was an opportunity for Peter to be able to erase in his mind the terrible guilt he feels.

◆ **Jesus Further Encourages Peter by Telling Him That He will Have the Honor of Dying for the Gospel (v. 18).**

The tradition is that Peter died a martyr at Rome about AD 67, under the Emperor Nero, when he was about seventy-five years old. It is said that he was crucified head downward, at his own request, feeling himself unworthy to die as Jesus did. John penned his gospel around the late '80s to early '90s AD, meaning that Peter had already died by the time John wrote John 21:18. If

The probable intent of Jesus in this dialogue with Peter was not to embarrass or chastise him, but to encourage him and to help Him learn from his previous failure.

tradition is correct, the "follow Me" in John 21:19 was literally fulfilled in that Peter followed Jesus to the cross.

♦ **Peter Wants to Know John's Fate, But Jesus Tells Him Not to Worry About John, Just Follow the Lord.**

DAY 90

JESUS' EIGHTH APPEARANCE IS TO THE FIVE HUNDRED ON A MOUNTAIN IN GALILEE.

READ: Matt. 28:16–20; Mark 16:15–18; 1 Cor. 15:6

Were all of the five hundred who saw Jesus convinced at this point?

♦ **Jesus Gives the Second of Three Commissions, What Has Been Labeled the Great Commission (Matt. 28:18–20; Mark 16:5).**

If the disciples as well as you and I are to go into all the world, who is going to need the power to go? _____. Does your answer match up with what Jesus says in Matthew 28:18? _____. Jesus wants them (and us) to be His instruments in three things: _____ _____, _____, and _____.

Though it is not mentioned by the gospel writers, Paul tells us in his first letter to the Corinthians that Jesus appeared to his half-brother James prior to His final appearance to all of the apostles.

This is probably one of the top two or three favorite verses of the evangelical church, but it is alarmingly misunderstood. The emphasis of the passage is not on "go," but on "make." The word *go* here is *not* an imperative verb, but a participle. The passage is more accurately rendered, "As you go, make disciples." We are all going somewhere all of the time. So, as you go, make disciples. As you drive along with your kids, make disciples. As you golf with friends, make disciples. The power and authority are not given to us, but to Jesus. As we have seen throughout our study, Jesus is not a gas station where we fuel up each week with power. He had all power and authority and because He is in us, we need no power whatsoever; we simply need Him! As you go, with His power and authority resident within you, make disciples. Jesus pulls it altogether by saying that He will always be with them.

♦ **Jesus' Ninth Appearance Is to His Half-Brother James (1 Cor. 15:7).**

JESUS' TENTH APPEARANCE IS TO THE ELEVEN. HE GIVES THEM THE THIRD OF HIS FINAL COMMISSIONS.

READ: Luke 24:44–49; Acts 1:1–8

During the forty days between His resurrection and ascension, Jesus spent a significant amount of time teaching the disciples two basic things. First, all the things written about Him in the law, the prophets, and the psalms must be fulfilled (Luke 24:44). Second, He taught the things concerning the kingdom of God (Acts 1:3).

James, thought to be Jesus' half-brother, became the head of the church in Jerusalem (Acts 15:13; 21:17–18). He is also believed to be the author of the book of James.

♦ **Jesus Opens the Disciples' Minds to Understand the Scriptures (v. 45).**

What two basic things does He want them to understand (vv. 46–48)?

What are they still confused about (Acts 1:6)?

What will enable them to be His witnesses throughout the world (Acts 1:8)?

Does Acts 1:8 appear to be a contradiction to what we said concerning who the *power* belongs to back in Matthew 28:18? It might be, except for two very important words: *Holy Spirit.* "You will receive power when the Holy Spirit comes upon you." Where will the power come from? The Holy Spirit. Where will the Holy Spirit reside? In the believer. All power is given to Jesus and His Spirit. He lives in us. Therefore because we have Him, we have power.

♦ **Jesus Gives His Third and Final Commission (Luke 24:49; Acts 1:8).**

The third and final commission is _____

THE ASCENSION OF JESUS CHRIST

It is important to note that the angels said Jesus would return in the same way in which He departed, but there is *nothing* in Scripture that says He will return to the same place (the Mount of Olives).

READ: Matt. 28:19–20; Luke 24:50–53; Acts 1:9–12

As they stand together on the Bethany side of the Mount of Olives, Jesus lifts up His hands and blesses His beloved disciples. Suddenly, He is lifted up into the air into a cloud (Luke 24:51). As they gaze into the sky, two angels in white stand beside them. They tell the disciples that Jesus will return in the same *way* as they have watched Him go to heaven.

♦ **The Eleven Return to Jerusalem with Great Joy, Continually Praising God in the Temple.**

Paul tells us that most of the 500 were still alive at the time Paul wrote his epistle (1 Cor. 15:5–6) in around AD 55. No record in all of church or secular history exists of any believer who saw Jesus ever recanting His story.

Their fear and confusion is now gone. Ten days later, on the Day of Pentecost (Acts 2), the New Testament church is born. Believers would be filled with the Holy Spirit and their passion and tenacity would keep the Roman Empire up late at night trying to stop an unstoppable revolution of love as it washed across the known world. For centuries to come, the hearts of men and women would be set ablaze with the love of God, and what happened on two pieces of wood in AD 30 would give significance and meaning to all of human history.

POSTSCRIPT

These biographies that we have studied are just the beginning of God's continuing pursuit of intimacy with humankind. My fervent prayer is that as you study the Gospels for the rest of your life, you will see them in a new and refreshing way. My prayer is also that you have come to appreciate God's great love for His people, Israel. Though they suffered great lapses in moral and spiritual leadership, especially during the time of Jesus, they are God's beloved bride that He has refused to let go.

Who, then, bears responsibility for Jesus' death? Was it the Jews? Was it Caiaphas and the Jewish leaders? Was it Judas or Pilate and the Romans? The reality is that you and I are the real culprits. It was because of our sin and the sin of humankind, beginning with Adam, that set in motion God's great plan to redeem us by the substitutionary death of His Son on the cross. The Jews and the Romans certainly played a role. They were catalysts in this great drama we have studied. Each one, even Judas, played a part, but the death of Jesus Christ was the result of a decision made by the Father and the Son long before any of us were born. Jesus said that no man could take His life, but that He voluntarily laid down His life for us. Jesus' death was an act of His own volition. It was intentional because it was the only way that God's great love, compassion, and justice could be satisfied simultaneously.

Persecuted beyond measure, the Jews have suffered greatly through the centuries. We would make a great mistake to harbor any animosity toward the Jews. They are still God's beloved people, and God is doing great things today among the Jews as many are turning to Jesus the true Messiah. Please pray for and support the Jewish people and read and study these wonderful accounts over and over for the rest of your life. Teach others these great truths as they make their home in your heart. Shalom.

Primary Resources Used in This Book

A Harmony of the Gospels by A. T. Robertson (HarperOne).

The Life and Times of Jesus the Messiah by Alfred Edersheim (Hendrickson).

The First Century by William K. Kingman (Harper).

Jerusalem in the Time of Jesus by Joachim Jeremais (Fortress).

The Mishnah, A New Translation by Jacob Neusner (Yale University).

The Works of Josephus translated by William Whiston (Hendrickson).

Life of Christ Series by Arnold Fruchtenbaum (Ariel Ministries).

The Pharisee's Guide to Total Holiness by William L. Coleman (Bethany).

Ecclesiastical History by Eusebius (Loeb).

Exploring Bible Times Syllabus (Studies in Israel) by James Martin (Bible World Seminars).

The Gospels from a Jewish Perspective by Bob Warren (Life on the Hill Ministries).

A Commentary on the New Testament from the Talmud and Hebraica by John Lightfoot (Hendrickson).

Manners and Customs of the Bible by Fred H. Wright (Moody).

The Wycliffe Historical Geography of Bible Lands by Charles Peterson and Howard Voss (Moody).

The Cross and the Prodigal by Kenneth Bailey (Bethany; InterVarsity).

Jesus Through Middle Eastern Eyes by Kenneth Bailey (InterVarsity).

Note: Beginning to understand something of the Jewish mind-set in the first century took me on a circuitous route, not only through the above-mentioned references, but also through personal interviews with rabbis and those who studied Jewish culture and history. Three separate journeys to Israel with Dr. James Martin, each for over two weeks, gave me the inquisitiveness to pursue my own personal study. I discovered that it was much more than information, but an intuitive *feel* and appreciation of the yearnings and perspective of the Jewish people that began to overtake me.